ENGLISH
for Cambridge Proficiency

Margaret Archer   Enid Nolan-Woods

Nelson

Thomas Nelson and Sons Ltd
Nelson House   Mayfield Road
Walton-on-Thames   Surrey KT12 5PL

51 York Place
Edinburgh EH1 3JD

Thomas Nelson (Hong Kong) Ltd
Toppan Building 10/F
22A Westlands Road
Quarry Bay   Hong Kong

Distributed in Australia by
Thomas Nelson Australia
480 La Trobe Street
Melbourne   Victoria 3000
and in Sydney, Brisbane, Adelaide and Perth

This edition first published by Thomas Nelson and Sons Ltd
1984
Reprinted 1984, 1985(twice), 1986
ISBN 0-17-555338-6
NCN 71-ECE-9207-05

Printed in Hong Kong

Acknowledgements

The publishers are grateful to the following for permission to
reproduce copyright material:

The Bodley Head for an extract from *Eustace and Hilda* by L. P.
Hartley; The Hogarth Press Ltd, Harcourt Brace Jovanovich Inc.
and the author's literary estate for an extract from *The Duchess and
the Jeweller* by Virginia Woolf (taken from *A Haunted House and
Other Stories*). Copyright 1944, 1972 by Harcourt Brace Jovanovich
Inc.; The Society of Authors, Jonathan Cape, Viking Press Inc. and
the author's literary estate for an extract from 'Two Gallants' from
Dubliners by James Joyce. Copyright 1916 by B. W. Huebsch.
Definitive text copyright © 1967 by The Estate of James Joyce; A. P.
Watt and the author's literary estate for an extract from *Kipps* by
H. G. Wells; The Post Office for the customs label; The Inland
Revenue for the tax return form.

All photographs by D. Lewcock except the following:
Bournemouth News and Picture Service, page 226 bottom right;
British Museum, 142; Camera Press Ltd., 74; Dean and Chapter of
Durham, 163; Flax & Kingsnorth, 117; Carole Hay, 77; David
Hoffman, 226 top right; Ice and Roller Skate Magazine, 226 top
left; Keystone Press Agency, 9, 17, 36; National Portrait Gallery,
145; National Westminster Bank, 114; Popperfoto, 213; Ronald
Sheridan, 192; Chris Steele-Perkins, 226 bottom left; Stock
Exchange, 138; U.N. High Commissioner for Refugees, 95; VRU,
178, 185.

The drawing on page 170 is reproduced from *Beardsley's
Illustrations for the Mort d'Arthur* in the Dover Pictorial Archive
Series.

Foreword

This book is intended to provide students preparing for the new (1984) syllabus of the Cambridge Certificate of Proficiency in English examination with the essential skills and background knowledge necessary to reach the required standard.

It is divided into eight units, each dealing broadly with a general theme – Space, Ecology, Money, etc. The units are subdivided into Oral Skills, Use of English, Written Skills and Reminders, including practice in comprehension, information retrieval and summary, composition and recognition of register and style. There are guidelines on how to approach particular problems and each unit also revises a common structure.

ORAL SKILLS

Intensive Listening
Extracts from discussions, radio programmes, talks and essays on the general themes of the units are followed by comprehension questions, which can be done orally, or written. Notes and practice exercises are given on the expressions and vocabulary used in the texts. The language used in various situations is also practised.

Dialogues
These relate to the themes of the units but are generally in a more colloquial register, and introduce phrasal verbs and common idioms. Vocabulary notes and practice exercises are included, together with some multiple-choice questions.

Listening Comprehensions
These provide practice for the Cambridge Proficiency Examination.

Photographs
Photographs relating to the themes occur in each unit, and questions and suggested topics similar to those in the Cambridge Examination are included.

Reading Aloud and Group Discussion
Passages for reading aloud, with questions, and topics for group discussion are given to provide practice for the examination.

USE OF ENGLISH

Structures
Each unit revises a common structure with which a student at this level is expected to be familiar. Practice and exercises are included.

Special Uses
Particular uses of certain structures which give general difficulty are also included. As far as possible the structure exercises have been designed to fit in with the requirements of the Cambridge Proficiency Examination.

WRITTEN SKILLS

Note-taking and Expansion of Notes
A guide and suggestions for making and expanding notes from both written and spoken material is given.

Reading Comprehension
There is a variety of passages and extracts with multiple-choice questions, and suggestions on how to tackle them. The questions are designed to test gist, detailed context and implied meaning as well as recognition of form, register and intention.

Reading for Information
Various charts, diagrams and texts are given from which the student has to extract certain information and then write it up.

Composition
Both narrative and descriptive forms are given and the student is also shown how to present a debate or logical discussion.

Register and Style
Register and style are defined and practice and exercises are provided to help the student in this difficult but important area.

Reading for Language
Literary figurative language and literary style are discussed, with extracts from classical and modern writers and poets for literary appreciation.

Expositions
The student is encouraged to give an opinion backed up by facts.

REMINDERS

Reminders
Punctuation, definite/indefinite articles, and other points on which the student, even at Proficiency level, often makes careless mistakes are revised in the Reminders at the end of each unit.

The book includes a variety of authentic material with information in graphic form, charts, timetables, forms and advertisements, as well as radio and public announcements and instructions. The range of English required for the examination is extensive. We have therefore tried to provide as wide a selection of material as possible. It is hoped that students will be encouraged to follow this up by further reading, class projects, debates and similar activities.

As a mixture of 'light' and 'heavy' material is contained in each unit, the student may benefit from turning to one of the lighter dialogues or passages after tackling one of the heavier, more concentrated sections. The material can, in fact, be used in any order preferred.

Recorded material is available from the publishers; the sections recorded are marked in the margin.

Contents

Unit one Space – Fact and Fiction

Unit two Employment

Unit three Ecology

Unit four Health and Fitness

Unit five Money

Unit six The Language of Literature

Unit seven Government and Law

Unit eight Relationships

Unit one Space-Fact and Fiction

In the Oral section of this and following units, you may be asked to distinguish
the different kinds of English that people use. More formal and correct English is used
when people are, for instance, giving a lecture or being interviewed for a job, than when
they are talking to their friends or colleagues at work. Language also varies according to
social background, regional areas, occupation or education. Its idiom, too, is constantly
changing in line with development and life-styles in the modern world. You should,
however, be careful not to make too rigid a distinction as this may result in your
English sounding over-precise, pompous and old-fashioned or, on the other hand,
being so peppered with slang and catch-phrases as to lose its meaning.

ORAL SKILLS A

Intensive Listening

Listen to this extract from a radio programme on the existence or non-existence of life
forms in outer space.

Presenter Are We Alone? This is the first in our series of programmes on the
possibilities of life on other planets, and tonight we are privileged to
have in the studio with us Professor Wilbur T. Betts, Professor of
Astrophysics at the North American State University; Dr Morgan
5   Barry, well known to most of our listeners for his contributions to that

very popular TV Programme, 'Astronomy for All'; and, last but not
least, Stewart Rider, whose science fiction books have sold half a
million copies in this country alone and whose latest book, 'The Lost
Galaxy', has recently been the subject of a highly successful film.

10   Professor Betts, would you like to begin?

Betts   Well, first of all, I'm going to put the cat among the pigeons and state
quite categorically that I am convinced there is life, intelligence, call
it what you will, in other parts of the universe. I feel there is an
immense arrogance in assuming that we are the only intelligent beings

15   in creation.

Barry   I find that a rather facile assumption. It leads the way to a belief in
all kinds of mumbo-jumbo, celestial beings with incomprehensible
powers, UFOs, all that kind of thing, to say nothing of astrology with
all its attendant superstitions. As a scientist, I am prepared to concede

20   that our knowledge of the universe is still painfully limited, but the
most patient research with highly sophisticated instruments has failed
to reveal any evidence of life, as we understand it, outside our own
planet.

Betts   When you say 'life as we understand it', you're making the classic

25   error of thinking of life in terms of humanoids. There are already
well-substantiated reports of signals being received from a planet
outside our own galaxy. The interpretation of such signals is, of
course, extremely complex but it is a dangerous fallacy to assume that
the intelligence sending such signals necessarily resembles ourselves.

30   I'm not talking about little green men with antennae or anything of
that sort, but you have to remember that life forms on Earth have
evolved largely as a result of adaptation to the conditions on this
planet. We are so restricted by our concept of time, the speed of light,
Einstein's theory of relativity, and so on, that we have not yet

35   acquired the knowledge or the mental capacity to comprehend a
universe where such barriers do not exist.

Presenter   What do you think of all this, Stewart? You put forward some pretty
advanced ideas on time and intelligence in 'The Lost Galaxy', I
believe.

40   **Stewart**   Well, yes, but then I'm not a scientist, I'm a writer. I suppose you
could say I earn my living frightening people out of their wits. As a
matter of fact, I had quite a few worried letters from people who'd
seen the film. They didn't seem to be too upset about breaking the
time barrier, but they were afraid of their brains being taken over by

45   alien intelligences. It happens in the story, you see. Cosmos, the chief
character, is a humanoid time traveller – his mission is to find the
Lost Galaxy – and he can in fact take control of people's brains by
means of a kind of electro-magnetic ray. Quite a lot of people come
out of the film complaining of pins and needles in their heads. It's

50   auto-suggestion, I suppose.

Barry   I haven't read your book, Mr Rider, but it sounds like an excellent
piece of escapism. I assume you don't really expect people to take it
seriously. I mean, you don't really believe in it yourself?

Stewart   I'm not sure. It seems real enough to me when I'm writing it. I get a

55   bit worried sometimes in case I haven't got the sci-fi jargon quite
right, but I've always been interested in the subject. There's a grain

of truth somewhere in most science fiction books, that's one of the reasons people read them, I suppose. It's all a bit fantastic, but it might just be true.

60 **Betts** I have to agree with you there, Stewart, but I'm not so sure about it all being so 'fantastic'. It seems to me that the universe is infinitely more fantastic – if that's the right word – than you or I, or even Barry here, can even begin to imagine.

Barry I think Shakespeare said the same thing, Betts, only rather better:
65 'There are more things in heaven and earth, Horatio, than are dreamt of in your philosophy. . . .'

Betts Well, of course, if you're going to start quoting Hamlet, there's no knowing where this discussion will end. . . .

Read or listen to the discussion again. Note the style of language used by the three speakers: not too formal or scientific, using a fairly simple range of vocabulary that would be easily understood by a listener interested in the subject.

Match the following expressions used in the discussion to their meaning. Put the letter of your choice in the box.

☐ **1**	*to put the cat among the pigeons*	*A* tingling sensation when recovering from numbness
☐ **2**	*quite categorically*	*B* Unidentified Flying Objects; Flying Saucers
☐ **3**	*mumbo-jumbo*	*C* form of entertainment during which worries are forgotten
☐ **4**	*UFOs*	*D* stir up trouble
☐ **5**	*humanoids*	*E* object of foolish veneration or fear
☐ **6**	*frightening people out of their wits*	*F* without fear of contradiction
☐ **7**	*pins and needles*	*G* terrifying people to the point of madness
☐ **8**	*escapism*	*H* expressions used in science fiction stories
☐ **9**	*sci-fi jargon*	*I* beings which physically resemble humans

Exercise 1

Discuss the answers to the following questions.

1 What do we know about the three speakers taking part in the discussion?
2 What are Professor Betts' views on extra-terrestrial intelligence?
3 Why does Dr Barry describe Professor Betts' statement as 'a rather facile assumption'?
4 In what way have the 'highly sophisticated instruments' referred to by Dr Barry proved disappointing?
5 What does Professor Betts mean by the phrase 'thinking of life in terms of humanoids'?
6 What has been one of the major factors in the evolution of Man?

3

7 Why does Professor Betts believe that Man is incapable of understanding the universe?

8 What do people seem most concerned about when they have seen the film, 'The Lost Galaxy'?

9 Who is Cosmos?

10 How does Stewart Rider feel about science fiction in general?

Exercise 2

Using a Present Tense (including the Present Perfect) of the verbs given, ask someone questions about the following subjects. For example:

Astronomy (study)	*Have you ever studied astronomy?*
Life on Mars (think)	*Do you think there is life on Mars?*

1 Life in outer space (believe) ....?
2 The film, 'The Lost Galaxy' (see) ....?
3 The speed of light (know) ....?
4 Signals from space (receive) ....?
5 Science fiction (read) ....?
6 The time barrier (break) ....?
7 Flying Saucer (photograph) ....?
8 Astrology (study) ....?
9 Einstein's theory (understand) ....?
10 Extra-terrestrial activity (record) ....?

ORAL SKILLS **B**
Dialogue

 Now listen to this dialogue between two young people walking home down a country road on a clear, still night. Note particularly the informal style and limited vocabulary of the speakers, which make it difficult for them to describe unfamiliar objects.

Listen to the dialogue again and then do exercises 1 and 2.

Exercise 1

Rephrase the following expressions from the dialogue in more formal language.

1 That sort of big orange blob
2 Looks more like a soup plate wrong way up
3 It's got a kind of aerial or something sticking out of the top
4 It looks ever so funny
5 What on earth can it be?
6 It's not much to look at
7 It's a bit scarey
8 It's all yellow now
9 You'd better look out
10 I didn't like the look of it

Exercise 2

Work in pairs.

You are Oris. Continue the conversation with Joe *or* his girlfriend.

Exercise 3

In the Proficiency Paper 5, Interview, you will be asked to look at a short passage, answer a few questions about it – where it comes from, who is speaking, what the situation is and so on – and then read it aloud. The passage may be in the form of an announcement, advertisement, instructions, warning, news report, etc.

Note carefully the kind of language used – formal/informal. Try to read fluently at an even pace, giving the right emphasis to what is important in the text. Allow a brief pause before beginning a new sentence. Try not to break up phrases. Identify with the speaker as far as possible.

Study the following passage:

Good evening and welcome to another edition of 'In Our Stars'. Tonight, in response to numerous requests from our regular listeners, our special guest is Dr Humphrey Wilde, lecturer in astrophysics at Brook University. He is going to answer some of the questions you have sent in, and tell us something of the chemical nature of the stars and the natural forces that influence them. Over to you, Humphrey ...

Answer these questions: Where do you think the speaker is?
What is his job?
Who is he speaking to?
What information does he give about Dr Wilde?

Now read the passage aloud.

ORAL SKILLS **C**
Listening Comprehension

In one or more of the parts in the Cambridge Proficiency Paper 4, Listening Comprehension, you will be asked to select the correct answers, A, B, C or D, after listening to a recorded text. These texts will frequently be in dialogue form, but may also include announcements, newspaper reports, extracts from radio programmes, books and so on. It is unwise to assume too quickly that what looks like the obvious answer is necessarily the correct one. It is important to read carefully, not only the choice of answers, but also the 'stem' or sentence that leads into them. In some cases you may have to deduce a fact that is not precisely stated in the text or assess the mood – angry/sympathetic/distressed, etc. – of the speaker.

Now listen to this extract from a lecture on 'Early Man and the stars' and study how the correct answers to the questions are selected.

The earliest writings record the instinct of Man to look to the heavens for guidance. Stars guided explorers across uncharted seas and desert wastes. To Man the Sun rose and set, bestowing the warmth of its rays apparently according to

5   some immutable Will, while the Moon appeared to wax and wane with a perplexing inconstancy. Rain, snow, gales, or refreshing breezes all came from the sky, as did violent thunderstorms, the last usually taken to communicate the displeasure of the gods. In a universe that contained so much beyond his understanding, it is small wonder that Man looked upward, seeking to identify and, if possible, placate his heavenly masters. Religion has taught that God made Man in his own image, but

10 the reverse might also be said to be true. Primitive Man's concept of intelligence was limited to himself and the animals around him. It followed, therefore, that his representations of the gods he worshipped depicted either a superior form of human, or some animal of exceptional strength or wisdom such as the bull, or the serpent. Man recognised his own nature and, vaguely conceiving it as part divine,

15 attributed to the celestial beings he venerated the same lusts and passions to which he himself was subject.

1   The lecturer explains how even the earliest writings
   A   stressed the importance of instinct
   B   revealed Man's need for guidance
   C   revealed the origin of the stars
   D   were inspired by heavenly guidance

A	
B	✓
C	
D	

Correct answer

B   revealed Man's need for guidance

   The need for guidance is recorded, if not explained, in these early writings.

Wrong

A   There is no suggestion that the writings laid any particular emphasis on the importance of *instinct*.
C   No reference to the *stars*, charted or uncharted; only a brief reference to uncharted *seas*.
D   It would be merely an assumption to suppose those early writings were inspired by some heavenly agent.

2   Why was the Moon thought of as 'inconstant'? It
   A   was apt to change its course
   B   could only be seen from one side
   C   continually altered in size
   D   appeared to vary in size

A	
B	
C	
D	✓

Correct answer

D   appeared to vary in size

   Man thought of the Moon as *inconstant*, i.e. *capricious* (see line 5) because of the variations he noticed between the New Moon and Full Moon (waxing and waning).

Wrong

A   The Moon does not change its course. It is a satellite of the Earth.
B   It is true that only one face of the Moon is visible, but this would suggest *constancy* rather than *inconstancy*.
C   The Moon does not alter in its *actual* size.

6

3 One of the reasons that Man believed in celestial power was that
  A he could not control the elements
  B nothing beneficial came from the sky
  C life offered little pleasure
  D he was able to communicate with the gods

A	✓
B	
C	
D	

Correct answer

A he could not control the elements

Since he did not understand the reasons for changes in weather conditions, he naturally assumed they were caused by some celestial power.

Wrong

B Incorrect because some good things such as sunshine and soft winds come from the sky.
C His life may have been hard, but the text does not give this as a reason for his belief in heavenly gods.
D It is obvious that he was unable to communicate in person with the gods.

4 It was natural for Man to think the gods must resemble life forms on Earth because he
  A worshipped all animal life
  B had seen idols of the gods
  C was unable to imagine anything different
  D had only a limited intelligence

A	
B	
C	✓
D	

Correct answer

C was unable to imagine anything different

His concept of intelligence was limited to himself and the animals around him.

Wrong

A He didn't worship *all* animal life.
B The only representations of gods he could possibly have seen had been made by Man and not by the gods.
D It was not his *intelligence* that was limited but his knowledge.

5 Man believed that
  A the gods recognised his divinity
  B he was destined to become a god
  C he had some affinity to the gods
  D his feelings were divinely inspired

A	
B	
C	✓
D	

Correct answer

C he had some affinity to the gods

Line 14: 'Man recognised his own nature and, vaguely conceiving it as part divine ...'

Wrong

B There is no suggestion in the passage that Man believed he would eventually become a god.
A The line 'Man recognised his own nature' does not mean that *the gods* thought Man was divine.
D Man did not believe that his feelings *were inspired* by the gods, but only that the gods had the same sort of feelings as himself.

Unit one

Listening Comprehension Practice

Listen to the recorded texts and choose the correct answers from the following questions. Tick the box A, B, C or D for the answer of your choice.

Passage I

1 Jane's information comes from a

A   science fiction book

B   newspaper reporter

C   scientific journal

D   reliable journalist

A	
B	
C	
D	

2 Some people may think that Arthur Clarke's revolutionary idea for space travel is merely

A   a hallucination

B   an imaginative exercise

C   a castle in the air

D   an overstatement

A	
B	
C	
D	

3 Jane points out that one of the advantages of cable car space travel would be

A   reduced cost

B   increased speed

C   room for freight

D   greater comfort

A	
B	
C	
D	

4 If the cable became detached from the satellite, it would

A   gravitate to Earth

B   fall upwards

C   encircle the Earth

D   remain in position

A	
B	
C	
D	

5 Disastrous consequences would result from a break in the middle of the cable if it was

A   at an altitude of over 15,000 miles

B   less than 23,000 miles long

C   made of heavy metal

D   not made of steel

A	
B	
C	
D	

6 Tom's attitude towards Arthur Clarke's proposal is

A   disbelieving

B   unenthusiastic

C   disinterested

D   ironic

A	
B	
C	
D	

Passage II

1 The watchers at Warminster are

A   dedicated to making inter-planetary history

B   remarkably dedicated to their belief

C   answerable to world-wide planetary organisations

D   mostly highly trained observers

A	
B	
C	
D	

2 A visitor entering the village of Warminster

A   may notice a smell of fading flowers

B   immediately makes his peace with the world

C   finds the villagers strange and unworldly

D   is impressed by the unusual atmosphere

A	
B	
C	
D	

3 The name 'Warminster' is sometimes thought to derive from the belief that

A   the village was once the site of a convent

B   an ancient chief was drowned there

C   the sky god was protected by a dragon

D   the village was the grave of the sky god

A	
B	
C	
D	

4 It seems to be an established fact that beneath the village of Warminster there
    A are a series of catacombs
    B is an underground reservoir
    C are numerous underground streams
    D is a planned waterway system

A	
B	
C	
D	

5 The UFOs sighted at Warminster are reported to be
    A readily able to vanish
    B uniform in shape and size
    C encircled with fire
    D of no recognisable shape

A	
B	
C	
D	

ORAL SKILLS **D**

Space Travel: Expressions

Listen to the following extract from a dialogue between Mission Control and an astronaut just prior to the launching of the spacecraft, Hermes II.

Unit one

	Mission Control	Hello, Hermes II. This is Mission Control. Are you reading me?
	Captain Daniel Blake	Captain Blake here. Reading you loud and clear.
5	**Mission Control**	Well, hi, Dan. This is Hank. How's it going? You all in good shape?
	Captain Daniel Blake	You better believe it. Everything's looking good.
	Mission Control	No problems with those fuel cells?
	Captain Daniel Blake	No problem. All systems go.
10	**Mission Control**	We're sure glad to hear that, Dan. I guess you don't need me to tell you everyone here sends their best wishes for a successful mission. We'll be with you all the way from count-down to splash-down. Don't forget to bring back a bit of that moon-rock for my back yard.
	Captain Daniel Blake	Sure will, Hank.
15	**Mission Control**	Here we go then. Stand by for count-down: TEN – NINE – EIGHT – SEVEN – SIX – FIVE – FOUR – THREE – TWO – ONE.... We have lift-off! We have a perfect lift-off! Just watch her go! Boy, oh boy, isn't that something!

Note the phrases in the dialogue which have the same meaning as the following:

Can you hear me?
I can hear you perfectly.
Is everyone fit and well?
Of course we are.
We've no problem.
We're ready when you are.
After re-entry into the Earth's atmosphere, the
moment when the module/capsule makes contact with
the sea
Wait – be ready for launching now.
The ten seconds counted aloud to the moment of
launching
The launching of the rocket from its base
Isn't that wonderful, impressive!

Exercise 1

Pair work.
One of you is an astronaut who has just landed safely on another planet. Report your situation and impressions to Mission Control.

ORAL SKILLS **E**
Group Discussion

Space Exploration

scientific research
benefits v. cost
the space race

USE OF ENGLISH **A**
Revision of Present Tenses

N.B. These are Active forms; for Passive forms, see Unit five.

1 Simple Present   Do/Does   Don't/Doesn't do   Do/Does … do?

a	Habitual actions	*I go to Warminster every week-end.*
b	Simple fact	*Does that road lead to Brighton?*
c	Natural and scientific laws	*The sun rises in the East.*
d	For verbs with no Present Continuous form	*I know you believe in UFOs.*

2 Present Continuous   Am/Is/Are doing   Am not/Isn't/Aren't doing
Am/Is/Are   … doing?

a	Action happening now or about this time	*That plane is flying to Los Angeles.*
b	Certain future	*I'm going to Warminster for my holiday.*
c	Temporary habit	*He is revising for his exams this month.*
d	Frequently recurring action	*He is always reading science fiction books.*

3 Present Perfect   Have/Has done   Haven't/Hasn't done   Have/Has … done?
(See also Unit two)

a	Indefinite past	*I have travelled all over the world.*
b	Incomplete action	*We have lived here all our lives.*
c	With 'just' for completed action	*I've just seen a strange object in the sky.*
d	With 'for' for incompleted period of time	*He has studied astronomy for five years.*
e	With 'since' showing when incompleted action began	*They have lived here since Christmas.*
f	With 'ever' expressing any time in the past till now	*Have you ever seen a Flying Saucer?*
g	With 'yet' for questions and negatives	*Have they answered your question yet? They haven't seen a UFO yet.*
h	Completed action which may recur	*He has written several books on the Mayan civilisation.*

Unit one

4 Present Perfect Continuous Have/Has been doing Haven't/Hasn't been doing
Have/Has ... been doing?

Uses are similar to those of the Present Perfect, but this tense is naturally used with
verbs that imply continuity of action, i.e. *watch*, *wait* etc., or with an action that the
speaker feels has been continuous even though it is already completed.

He's been watching TV all day, so it's no wonder he has a headache now.
I've been learning English for two years.
They've been waiting for news of the astronauts for two hours.

Exercise 1

Put a correct Present Tense form of the verb in these sentences.

1 You ever (meet) an astronaut?
2 Mr Bates (say) he often (see) a UFO hovering over his garden shed.
3 What you (think) those flashing lights (be)?
4 The planet Earth (belong) to the galaxy known as the Milky Way.
5 What (be) the markings on that plane which (circle) over the airfield?
6 The pilot (report) that he just (see) a cigar-shaped object over the coast of
California.
7 Research scientists at the Space Laboratory (carry out) investigations into the
possibilities of extra-terrestrial life for the past four years.
8 In spite of the evidence to the contrary, many people still (believe) that some form
of life (exist) on the Moon.
9 An American scientist (state) that he (make) contact with a Venusian who (tell)
him a great deal about inter-planetary communication.
10 (Believe) you that the human remains which Professor Simpson (find) in Central
America (be) those of pre-historic man?
11 The lost city of Atlantis (remain) one of the great mysteries of all time, but in the
book I just (read), it (say) that all the stories about Atlantis (be) nothing but myths.
12 He always (ask) me if it (be) true that the stars (control) our destiny.
13 Mrs Bates (say) she (hope) to see a UFO when she (stay) in Warminster.
14 What you (do) all this time? I (stand) in the garden watching that light which
(keep) flashing on and off over there.
15 The author of this book (advance) a startling theory that there (be) many visitors
from Outer Space who (live) among us today.
16 Why you (not want) to tell me what you just (see)?
17 That TV programme on astrology (not finish) yet?
18 Archaeologists (discover) cave drawings of men who (wear) helmets and shoes.
19 During the last twenty years there (be) a vast increase in the interest people (show)
in popular science.
20 He (not be) ready to publish his thesis yet as he (wait) till he (receive) further
reports on the UFO sightings in Nevada.

Exercise 2

Complete the following passage with a suitable Present Tense verb for each blank.

The National Museum of Mexico ....(1) a quantity of figurines who ....(2) to be
wearing a helmet and a little box on their chest. When you ....(3) them closely, they
.........(4) an astonishing resemblance to our idea of a spaceman. There is also a
similarity between them and the clay figures which archaeologists ....(5) in prehistoric tombs in Japan. Even more intriguing, in the Vera Cruz jungle huge monolithic

heads of black basalt and stone altars ....(6) to light after they had lain buried under the soil and dense undergrowth for thousands of years. One head, nine feet high, ...(7) sixteen tons. The quarry from which the stone ....(8) is over 60 miles away across difficult country and over a 60-foot gorge. Today we ....(9) highly sophisticated equipment to move stone of this weight and size. Archaeologists ....(10) that, like all the figures which they ....(11) in this area, they ....(12) no known American race. The faces ....(13) a look of serenity as though they ....(14) to a different world. They ....(15) close-fitting helmets, a fact which some people ....(16) proves that they ....(17) representations of visitors from space. The sculptors ....(18) them with exquisite care and artistry, and informed opinion ....(19) that they are in fact meant to represent the Sun God, but, if so, the question ....(20), why are they dressed as spacemen?

USE OF ENGLISH **B**
Special Uses

1 'To be' + Infinitive   Am/Is/Are to do

This form is used to express: orders, instructions, facts, enquiries relating to future facts or arrangements:

You are to be in the control room at 8 a.m. precisely.
Peter Hubbard, the archaeologist, is to be one of the team investigating the fossil remains recently found in Central America.
The scientists on board the nuclear submarine are to wear protective clothing.
What am I to do if the machine breaks down?

2 Simple Present   Do/Does

a As firm statement of future fact or arrangement:

Count down begins at 4.25 GMT tomorrow.
Professor Bates and his team leave for Peru early next week.

b With 'if' and 'when' for parallel facts and conditions:

When you pull this switch, the machine stops working.
If Mary starts talking about astrology, I go out of the room.
If George wants to watch TV, we all watch.

c For explanations and information, except when given in the Imperative:

Star-maps help us to learn about the stars, but there is a difficulty owing to the way in which the constellations appear to change when you look at them against the background of the sky during the course of a year. For instance, you look at a star-map for the month of January and see that the constellation Orion is midway between the south-eastern and southern horizon on January 5th at 9 o'clock, but if you look at it at the same time in May, Orion is no longer visible and does not reappear in the evening sky until early November.

d **Dramatic Present,** to describe the sequence of events in a film, play or book:

'The Lost Galaxy' is about a space traveller who visits Earth in the year 2000.
He makes his appearance in a lonely part of the desert in California where he meets a party of tourists and hitches a lift in their car....

3 Present Continuous   Am/Is/Are doing

a For a temporary situation:

The Government is cutting down on the Defence estimates this year.

b For running commentaries on actual events:

Everyone here is waiting expectantly for the first sight of the astronauts. Now the hatch is opening. Someone's coming out. Yes, it's them. They're smiling and waving. Now they're walking up the gangway....

Use the appropriate form of a Present Tense in the following exercises.

Exercise 1

Using **'to be' + Infinitive,** explain from the notes given below the arrangements that have been made for a party to visit a historic castle next Saturday.

Meet 10 a.m. / coach 10.15 a.m. / arrive Castle 11.30 / no cameras or tape-recorders / own packed lunch / introductory talk by Castle Curator / bring notebooks / make notes discuss at next meeting / assemble 5.30 Castle entrance / return coach 5.45 p.m.

Exercise 2

Write sentences using a **Present Tense** form stating the following future facts and arrangements.

1   Speaker – time – place: forthcoming lecture on the Stone Age in Britain
2   Date of closure of current exhibition of Mayan relics
3   Meeting of Geological Society at Canford Caves next month

Exercise 3

Write a running commentary on
either :   the launching of a spacecraft
or :   the sighting of a UFO

Exercise 4

Explain what happens
either :   when you look through a telescope
or :   when you use a camera

USE OF ENGLISH **C**

Expressions of Reassurance

1   Read the following extract from a newspaper report and note the *formal* expressions of reassurance that occur in it.

It is reported that the two astronauts on their way back to Earth from Mars in Hermes II have lost touch with Mission Control. We are assured, however, that *there is no need for alarm.* The trouble is due to a temporary fault in the communications system. *Steps are being taken to rectify this* with the least possible delay and it would appear that *everything is under control*. The situation of these two brave men in their spacecraft *does not give rise to undue anxiety* and Mission Control have announced that they *will take full responsibility* for the safe re-entry of Hermes II and her crew.

There is no need for alarm

Steps are being taken to rectify ...

Everything is under control

... does not give rise to undue anxiety

... will take full responsibility

Exercise 1

Using these expressions in a suitable form, write short paragraphs for a newspaper reassuring readers about the following situations.

a A nuclear submarine is grounded on the sea-bed in the Arctic Ocean. Four men are trapped in the engine room.

b There has been an explosion at a chemical factory in the North of England. Dangerous gases are escaping over the countryside.

2 Read the following dialogue and note the *informal* expressions of reassurance used by Mr Anderson to his young daughter, Mary.

Mr Anderson and Mary are sitting on the beach at a small coastal resort.

Mary	What's that funny light out to sea, Dad?
Mr Anderson	[without looking up from his newspaper] *It's nothing.* Just a flare from some aircraft, I expect.
Mary	It's not a flare. It keeps going on and off.
Mr Anderson	*It isn't anything,* I tell you. Probably just a reflection or something.
Mary	A reflection of what?
Mr Anderson	How should I know? Might be a fisherman signalling. Anyway, *there's no need to worry.* The coastguards'll take care of it, whatever it is.
Mary	I don't like it, Dad. It seems to be going round and round now.
Mr Anderson	*Stop worrying.* I told you, it's only a light from a ship or a plane.
Mary	I'm sure it's getting bigger.
Mr Anderson	Well then, *what are you worrying about?* It must be a plane.
Mary	Please, Dad, do put down your newspaper and look at it properly. You don't think it could be one of those UFO things, do you? Please, have a look.
Mr Anderson	Oh, all right, but it's getting a bit dark to see anything much. Wait a moment – where are my binoculars?
Mary	Here – under your chair.
Mr Anderson	Right. Now, just let me adjust them.... There! What did I tell you? *It's all right – nothing to get in a state about.* It's just the lighthouse out there on the point.

It's nothing

It isn't anything

There's no need to worry

Stop worrying

What are you worrying about?

It's all right

... nothing to get in a state about

Exercise 2

Using as many of these expressions as possible, complete the following dialogue.

Harry It says in the paper that some sacks of radioactive waste material have been dumped on a rubbish heap somewhere near here.

Bob ....

Harry What do you mean – 'it's nothing to do with us'? Unless we know exactly where it is, we might get contaminated.

Bob ....

Harry I know we're only sitting in a field eating sandwiches, but there's a heap of something over there in that corner. What do you think it is?

Bob ....

Harry How can you say it's nothing? It must be something.

Bob ....

Harry You can't say turnip tops and bits of wood aren't anything. Anyway, there's a tarpaulin over most of it. The sacks may be underneath that.

Bob ....

Harry I'm not getting in a state. I know the farmer knows what he's doing, I just think we oughtn't to take any unnecessary risks, that's all.

Bob ....

Harry If you're so sure it is the farmer, and you've just said there's nothing to worry about, what are you getting up for?

Bob This is a private field. Didn't you see that notice on the gate as we came in?

Exercise 3

Fill each of the numbered blanks in the following passage with one suitable word.

Searchers for other intelligent ....(1) in the universe are perpetually ....(2) with the problem of finding the most effective means of ....(3) with them. How ....(4) we send the message? What ....(5) can we provide about ....(6) that will be immediately understood by intelligences to ....(7) our form of spoken ....(8) may be completely ....(9)? In 1972 a plaque was ....(10) to the stars on Pioneer 10. This, drawn by Professor Drake, Professor Carl Sagan and his wife, Linda, showed a naked man and woman and indicated the ....(11) of the Earth in ....(12). However, ...(13) to the relatively slow speed of the Pioneer spaceship, the chance of the message being picked ....(14) by an alien in the first ten million years of its ....(15) was minimal. A message sent by radio offers the most ....(16) chance of success. Such a message can be sent ....(17) the speed of light, ...(18) is nearly 26,000 ....(19) faster ....(20) the Pioneer spacecraft.

'A small step for a man, a giant leap for mankind' (Neil Armstrong – 21 July 1969)

WRITTEN SKILLS **A**

Note-taking

Information from many sources such as textbooks, TV, radio and tapes, as well as from lectures, talks and discussions, can be systematically tabulated in note form for future reference. The note-taker requires the ability to recognise and extract the main points and to be able to set them down clearly using the minimum number of words while keeping the notes intelligible. Therefore a strict discipline has to be kept to and all inessential details ignored and superfluous words eliminated. The following points are offered as a guide to note-taking.

Unit one

From Speech

1 Listen to each complete sentence.

2 After each group of sentences, often indicated by speaker pausing, get down main points/facts.

3 Number and underline all main points.

4 Jot down any relevant details under the main points.

5 At the end of the lecture/talk, write down a title which clearly states the topic/subject. Underline.

6 Systematically arrange the points/facts in order of importance so that they can be read and understood easily.

From Written Texts

1 Read each complete sentence.

2 At the end of each paragraph, select and write down all main points/facts.

3 Number and underline all main points.

4 Recognise and write down any relevant details under the main points.

5 At the end of the chapter/paper, write down a title, if one is not already given, which clearly shows the subject matter. Underline.

6 Systematically arrange the points/facts in order of importance so that they can be read and understood easily.

The following is an article from a magazine.

Man has always been curious and since prehistoric times he has looked for new lands to conquer. First he explored his cave, then the land, next the sea and eventually the air. Now, finally, Man is exploring space and his dream of leaving the Earth has come true.

5   This wish to leave the Earth and reach other planets was first mentioned in the second century AD, when a Greek, Lucian of Samos, wrote two fantasies about men who went to the Moon; one used a pair of wings made by himself while the other was carried there by a waterspout during a storm. The Moon was the obvious destination in early literature as it is the nearest planet to the Earth and

10 has clearly visible markings which led to imaginative conjecture about life there.

    But after Lucian, for the next 1,400 years no other writings about travelling to the Moon have survived. Man seemed content in his belief that the Earth was the most important planet in the centre of the universe and therefore there was no

15 necessity to leave it. This view was reinforced by the Christian Church and in 1543 Copernicus was condemned as heretical when he published his revolutionary theory that the Sun was the centre of the universe and the Earth, Moon and other planets revolved about it. Although this theory was criticised it started men thinking about the stars again.

20   Not long afterwards the first telescope was invented in Holland and Galileo, the brilliant Italian astronomer, used one to explore the heavens and discover much new information about the planets. When his observations were published in 1610 the Church threatened to excommunicate him so he retracted most of his statements. But Man's imagination had been stirred by this new knowledge and in

25 1634, Kepler, the German astronomer who had discovered how the planets moved round the Sun, published a story about a journey to the Moon. His hero was transported there by 'magic moon people' who could fly through space. Included

in the story was a detailed description of the Moon's surface which Kepler had
seen through his telescope.

30 After Kepler's book, there were many more stories about space travel and
voyages to the Moon. Mostly they were fantasies but some contained attempts at
scientific reasoning. Then in 1640, Bishop Watkins wrote the first serious
discussion of space travel, describing physical conditions on the Moon and
proposing ways in which Man could possibly live there. Rockets were first

35 suggested as spaceships by Cyrano de Bergerac in two space adventures
written in 1649 and 1652. He was also the first writer to send his space travellers to
the Sun as well as to the Moon.

But when these books were written over 300 years ago, no one seriously thought
that it would be possible to travel in space. It was not until Jules Verne, the French

40 novelist, wrote his famous story 'From the Earth to the Moon' in 1865 that any
attempt was made to apply known scientific principles to spacecraft. Man had been
experimenting with flying ever since 1783 – the advent of the first hot air balloon.
But although various gliders and airships were invented, it wasn't until 1903 that
the first powered flight was made by the Wright brothers in a wooden biplane. By

45 this time H. G. Wells had already published his famous space stories, 'The Time
Machine' and 'The First Men on the Moon', so once again writers were leading
the way. Wells' prophecy, in the latter story, wasn't to come true until 1969 when
the two Americans, Armstrong and Aldrin, finally stepped out on to the Moon's
surface.

50 Since then rockets have landed on Venus and Mars and with the launching
of the space shuttle, it will not be long before men visit other planets.
Then it will be interesting to see if Wells' other prophecy will come true and
man will travel faster than light. Will he, in fact, build his own time machine
and travel through time as well as space? Many modern science fiction writers have

55 gone far beyond this speculation and have their heroes teleporting from spaceship
to planet with the greatest ease, dematerialising and materialising again at will,
and making loops with time to unite past and future without effort. How much of
this will come true we can only guess. But one thing we can be sure of is that
writers will continue to stimulate our imagination with marvellous adventures,

60 spectacular prophecies and astounding ideas, some of which, no doubt, will come
true and change fiction to fact.

Now let us apply the points of the suggested guide to note-taking.

1 Read each complete paragraph.

2 Select and write down all the main points/facts.

Para. 1 Man curious – explores all possible places – now exploring space – dreams of
leaving Earth

Para. 2 C2 AD first space fantasies – Lucian of Samos. Moon earliest destination –
proximity to Earth

Para. 3 Writers silent for next 1,400 years. 1543 Copernicus theory – planets revolve
round Sun – stimulates thought

Para. 4 Telescope invented – 1610 Galileo published observations of planets –
writer's imagination stirred. 1634 Kepler published story of journey to Moon –
incorporated details seen through telescope

Para. 5 C17 many stories about space travel (to Moon). 1640 Bishop Watkins – first
serious discussion. 1649/52 Cyrano de Bergerac first used rockets as
spaceships in fantasies – sent travellers to Sun & Moon

Para. 6   C19 actual space travel not taken seriously. 1865 Jules Verne applied known scientific principles to spacecraft in story. 1783 – first hot air balloon, 1903 – first powered flight, 1969 – first men on Moon – prophesied by H. G. Wells

Para. 7   C20 – rockets to Venus & Mars. Modern writers prophesy time travel, time loops, dematerialisation. Will fiction become fact?

3   Number and underline each main point.

1   Man curious – began exploring
2   C2 AD – first space fantasies
3   Writers of space fantasy silent for 1,400 years
4   Early 1600s – telescope invented
5   C17 – many stories about space travel
6   C19 – space travel not taken seriously
7   C20 – first men on Moon – space exploration

N.B. Although the information about the first men on the Moon actually came in para. 6, when making main headings it more logically goes in para. 7 with C20 space exploration.

4   Recognise and write down any relevant details under the main points.

1   Man curious
Explores all possible places
Now exploring space
Has always dreamt of leaving Earth
2   C2 AD – first space fantasies
Lucian of Samos – Greek
Moon earliest destination – proximity to Earth
Visible markings led to imaginative conjecture
3   Writers of space fantasy silent for 1,400 years
Earth thought to be centre of universe – Church support
1543 – Copernicus theory – planets revolve round sun – heretical
Thought of stars again stimulated
4   Early 1600s – telescope invented
1610 – Galileo used telescope – published observations of planets – writer's imagination stirred
1634 – Kepler published story of journey to Moon – incorporated details seen through telescope
5   C17 – many stories about space travel
1640 – Bishop Watkins – first serious discussion
1649/52 – Cyrano de Bergerac used rockets as spaceships in his fantasies – first writer to send travellers to Sun as well as Moon
6   C19 – actual space travel not taken seriously
1865 – Jules Verne first writer to apply known scientific principles to spacecraft in story
Man's exploration of flight – 1783 – first hot air balloon
                                                    1903 – first powered flight – Wright Bros. – biplane
H. G. Wells – prophesied men on the Moon – time machines
7   C20 – first men on Moon – space exploration
1969 – First men on the Moon
Rockets to Venus and Mars
Modern writers prophesy time travel, time loops, dematerialisation
Will fiction become fact?

5   At the end of the paper or text, write down a title that clearly shows the subject matter. Underline.
Possible title: <u>Writers lead the way in space exploration.</u>

6   Systematically arrange the points in order of importance so that they can be read and understood easily.

In this case the points lead on logically from each other so no rearrangement is necessary (see **3** previous page). The title of course goes first.

This information could, in fact, be tabulated even more precisely as a Time Chart:

Time Chart

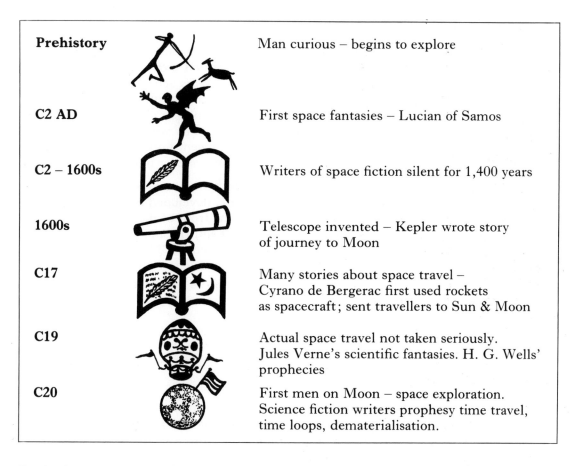

Prehistory		Man curious – begins to explore
C2 AD		First space fantasies – Lucian of Samos
C2 – 1600s		Writers of space fiction silent for 1,400 years
1600s		Telescope invented – Kepler wrote story of journey to Moon
C17		Many stories about space travel – Cyrano de Bergerac first used rockets as spacecraft; sent travellers to Sun & Moon
C19		Actual space travel not taken seriously. Jules Verne's scientific fantasies. H. G. Wells' prophecies
C20		First men on Moon – space exploration. Science fiction writers prophesy time travel, time loops, dematerialisation.

Study the above note-taking carefully and then apply the same principles in the following exercises.

Exercise 1

Consider the following paragraphs carefully and then make brief notes on each one.

1   In recent years UFO spotting has become a serious pastime for many people; young and old, scientists, artists, government officials, housewives and children, clutching cameras, tape recorders and notebooks, all ascend hills and solemnly perch on

the tops, sometimes all night, waiting for a sighting. Hundreds of unexplained bright lights, weird shapes and strange noises have been reported, but so far the definitive, irrefutable, scientifically proved sighting has not occurred. However, the spotters are not discouraged and are convinced that encounters of the third kind are not far in the future. Perhaps the beliefs of present-day spotters are not so new, for in 1670 John Aubrey reported a sighting as witnessed by a Mr W. Lilly as follows: 'Not far from Cirencester was an Apparition. Being demanded, whether a good spirit or a bad, returned no answer but disappeared with a curious perfume, and a melodious twang. Mr W. Lilly believes it to be a fairy.'

2   When Russia's Cosmos 954 satellite broke from its orbit to plunge earthwards on to Canada in January 1978, it wasn't the first nor the largest object to fall from space to land on Earth. Natural missiles, such as meteorites, also bomb the Earth. Thousands of rock fragments enter the Earth's atmosphere from space every day. Most are burnt out during their descent – sometimes their 'deaths' can be seen as pin-pricks of light shooting across the sky. We call them shooting stars. But the fragments that do survive and reach the Earth are called meteorites. Their origins are not clear, but the most widely accepted theory is that they are the remains of asteroids that disintegrated thousands of millions of years ago. Some 2,000 sites of meteorite falls have been found and evidence of giant meteorites comes from the craters made by their impact. In 1976 an American geologist claimed he had found a 150-mile-wide crater in Antarctica, which was caused by what he believed to be the largest meteorite ever to strike the Earth. More recent finds in Antarctica have included a meteorite weighing 900 lb., one of the largest ever uncovered.

3   A setback recently occurred in the USA's plans to fly the first shuttle. The Enterprise, which was to have been the first shuttle, developed major faults in the pumps, and was also found to be too heavy. The front of the Enterprise, therefore, is to be joined to the back of another test shuttle, and the resultant hybrid carries a space lab and the first European spaceman. The number of shuttles to be put into service has been reduced from five to four owing to cuts in NASA's budget. The Russians, who are also developing a space shuttle, hope to fly it before the Enterprise.

Exercise 2

Make brief notes on the following article.

Ever since October 1957, when the Russians sent up the first artificial satellite, Sputnik I, to orbit the Earth, there has been an escalation of interest in space exploration. Only four months after Sputnik I the Americans launched their first satellite, Explorer I; and then the space race began. For many years the Russians
5   and Americans competed with each other and it has only been recently in the seventies that they have agreed to co-operate on some projects.

After the achievement of the early satellites the next landmark in space travel was the putting of the first man into space. Once again the Russians were first, and Yuri Gagarin orbited the Earth in a Vostok spacecraft in April 1961, a mere three
10   and a half years after the launching of the first satellite. The Russians then went on to achieve their triple first with the landing of a robot explorer, Luna IX, on the Moon in 1966. It was from Luna IX that the first TV pictures of the Moon were transmitted to Earth.

15 Several more robot spacecraft explored the Moon's atmosphere and surface until finally, in July 1969, the first men landed and walked on the Moon's surface. These were of course, the famous Americans, Neil Armstrong and Edwin Aldrin, and probably everyone has seen TV pictures or photographs of this historic event.

20 Since then robot spacecraft have been sent to photograph other planets in the solar system, and spacecraft packed with scientific equipment have landed on Mars and Venus and relayed information back to the Earth. Pioneer X, an American spacecraft, passed the planet Jupiter in 1973 and sent back pictures and information to the Earth before moving on to the outer planets and the limits of the solar system, which it finally left altogether. Two more spaceships, the Voyagers I and II, were sent to the outer planets to transmit information and photographs

25 of Jupiter and its 13 moons before passing on to Saturn and its rings. The Voyager II will then continue its journey to reach Uranus in 1986 and finally Neptune will be approached in 1989.

More recently the trend has been away from exploring the furthest limits of the solar system and attention has been centred on putting space stations into orbit

30 round the Earth, in the hope that they will eventually become permanent and so provide Man with a jumping-off stage for reaching other planets. In September 1977 the Russians put up the Salyut VI space station, which was the first to be fully operational. The two Russian cosmonauts, Yuri Romanenko and Georgi Grechko, lived in the station from its launching until March 1978, a period of 94

35 days, thereby setting up a new space endurance record. The Russians have since completed a 180-day mission, the two-man crews only being changed every six months.

The Salyut VI is expected to remain in space for as long as five years, being refuelled and supplied by the unmanned Progress I spacecraft. Eventually, the

40 Russians hope to join several Salyut spacecraft in modules to assemble a truly permanent space station.

The Russians also intend to send cosmonauts from all the Intercosmos countries into space by 1983. The first step has been taken by sending a Czechoslovak cosmonaut to Salyut VI and they are planning to send a Polish cosmonaut into

45 space this year. Eventually representatives from all the Eastern European countries, Mongolia, and Cuba will have made space flights. This will break the US/Soviet monopoly of space.

The Americans expect to launch their four-man space lab, which has been developed in co-operation with the European Space Agency, in 1981. They intend

50 to man it with mixed American/European crews. Space will then become really 'international'.

Notes, of course, can also be made from spoken material. It is not quite so easy, as you cannot check back if you miss something; but remember, most lectures or discussions have a question period at the end when you can ask the speaker to clarify any points you are not clear about, or to fill you in on any information you may have missed. Apply all the points as offered in the guide to note-taking under the heading 'From Speech' and you should be able to produce a result as clearly as from written material.

Read or listen to the following lecture; take notes and arrange them systematically at the end of the lecture.

(The lecture will be found in the Appendix)

WRITTEN SKILLS **B**

Expanding Notes

In the Cambridge Certificate of Proficiency Paper 2, Composition, you will be asked to write two out of five compositions. One of these may require you to expand notes into a coherent and well-written piece of English. These notes may, for example, be in the form of factual lists, brief personal comment, lecture notes, telephone messages, etc. for expansion into an article, letter or report. The principle of expansion is opposite to note-taking, and you will probably have to use your imagination to expand the notes successfully. Keep the following points in mind when you begin.

How to expand notes

1   Read the question carefully and make sure you know what to do.
2   Study the given information and decide which are the most important points/facts.
3   Make sure you include all the information given, if asked to do so.
4   Write down the points/facts and underline.
5   Jot down under the main points any details or extra information that you can think of.
6   Join up all the details/information into well-constructed sentences. If necessary, leave out some points in order to keep within a given word limit.
7   Link the sentences logically, forming paragraphs.
8   Check through for correct structures and punctuation.

The following is a comparison of the planets in our solar system. The specimen exercise shows how to write approximately 250 words giving a brief introduction to the solar system, using the information given.

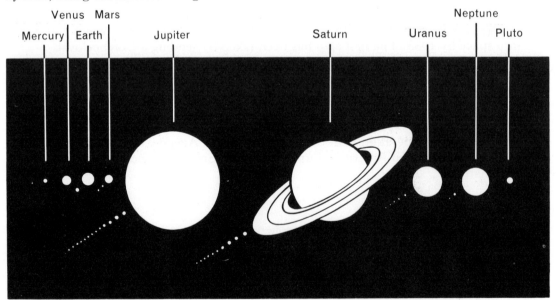

The Solar System (part of Milky Way galaxy)
9 planets, 33 moons or satellites, thousands of asteroids

Sun – centre of system, star, one of millions in galaxy. 865,000 miles in diameter – million times larger than Earth. Ball of gases – hydrogen and helium – react like H-bomb explosion. Very hot. Supplies heat and light to maintain life on Earth.

Planetary Information

Planet	distance in millions of miles from sun	satellites	diameter in miles	maximum surface temp. (degrees centigrade)	special characteristics	information sent back by
MERCURY	36		3,100	400	craters on surface	Mariner X 1974
VENUS	67		7,700	350	dense dust clouds	Mariner X 1974
EARTH	93	1 (Moon)	7,926	60	life, vegetation	–
MARS	141	2	4,200	25	red soil	Vikings I & II 1976
JUPITER	483	13	88,700	– 140	liquid	Pioneer X 1973
SATURN	886	10	75,100	– 160	rings (ice chips)	Voyagers I & II 1979
URANUS	1,783	5	29,600	– 210	spins on axis side on	Voyager II 1980s
NEPTUNE	2,793	2	27,700	– 230	very dense	
PLUTO	3,666	halo of comets	thought to be about 3,600	not known	eccentric orbit	

Now let us apply the points of the suggested guide to note expansion.

1 Read the question carefully:
   Write about 250 words – giving a brief introduction to the solar system

2 Study given information – decide most important points/facts:
   Brief description of sun and planets; comparison of information given

3 Include all information given if asked to:
   In this exercise you are not required to include everything

4 Write down/consider points/facts – underline

5 Look at given information again. Add extra relevant information.

   a Solar System
      In Milky Way galaxy – contains 9 planets, 33 satellites, thousands of asteroids.

   b Sun
      Star, one of millions in M.W. galaxy. Centre of solar system. Composed of gases – helium and hydrogen – react like H-bomb explosion producing intense heat/light which maintains life on Earth. V. large in comparison with planets.

c Mercury
Smallest planet in system, nearest to Sun therefore very hot with surface temp. 400°C. Has craters on surface similar to the Moon. Visited in 1974 by Mariner X, which also sent back information about Venus.

d Venus
Similar in size to Earth, but much hotter (350°C). Very difficult to see as covered by dense dust clouds.

e Earth
Supports many life forms. Has one satellite, the Moon. Roughly the same size as Venus.

f Mars
Known as the Red Planet because of colour of the soil. Most Earth-like of planets but colder and much smaller. Visits of Vikings I and II in 1976 confirmed life unlikely.

g Jupiter
Largest of the planets, composed of liquid and gases. Is extremely cold and has 13 satellites, 4 of them as big as Mercury. Information sent back by Pioneer X in 1973, Voyagers I & II in 1979.

h Saturn
Large planet, extremely cold. Most interesting feature is the rings which circle it, composed of ice particles. 10 satellites, largest as big as Mars.

i Uranus/Neptune/Pluto
Planets on fringe of solar system. All extremely cold as farthest from Sun. Uranus spins at an angle to its orbit, Neptune is very dense and Pluto has an eccentric orbit. More information about them will come from Voyager II in the 1980s.

6 Join up all the information/details into well-constructed sentences. If necessary, leave out some points in order to keep within given word limit:

The Sun, a star, one of many millions in the Milky Way galaxy, is the centre of the solar system. It is composed mainly of the gases helium and hydrogen, which react together causing H-bomb type explosions. The resulting heat and light maintain life on the planet Earth. The Sun is very large in comparison with its 9 orbiting planets which, in turn, are circled by a total of 33 satellites. Jupiter, the largest of the planets, has the most satellites, 13 in all, 4 of which are as large as the smallest planet, Mercury. Being 483 million miles from the Sun, Jupiter is very cold and consists of liquids and gases which have never solidified. Even further from the Sun, the planet Saturn is consequently colder and is circled by rings made up of ice particles. At the fringe of the solar system, the outer planets, Uranus, Neptune and Pluto have temperatures as low as −200°C. Little is known of these planets, but more information will be available after the visits of Voyagers I & II in the 1980s. The two hot planets are Mercury, the smallest and hottest with a surface temperature of 400°C and a strange cratered lunar appearance, and Venus, which is covered in dense dust clouds. Both were visited by Mariner X in 1974. Earth, as we know, has a more equable climate and supports a rich life system. Originally, Mars, the most Earth-like of the other planets, was thought to be the most likely to support a form of human life as well, but since the visit of Vikings I and II this now seems unlikely. It is both smaller and colder than Earth.

7 Link the sentences logically, forming paragraphs – add a title.

possible title: **The Solar System**

suggested paragraphs: *1* The Sun, a star ....

2 Jupiter, the largest of the planets.........................

3 The two hot planets ....

8 Check through for correct structures and punctuation.

Exercise 1

Study the following diagram carefully; then apply the principles of note expansion and write 200–250 words about the problems of wearing a lunar spacesuit.

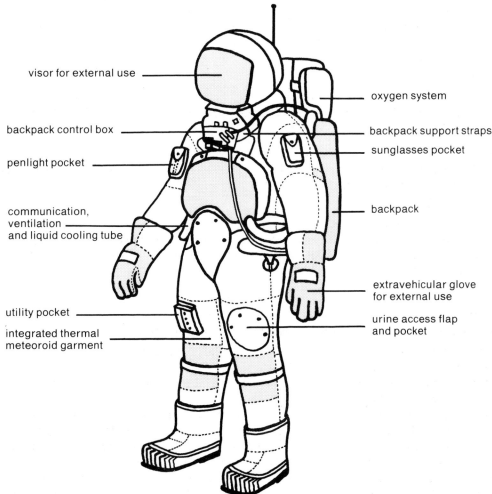

Exercise 2

From the following notes on a science fiction book, write a newspaper review of 2 or 3 paragraphs (about 200 words).

Set in the 21st century – people living on Mars – adapted to climate – resisting attacks from Earth – a dying planet – inter-planetary war – sophisticated weapons – laser guns – microwave guns – death rays – unexpected help from aliens from Andromeda galaxy – sinister motivation – control of Mars – plot discovered – Earth and Mars unite – defeat Andromedans – co-existence on Mars.

REMINDER 1
Capital Letters

don't let your words all look like these
use some CAPITAL LETTERS please

Capital Letters: fourteen points to remember

Use a Capital Letter for the first letter of:

1 Names of people and titles — Peter, Mr Brown, King George VI, Colonel Stevenson, Dr Jones

2 Countries, islands, continents — France, Crete, Asia

3 Counties, cities, towns, villages Districts, streets — Sussex, Paris, Richmond Westminster, Oxford Street

4 Rivers and seas Mountains and hills — the Thames, the Pacific Ocean the Alps, Mount Everest, the Sussex Downs

5 States and named geographical areas — Alabama, the Lake District, the Sahara Desert

6 Months, days of the week (but not usually seasons, e.g. winter) Festivals — March, April Wednesday, Friday Christmas, Easter

7 Historical periods and events — the Middle Ages, World War II

8 Languages, names and adjectives of nationality — French, Italian, Spanish a Spaniard, an Indian, a German lesson, an English teacher

9 Planets, stars, galaxies, constellations, etc. BUT only for the sun and moon when personified, or when referred to as planets — the Earth, Mercury, the Milky Way the sun sets in the west the Sun in all his glory rises ...

10 Stations, airports, historic buildings — Victoria, London Airport, the Tower of London

11 Titles of books, plays, films, poems, etc. — the Bible, Romeo and Juliet, Star Wars, The Waste Land

12 Organisations (also in abbreviated form) and political parties — the British Broadcasting Corporation (the BBC), the Labour Party

13 At the beginning of every sentence — He looked up. There was a strange red light in the sky. It seemed to be getting bigger....

14 At the beginning of speech — He said, 'Come in'.

N.B. Capital letters are NOT used to describe occupations or general subjects of study, unless they form part of a specific title:

He is a well-known archaeologist
He is Professor of Archaeology at the State University

Exercise

Insert the necessary capital letters in the following passage.

Professor Arnold Smith, who has spent a lifetime studying prehistoric remains, claims that the bones he unearthed in the Californian desert area last May are those of a man-like creature existing millions of years ago, probably at a time when the Pacific Ocean covered much more of the surface of this part of the American continent. Professor Smith is to give a talk on the subject on BBC television on Monday, 4th April, in the series, 'Where Did We Come From?' This is to be followed by a discussion with members of the Lost Atlantis Society whose president, Colonel Arthur Stone, contends that California is in fact part of the legendary city, the remainder of which lies hidden under the sea. He is urging the U.S.A. government to conduct research into this theory, but the project has not met with much enthusiasm from scientists who say that if Atlantis ever existed, it is far more likely to be found in the area known as the Bermuda Triangle. In the meantime Steven Hughes, professor of antediluvian history at Aberdeen University, has come up with the theory that Atlantis was in reality an area of land joining the east coast of Ireland to Britain and that many of the Scottish islands, notably the Hebrides, provide conclusive evidence that Atlanteans once lived in this area.

Unit two Employment

ORAL SKILLS A

Intensive Listening

A small factory making electrical components has been taken over by a large nation-wide company. As a result 300 men and women have lost their jobs. Mrs Sally Jenkins, Shadow Minister for Industrial Expansion, has been asked to address a meeting of the redundant workers. Listen to this extract from her speech.

Mrs Jenkins First of all, I want you to know I'm on your side. When I came here a few months ago, I promised to do everything in my power to ensure that there were no redundancies as a result of the take-over. I raised the question both in the House of Commons and in

5 committee. Those responsible assured me that there were guide-lines laid down to prevent the redundancy or re-deployment of workers who wished to remain in their jobs. I told them this was a small factory employing a high proportion of local workers, who had lived in the district all their lives, and were justly proud of

10 their reputation for high-speed production and loyal service. I laid the facts fairly and squarely before them. They listened, they nodded, they promised. The matter gave rise to long-winded discussions on the question of take-overs in general. But as far as this factory is concerned, they did nothing – absolutely nothing.

15   I am forced to the conclusion that they did not want to do
anything, that they never had any intention of doing anything!
    Let me say to you, here and now, that we, the members of my
party, are not going to take this lying down. Three hundred men
and women, some of whom were working in this factory before
20   some of the members of the present Government were born, are
today walking the streets having been made redundant without even
the prospect of another job. 'But we gave them redundancy pay,'
they say, 'we patted them on the back and thanked them for all
their hard work, what are they grumbling about?' Well, it was
25   hardly a golden handshake they gave you, was it? Six months' pay
without overtime – the company that's in control of your factory
now spent twice that on car allowances for their executives alone
last year, to say nothing of increases in salary. When did you last
get a rise? Not much chance of getting one now, is there?
30   I'm not going to lie to you. Unemployment rose by 2,500 last
month. Fifteen hundred of those laid down their tools in the name
of redundancy. Three hundred of that number are, guess who ...
YOU. The remedy lies in positive action ...

Exercise 1

Listen to the speech again and then answer questions 1–4 by putting a tick (✓) in one
of the boxes A, B, C or D.

1   Mrs Jenkins tried to prevent redundancies at the factory by

   A   having the problem discussed in Parliament
   B   getting the workers on her side
   C   questioning the committees in the House of Commons
   D   discussing the take-over with the workers

A	
B	
C	
D	

2   To support her argument, Mrs Jenkins mentions that the factory

   A   only employs people who live in the district
   B   has a reputation for loyalty to the workers
   C   had a good record of high productivity
   D   employed a lot of workers for its size

A	
B	
C	
D	

3   Why was it particularly shameful, in her eyes, for some of the workers to be made
redundant?

   A   They were incapable of getting another job
   B   They had given good service for many years
   C   They were too old to ever work again
   D   They got no help from the Government due to their age

A	
B	
C	
D	

4   The redundant workers were not given a 'golden handshake' because

   A   they refused to work 6 months' overtime
   B   the company didn't think they were worth it
   C   they were always complaining about the work
   D   the company preferred to spend the money elsewhere

A	
B	
C	
D	

ORAL SKILLS **B**

Expressions with Raise/Rise and Lay/Lie

Note the meanings of the following expressions used by Mrs Jenkins in her speech.

1 *I raised the question*   I asked for the problem to be considered
     The matter gave rise to   It caused
     When did you last get a rise?   An increase in salary or wages
     Unemployment rose by 2,500   The number of unemployed increased by 2,500

2 *I laid the facts fairly and squarely before them*   I gave an honest explanation of the matter
     We ... are not going to take this lying down   We are determined to do something about it
     The remedy lies in positive action   Our best course is to do something positive about the situation

See also Use of English C, page 41.

Exercise 1

Using one of these expressions in a suitable form, re-phrase the following sentences. For example:

He never had any increase in wages all the time he worked for that firm.
He never had a rise all the time he worked for that firm.
She always protested strongly about any criticism of her work.
She never took any criticism of her work lying down.

1 The wages dispute has caused considerable unrest among the staff.

    ....

2 The Union spokesman explained to the Management the exact reasons for the workers' present dissatisfaction.

    ....

3 Since last year there has been an increase in unemployment of approximately 50,000 workers.

    ....

4 It was agreed that the workers should get an increase of 10% of their gross earnings.

    ....

5 The Managing Director introduced the subject of expense accounts at the last Board Meeting.

    ....

6 The electricity workers were mistaken in thinking that the public would accept further power cuts without protest.

    ....

7 The Minister said that the only way to decrease unemployment was to reduce Company Tax.

    ....

ORAL SKILLS **C**

Dialogue

Listen to this dialogue between the Managing Director of a company and the Personnel Manager.

Man. Director	Well, Saunders, how did you get on with those applicants for the Sales Rep. job this morning?
Saunders	Not a very promising lot, I'm afraid. There was only one graduate and the rest hadn't got half a dozen O-levels between them.
Man. Director	I can't work out why you personnel people make such a fuss about qualifications. I didn't have any when I joined the firm. I started on the factory floor, sweeping, making tea, being a general dogsbody. In my day you worked your way up the hard way.
Saunders	I'm afraid things don't work quite like that now, sir. Industry needs graduates.
Man. Director	Graduates in what?
Saunders	I don't think it's of prime importance what the person's graduated *in*. What I learnt at university was how to use my mind, exercise my own judgement, distinguish the essential from the inessential ...
Man. Director	Yes, yes. Don't get so worked up about it.
Saunders	Well, I do feel rather strongly about it, sir. Do you realise that there were more graduates out of work than in work last year? That can't be good.
Man. Director	All right, all right, Saunders. Now, what about this applicant you said had a degree? Do you think we should engage him?
Saunders	Yes, sir, I do. He's got a degree in applied psychology. He's a nice chap – he's fond of animals – in fact he started out by wanting to be a vet. What's more, he's working on a thesis.
Man. Director	A thesis? On what?
Saunders	Something to do with the influence of the subconscious on door-to-door selling. Could be quite good for a Rep., that.
Man. Director	Can't see how that helped him if he wanted to be a vet.
Saunders	Well, perhaps not, sir. Still, he took a job after that selling encyclopaedias, but at the moment he's got a job in the Haematology Department of the local hospital. He's quite presentable, about six foot, he's got a very slight squint but not so you'd notice – oh, and he did quite a lot of boxing at university ...
Man. Director	SAUNDERS! Do I understand that your idea of a promising Sales Rep. is a cross-eyed giant who spends his time analysing the office cat, taking blood samples from our customers and knocking them out when he doesn't get any orders?
Saunders	I'm sorry, sir, I was only trying to work out ...
Man. Director	Well, don't. I'll see the next bunch myself.

Listen to this dialogue again and then discuss the Managing Director's attitude.

Unit two

Note the following expressions with 'work' used in the dialogue and their meanings.

I can't work out	I am unable to understand why ...
You worked your way up	You started at the bottom and gradually got promotion
Things don't work quite like that	That is not the way things happen/are organised
Don't get so worked up about it	Don't get so excited/upset
out of work	unemployed
in work	employed
he was working on	doing some concentrated work

Here are some further expressions with *work*

work to death	make someone work excessively hard
work to rule	impede efficiency by adhering closely to every rule: a substitute for a strike
work up	gradually bring to an efficient state
work away at	work hard on a particular project
work on someone	exert influence on someone

Exercise 1

Using one of the expressions with 'work' in a suitable form, re-phrase the following sentences.

Example

The staff refused to do any overtime.
The staff insisted on *working to rule*.

1   The foreman has been trying to persuade Jones to join the Union.
    The foreman has been ....

2   My neighbour has not had a job for six years.
    My neighbour has been ....

3   I couldn't understand why Harris didn't apply for that job.
    I couldn't...

4   Why did John get so upset about going for that interview?
    Why did John get so ....

5   His self-confidence increased as soon as he got a job again.
    His self-confidence increased as soon as he ....

6   He was gradually promoted from post boy to Managing Director.
    He gradually ....

7   Don't interrupt Mr Barker, he's concentrating on the sales figures.
    Don't interrupt Mr Barker, he's ....

8   The Manager of that company makes his staff work excessively hard.
    The Manager of that company ....

9   Several trains have been cancelled because the staff are refusing to do any overtime.
    Several trains have been cancelled because the staff ....

10 The filing system isn't organised like that in our office.
    The filing system doesn't ....

34

ORAL SKILLS **D**
Passage for Discussion

Read or listen to this extract from an essay on 'Work' by the nineteenth-century
English author and art critic John Ruskin. Be prepared to discuss it.

    ... Here we have an inevitable distinction. There *must* be work done by the arms,
or none of us could live. There *must* be work done by the brains, or the life we get
would not be worth having. And the same men cannot do both. There is rough
work to be done and rough men must do it; there is gentle work to be done and
5   gentlemen must do it; and it is physically impossible that one class should do, or
divide the work of the other. And it is of no use to try to conceal this sorrowful
fact by fine words, and to talk to the workman about the honourableness of manual
labour, and the dignity of humanity....
    Rough work, honourable or not, takes the life out of us; and the man who has
10   been heaving clay out of a ditch all day, or driving an express train against the
north wind all night, or holding a ship's helm in a gale, or whirling white-hot iron
at a furnace mouth, that man is not the same at the end of his day, or night, as one
who has been sitting in a quiet room, with everything comfortable about him,
reading books, or classing butterflies, or painting pictures. If it is any comfort to
15   you to be told that the rough work is the more honourable of the two, I should be
sorry to take that consolation from you; and in some sense I need not. The rough
work is at all events real, honest, and generally, though not always, useful; while
the fine work is, a great deal of it, foolish and false as well as fine, and therefore
dishonourable; but when both kinds are equally well and worthily done, the head's
20   is the noble work and the hand's the ignoble....

(*ignoble*.... mean, base, dishonourable)

N.B. John Ruskin (1819–1900) helped to establish the Pre-Raphaelite school of
painters. He held strong views on social problems and tried to use his wealth for
education and non-profitmaking enterprises. Ruskin College at Oxford, the first
residential college for working people, is named after him.

ORAL SKILLS **E**

Photograph for Discussion

Look at this photograph of factory workers and be prepared to talk about it.

Questions

1 What can you see in the picture?
2 What does the man in the foreground seem to be doing?
3 Would you consider this skilled or unskilled work?
4 Do the men seem to be enjoying their work?

Topics

Skilled and unskilled work.

The threat of automation/unemployment.

The revival of certain industries (bicycles).

ORAL SKILLS **F**
Expressions of Encouragement

Listen to this dialogue between Anne, who has been trying to get a job for six months, and Maureen, who starts work in her first job next week. Both girls have completed a secretarial course.

Anne   Oh dear, that's the fifth job I haven't got today. The trouble is I've got no experience. They weren't interested in my shorthand and typing speeds; they just kept saying they wanted someone with experience.

Maureen   *Don't let it get you down.* I went to at least ten interviews before I got my job and each time I came away feeling like a squashed fly. I couldn't believe it when that girl at the Job Centre rang to tell me I'd got this job with the recording company.

Anne   I wish I had. They turned me down, remember?

Maureen   It was just a bit of luck, really.

Anne   Well, I'm not lucky like you are. I'm sick of looking for a job.

Maureen   *Oh, something'll turn up,* you'll see. I felt just like you do. I was looking for work for three months before I got this.

Anne   I feel like packing the whole thing in and living on Social Security.

Maureen   *Oh, don't give up now. It'll work out.*

Anne   I'm not so sure.

Maureen   Of course it will. Anyhow, you might as well *look on the bright side.*

Anne   What bright side?

Maureen   Well, if you had a job, you'd be sitting in an office pounding a typewriter instead of having tea with me, wouldn't you?

Note the expressions of encouragement Maureen uses and repeat them.

Don't let it get you down   It'll work out
Something'll turn up   Look on the bright side
Don't give up now

Exercise 1

Look at the passage and be prepared to answer some questions about it and then to read it aloud.

> Now remember, if you don't get the first job that you apply for, don't give up. Keep on sending in your application forms and something is sure to turn up. Then when you do get an interview, try not to become so nervous that you are unable to do yourself justice. Even if the interview board does appear unfriendly, don't let it get you down – after all they have all been applicants themselves at some time or another, so look on the bright side. Be optimistic and you'll probably do well. And if you don't get that particular job, well, don't worry! It'll all work out for the best – perhaps it wasn't the job for you after all.

What is this passage about?
Who might be speaking?
Who are they speaking to?
Where might it take place?

ORAL SKILLS **G**

Group Discussion

Unemployment

individual adjustment
effects on society
changing patterns of work and leisure

USE OF ENGLISH **A**

Revision of Past Tenses

N.B. These are Active forms; for Passive forms, see Unit five.

1 Simple Past   Did   Didn't do   Did … do?

a Complete past action – known time:
He applied for four jobs last month.

b With 'when' enquiring about definite past time:
When did he apply for that job?

c For a definite period of past time:
He worked in that firm for three years.
(N.B. He no longer works there now)

d Past action – time understood but not stated:
He took his degree at London University.

e Habitual past actions and states:
He never wanted to go into his father's business.
She always misread her dictation notes.

2 Past Continuous   Was/Were doing   Wasn't/Weren't doing   Was/Were … doing

a Continuous past action:
I was writing letters all day yesterday.

b Frequently repeated past actions:
He was always answering advertisements for jobs.

c Interrupted past action (combined with Simple Past):
She was writing when the telephone rang.

d Simultaneous past actions:
The Union leaders were meeting while the Management were having lunch in the Board Room.

e Past intention:
I was going to apply for that job, but I didn't have the right qualifications.

3 Past Perfect   Had done   Hadn't done   Had … done?

a For the first of two past actions (combined with Simple Past):
He had applied for the job before he heard about the firm's reputation.

b For an action that happened before a stated past time:
She had finished typing the letters by one o'clock.

c For a past situation before a time understood but not stated:
She had always been a most conscientious worker.

4 Past Perfect Continuous   Had been doing   Hadn't been doing   Had ... been doing?

a Repeated past action implying continuity:
She had been trying to get a job for six months and was feeling very depressed.

b Continuous past action completed before another past action:
The workers had been protesting about their time schedules for six weeks before they went on strike.

Note carefully

5 Present Perfect   Has/Have done   Hasn't/Haven't done   Has/Have ... done?
Although it is usual to list this tense under the Present Tenses, it is equally a Past, since it is used to refer to:

a an indefinite past

b a recently completed action (with 'just/already')

c an action not yet completed (with 'yet')

d an action begun and continuing in the present

The notes on the use of this tense are found on page 21, Unit one, and should be referred to in considering the uses of Past Tenses. Some of these uses are likely to occur in this Unit.

Exercise 1

Put a correct Past or Perfect form of the verb in the following sentences.

1 He (apply) for numerous jobs before he (succeed) in getting this one.

2 According to the report we (receive), the factory (close) last month.

3 After he (inspect) the workshop, he (discuss) a number of points with the foreman.

4 She (look) for a job for over six months now.

5 Some of these men (work) for this company before you (be) born.

6 When the whistle (blow), the men (down) tools.

7 I (know) at once it was the type of job I (look for).

8 The secretary (not answer) the phone, because she (type) an urgent letter.

9 When he (examine) the accounts, the auditor (find) that the firm (spend) twice as much on advertising this year.

10 When I (come) into the room, Mr Jones and Mr Simpson (argue) about the photo-copying machine.

11 He always (want) to be a policeman, ever since he (be) a child.

12 The telephone (ring) all the morning, so Mary (not able) to do much work before she (go out) for lunch.

13 When you (take) your degree and where you (study) for it?

14 I (write) six letters before I (see) I (put) the wrong date on each one.

15 What (happen) when the men (go) on strike?

Exercise 2

Complete the following dialogue.

Philip Well, I'm afraid I didn't get that job as Sales Assistant, after all.

Anna ....?

Philip No, it wasn't because I didn't have the right qualifications.

Anna ....?

Philip They said I didn't have enough experience.

Unit two

Anna Not enough experience? That's nonsense *tout à* .... *no have see working* ....

Philip Yes, but working in my father's firm didn't seem to impress them very much.

Anna ....?

Philip They said it didn't prove anything. They seemed to think it rather a joke *what* ....

Anna ....?

Philip I think it was about £5,000.

Anna ....

Philip I agree, it's not too bad for a start, but anyway I didn't get the job, did I?

Anna Have you got any other interviews lined up?

Philip No, not yet. I looked in the local paper yesterday but *there was anything* ....

Anna Nothing worth applying for? It was full of advertisements for jobs.

Philip ......*there were but it don't suit us* ......

Anna How do you know they wouldn't have suited you, if you didn't apply?

Philip I just know they wouldn't, that's all. Sorry, I can't waste any more time talking.
I've got to go to the launderette.

Anna Whatever for? You...yesterday.

Philip Yes, but someone told me ......*there was the job* .... as Manager.
I might apply.

USE OF ENGLISH **B**

Special Uses

1 Past Continuous/Past Perfect Continuous   Was doing/Had been doing

Past intention or hope – usually unfulfilled:

I was thinking of doing the filing this morning, but I shan't have time now.
They had been hoping to receive the contract before the weekend, but it didn't arrive.

There is very little difference in the choice of these two tenses, except that the use of the Past Perfect Continuous usually suggests a little more regret.

2 Past Perfect   Had done

Repeated past action or continuous state with 'often, always, never' etc.
She had often tried to learn shorthand, but had never succeeded.
He had always liked working in an office, so he made up his mind not to leave.

Exercise 1

Write sentences expressing:

i Your regret at not being well enough to attend the Staff Dinner
ii Your disappointment at being too busy to go away for a few days
iii Something you never wanted to do in the past, but are now doing
iv Something you are doing now and always wanted to do
v A past hope that has not been fulfilled

3 Notes on the use of the Simple Past

a In English the Simple Past is the basic Narrative Tense, that is, it is normally used for telling stories, or giving accounts of past events. Naturally other tenses may be used to describe events that happened before or during the events described, but the basic tense remains the Simple Past.

Example

When I opened the window, I saw a crowd of men outside the factory gates. They were obviously in an ugly mood. Some carried banners, a few even had sticks or metal bars in their hands. One man, who had brought an orange box, had climbed on to it and was now shouting at his fellow workers at the top of his voice. He had a broad flat-nosed face and seemed to be their leader. I was leaning out of the window to get a better view, when this man spotted me. He put his hand in his pocket and without warning, hurled a stone at me. I ducked just in time to avoid it. . . .

b The Simple Past is also naturally used to express a rapid series of past events, frequently happening in fast succession.

Example

The manager *slammed* down the receiver, *tore* up the contract, *shouted* for his secretary, *dictated* a furious letter of complaint, *and refused* to see anyone for the rest of the day.

Exercise 2

1 Write a paragraph of about 100 words giving an account of a business trip to Edinburgh. Use the following words, but make any necessary changes.
Monday 11 a.m./ plane late/ delay 2 hours/ arrive Edinburgh/ taxi strike/ late appointment/ firm's representative unfriendly/ discover leave briefcase on plane/ meeting unproductive/ return frustrated

2 Write sentences to show the rapid sequence in the following past events.
yesterday morning/ smell smoke/ dash office/ wastepaper basket/ burn/ seize fire extinguisher/ spray/ fire put out

3 Using your own words, write a paragraph of about 100 words describing a recent experience at work.

USE OF ENGLISH **C**
Lie and Lay, Rise/Arise and Raise

1	*To lie*	*lied*	*lied*	*lying*	not to tell the truth (to tell a lie)
2	*To lie*	*lay*	*lain*	*lying*	to be in a horizontal position (to lie down)
					to be situated
3	*To lay*	*laid*	*laid*	*laying*	to place or put
4	*To rise*	*rose*	*risen*	*rising*	to get up, come up, increase
5	*To arise*	*arose*	*arisen*	*arising*	old or literary form of 'rise', to result from, be discussed
6	*To raise*	*raised*	*raised*	*raising*	to lift something up, to bring up (a subject)

41

Unit two

N.B. Mistakes often occur in using these verbs because students do not remember:

1 **Lie/Rise/Arise** are intransitive: They do not take an object but say *where, when, how long, why*, etc.

He lied when he said that.
He lay in the garden all the afternoon.
Prices rose again last week.

The argument arose over a disagreement about night shifts.

2 **Lay/Raise** are transitive: They take an object and say *what* is laid or raised.
He laid the papers on the table.
She raised her hand to attract the speaker's attention.

Exercise 1

Put an appropriate past form of 'lay/lie' or 'rise/arise/raise' in the following sentences.

1 The problem of a reduction in manpower (never) .... at this factory.
2 The construction site .... in an open area about two miles away.
3 The letter ..lay.. on the floor for half an hour before anyone noticed it.
4 Production costs ..rose.. in line with inflation.
5 The manufacturers ..raised. the price of coffee again.
6 I knew from his expression that he ....lied.
7 The man (not) ..raised.. his head when the foreman spoke to him.
8 He ..laid. his tools on the work bench.
9 The door had been forced open and the keys ..lay... on the floor.
10 The sun (already) ..risen. when we left for work.

Exercise 2

Complete the blanks in the following passage:

Mr Parsons ....(1) awake most of the night, unable to sleep in anticipation of the threatened strike at the works. It was now 6 a.m. He got up, put on the dressing gown ....(2) on the bed, and went over to the window. He pulled back the curtains and saw that the sun (just) ....(3). He ....(4) the bottom of the window and looked out. A soft blanket of mist still ....(5) like a shroud over the grass and bushes. Before long it would ....(6) and evaporated in the warmth of the sun. It was going to be a hot day. He dressed slowly, pulling on the clothes he ....(7) ready the night before. He always ....(8) early, but today he was earlier than usual. Presently he went downstairs to the kitchen to get his breakfast. The cat, ...(9) curled up on the hearth, ...(10) its head, blinked and went to sleep again. Sipping his tea, Mr Parsons was unable to dismiss the worries that ....(11) so heavily on his mind. It was hardly his fault that the vexed question of redundancy ....(12) yet again. The responsibility ....(13) entirely with the Board of Directors. They were too pig-headed to admit that it was their own mismanagement that ....(14) to the general dissatisfaction. He thought of all the beautiful new machinery which ....(15) idle like a great sleeping monster waiting to be used and his anger ....(16) at the waste of it all. He finished his eggs and bacon and ....(17) his knife and fork neatly on his plate. He pulled out the notes of the speech he had planned to make to the workers. Already he felt defeated by the prospect that ....(18) before him. Who was going to listen to him anyway? The best he could hope for was to ....(19) a laugh. Coming to a sudden decision, he got up from his chair and thrust his notes into the kitchen stove. They blazed merrily. Immediately he felt his spirits ....(20). Outside the sunshine beckoned, dappling the trees. It was a beautiful day for staying at home.

USE OF ENGLISH **D**
Rewriting Sentences

In Question 4 of the Use of English Paper in the Cambridge Proficiency examination you may be required to rewrite a number of sentences using a word which is given.

Example

Many workers were made redundant when the factory closed down.
REDUNDANCIES
There were many redundancies when the factory closed down.

Rewrite the following sentences, changing them where necessary, but keeping the meaning as close as possible to the original sentence. Use the word given in capital letters.

1   Rising unemployment is causing concern in most of the Western European countries.
WORRIED

....

2   There is a shortage of places in many of the Government retraining centres.
ENOUGH

....

3   Job satisfaction is more important than a high salary.
SO

....

4   It is not easy to create new jobs in a stagnant economy.
EASILY

....

5   An unofficial strike started in the factory because the charge hand was sacked.
DISMISSAL

....

6   What do you think about your new job?
FEEL

....

7   There is no doubt that salaries will rise by more than 10% next year.
SURE

....

8   If you want promotion, you must work hard and prove your worth.
UNLESS

....

9   A drop in production resulted from the strike.
CAUSED

....

10   How many times do I have to tell you not to put your name at the top of a letter?
ALWAYS

....

'I like work; it fascinates me. I can sit and look at it for hours.' (Jerome K Jerome)

WRITTEN SKILLS A

Job Applications and Interviews

1 Advertisement

TRANSLATOR
to work in Switzerland

An opportunity has arisen for a translator to work for a major Pharmaceutical
Company in Geneva. The work will involve translation of a wide variety of
medical, pharmaceutical and scientific texts from French and German into
English. A certain amount of financial and commercial translation is also
required. The successful applicant will be a qualified and experienced
translator with an impeccable command of English and a sound knowledge of
German and French. At least two years' experience in scientific translation is
necessary. The successful applicant will be flexible and versatile. Only candidates
between the ages of 25 and 35 should apply. A high basic salary plus twice-
yearly bonus will be paid and the company provides excellent social, welfare and
working conditions. Short-listed candidates will be required to take a translation
test and to attend an interview which will be held in London. Application should
be by letter only addressed to: The Personnel Officer, Swiss Medico Ltd,
PO Box 1990, Geneva, Switzerland.

2 Applications

The three applicants who wrote the following letters were short-listed. Study the lay-out of the letters and notice where the date and addresses were placed, and the language used.

LETTER ONE

10 Winchester Avenue,
Coldharbour, Essex.

The Personnel Officer,
Swiss Medico Ltd,
PO Box 1990, Geneva,
Switzerland.

15 May 19--

Dear Sir,

With reference to your advertisement in the 'Daily Globe' I should like to apply for the position of translator with your company.

I have worked as a translator for the past five years with T. Simms & Sons, Ltd (Ipswich), Manufacturers of Scientific Instruments, translating texts and orders from French, German and Spanish into English.

Before working for my present company I lived in France, where I was educated, and I hold a degree in German and Spanish from the University of Paris. My father is French and my mother English so I am bi-lingual in these two languages.

I am 28 years old, unmarried and without ties. I enjoy living and working in different countries and I should welcome the chance of moving to Switzerland.

Yours faithfully,

Jennifer Dupont

(Miss) Jennifer Dupont

LETTER TWO

Immermannstrasse 5,
1603 Seelzel,
West Germany.

The Personnel Officer,
Swiss Medico Ltd,
PO Box 1990,
Geneva, Switzerland.

15 May 19--

Dear Sir,

I should like to apply for the position of translator as advertised in yesterday's 'Daily Globe'.

I have spent the last three years in Germany as the translator at the Solid State Technology Center, Frankfurt, where I translate a wide variety of scientific texts from German and French into English. Before moving to Germany, I worked for five years as a translator and research assistant in the Linguistics Department of Dunstans College, University of London. My work involved translating French and German texts into English in connection with the compilation of a Scientific Dictionary.

I am 30 years old, married with two children. I was educated at Eton and took a degree in French and German at London University. I also hold a translator's certificate of the Institute of Linguists.

If I am short-listed, both Dunstans College and my present employers would be pleased to supply you with references.

Yours faithfully,

Peter Simmons

Peter Simmons

LETTER THREE

21 Underhill Road,
Saleham,
Berkshire.

The Personnel Officer,
Swiss Medico Ltd,
PO Box 1990,
Geneva, Switzerland.

16 May 19––

Dear Sir,

Translator

I have seen your advertisement in the 'Daily Globe' and I should like to apply for the position.

I am at present employed as a translator in a medical research organisation and also act as interpreter there. I joined this organisation two years ago.

I am 26 years old and single. I read French and German at Howland College, Cambridge and stayed there to take my Ph.D. in the dialects of North-East France.

I should be interested in working for your company for two reasons: firstly, I should like to live abroad and secondly, the work would involve medical/scientific translation which is my particular field.

I shall look forward to hearing from you.

Yours faithfully,

Rupert Johnson

Rupert Johnson

In these letters the applicants have given most of the information necessary, but sometimes a curriculum vitae is requested or an application form has to be filled in. In these cases the information required is basically the same: age, marital status, education, qualifications, experience, work history and present job held. Some employers like to know why you wish to leave your present job or ask why you want to work for their company, although many of these points come up at the interview.

3   Interviews

Exercise 1

Read the letters again and then write to the applicants informing them that they have been short-listed and inviting them to an interview. Include the following information:

time, place and date of the interview
details of the translation test
notice that the interview will be before a selection board.

Remember that letters addressed to a person by name (e.g. Mr Johnson) finish 'Yours sincerely,'. Don't forget to make the time and date of each interview different.

Exercise 2

The following is a possible interview form that would be completed by a member of the selection board for each candidate that came before the board. Study it and then complete it for one of the candidates who appeared for an interview.

Name	Date of interview	Time

Age   Married / Single   Children

Education and qualifications

Present position

Previous positions held   *No previous position .*

Experience

Any special abilities

Social relationships / leisure activities

General manner and appearance

Initiative and motivation

Willingness to travel

Present salary

Date from which available   Expenses   paid
to be paid

Names and addresses
of 2 referees

1

2

4 Selection

Exercise 3

From the letters and any information you may have gained at the interviews, select one of the candidates and write a letter to him/her offering the position as translator. Write two other letters to the unsuccessful candidates informing them that they have not got the job and expressing your regret.

Supplementary Material

Exercise 4

Reply to the following advertisements, giving any information requested.

1   International engineering company require a Projects Manager to establish project teams and to control and co-ordinate their activities. Candidates should have an engineering background and have at least three years' experience in management of major projects with a consulting engineer or construction company. Age range 35–45. Salary will be negotiable and other benefits include a company car, a non-contributory pension scheme and free life insurance. Applicants should give brief details of their careers to date. Write to: Personnel Dept, Ronocol Ltd, Ronocol House, Star Place, London, EC1.

2   University of Suffolk. Applications are invited for two lectureships in (1) Textiles, (2) Industrial Design. Both positions are tenable from October 1 19––. Candidates for both posts should have considerable educational and/or industrial experience and will be working in teams answerable to the senior lecturers in their departments. Further details and application forms may be obtained from: The Registrar, University of Suffolk, Great Yarmouth, YA2 7AY.

3   Secretary for an American firm. Someone quick-minded, meticulous and able to work on own initiative. Typing, shorthand and dictaphone work. Electric typewriter. Promotion prospects to Personal Assistant. Hours 9–5 Monday–Friday. Benefits include LVs and 4 weeks' holiday. Attractive salary. Phone: 120 3420 or write Mr Hyman, Starcross Films, Wardour Street, London W1.

4   Part-time Sales Assistants required to work in Fashion Department, Hardy and Thomas of Oxford Street, London W1. The work is for three days per week including Saturdays. Excellent hourly rate. Clothing concessions and store discount. Telephone the Manageress of the Fashion Dept for an interview. Tel: 374 1007 or write to: Sally Brown, Top Fashion, Hardy and Thomas, Oxford Street, W1.

5   Barmaid/man required. Lunchtime and evening sessions. Live in – hours and salary negotiable. References required. Write: Bentleys, Old Whitechapel Lane, Limehouse, E2.

Exercise 5

1 Imagine you are applying for a job you are interested in. Complete the following curriculum vitae.

CURRICULUM VITAE

Name:

Marital Status: Age:

Address: Children:

Telephone Number:

Education:

1 Secondary   **2** Further _UNIVERSITY_   **3** Other

Previous experience:

Present position: Salary:

Name and address of employer:

References:

1   **2**

Special interests:

2   Imagine you are to be interviewed shortly for this job. How would you reply to questions on:

Salary/bonus   Holidays/benefits
Prospects/promotion   Responsibilities

Jot down any questions you would like to ask about these four subjects. Think of any other points you may want to raise at the interview.

3   Working in pairs and using the information from **1** and **2**, conduct the interview between the employer and the applicant. When you have completed the interview, change roles and repeat the exercise.

WRITTEN SKILLS **B**

Reading Comprehension

The Proficiency Reading Comprehension paper will include three or more passages with about five questions on each, from which you are asked to select the correct answer A, B, C or D, from the choices given. The type of question may be similar to that asked on Listening Comprehension passages, but this time you are *reading* and not *listening*, which means that both passage and questions are a good deal more difficult and the vocabulary range much wider. You may be expected not only to comprehend the meaning of sentences on the printed page, but in some cases to assess, deduce or comment on a particular set of circumstances.

Exercise 1

Following are five short paragraphs which, though quite simple in themselves, require careful reading to produce the right answer.

1   The 8.30 a.m. train was cancelled, so I had to catch the 8.45. Unfortunately this was ten minutes late which meant that I didn't get to London till 9.55 a.m. – twenty-five minutes later than I would have done if I had caught the 8.30 a.m. as usual.

   What time does the 8.30 train usually arrive in London?

2   Ann, Janet and Sarah work in the same office. On Tuesday and Wednesday last week, Ann and Sarah were off sick. On Thursday Janet had to attend an all-day conference with her boss and Friday was a public holiday, so of course she was free on that day.

   Which of the girls spent most time in the office last week?

3   Although the car was undoubtedly a bargain with a low petrol consumption and needing only minor repairs, running such a vehicle was still beyond my means, taking into account the tax and insurance.
   What decided the writer not to buy the car?

4   It was a large room which had been partitioned into four, more than a half of which was occupied by the Typing Pool. Mr Hobson's office was on the right of this and next to it, not much more than a cubby-hole, was his secretary's office. Even more minute and leading out of the section labelled Post Room, was Records and Filing where a young man sat all day reading newspapers.

Which was the largest room?
Which was the smallest?

5   I was ushered into a waiting-room on the first floor and after a brief interval, was conducted along a corridor and up two more flights of stairs to a room at the top of the house where my client was waiting.

How many floors did the house have?

Exercise 2

Read the two passages and the following questions or unfinished statements. Then choose the answers that you think fit best from A, B, C or D.

1   There are two things that stand at record level in today's world. One is unemployment. The other is spending on weapons of mass destruction.

The effects of unemployment are there for all to see: crippled communities, decaying cities and, for the young especially, long-term unemployment and despair. Often the only way of avoiding the dole queue is to join the armed forces.

But you can help bring down unemployment by demanding that the money now spent by Governments on weapons be redeployed towards more socially useful purposes.

What is the writer's intention?

A   To invoke sympathy for arms manufacturers
B   To persuade young people to join the armed forces
C   To encourage people to protest about unemployment
D   To rouse public opinion against dangerous weapons

2   CASTLE JOBS YOUTH TRAINING SCHEME
Castle Jobs Youth Training Scheme has six workshops offering a variety of work skills supported by a programme of social studies:

Silk Screen Printing	Pottery
Woodwork	Basic Engineering
Horticulture	Litho Printing

The objectives we are trying to achieve are to prepare young people to assume responsibility in society – as self-confident persons – whether employed or unemployed.

What are the CJYTS objectives?

A   To provide work for all young unemployed people
B   To develop young people's ability to think
C   To give a place in a workshop to all school leavers
D   To offer young people the chance to gain work skills

WRITTEN SKILLS **C**
Reading and Choosing the Right Answer

Read the following extract and note how the correct answer is arrived at.

> The Home Secretary has been asked to intervene in the growing disagreement between leaders of the Refuse Collectors' Union and their employers over the proposed shortening of the refuse collectors' working week.
>
> 5 The Union yesterday pressed him to support their contention that hours should be reduced from 48 to 42 a week, without change to manning patterns.
>
> The local authority employers have angered the Union by insisting that any reduction in hours must be matched by a more cost-effective use of manpower. Union negotiators told the Home Secretary yesterday that they interpreted this as an attempt to reduce the number of refuse collectors.

1 From the text we understand that
   A there has been disagreement among the Union leaders
   B the employees have rejected the Home Secretary's proposals
   C the disagreement appears to have reached a deadlock
   D the employers disagree with the Home Secretary's proposals

Correct answer
   C The Home Secretary has been asked to intervene because the two sides cannot agree on a course of action – i.e. a deadlock.

Wrong

   A   The Union leaders are not in disagreement with *each other*.

   B   No proposals have yet been made by the Home Secretary.

   D   For the same reason as B.

2   It seems that the Union leaders are concerned that

   A   the number of men employed should not be increased

   B   the men should not work more than a maximum of 48 hours a week

   C   present manning patterns should be adapted to a 42-hour week

   D   present manning patterns should remain unaltered

Correct answer

   D   The phrase in the text is 'without change to manning patterns'.

Wrong

   C   Very close to D, but *adaptation* must mean change of some kind.

   A   Obviously the Union do not wish the number of employees to decrease (not to be increased).

   B   The Union are campaigning for a 42-hour week, not a 48-hour week.

3   What is meant by the phrase 'a more cost-effective use of manpower'? (line 7)

   A   paying the employees at the lowest possible rate

   B   cutting down on the number of men employed

   C   using the available manpower economically

   D   showing a sizeable profit

Correct answer

   C   Making sure that any reduction in hours did not mean an increase in expenditure and that the existing employees worked in the most efficient and economical way possible.

Wrong

   A   No suggestion that the employers intended to pay the employees at the lowest possible rate. They are, after all, contending with a union.

   B   Although the Union interpreted the phrase as an attempt to reduce manpower, this is not in fact what it means in the text. It is simply an instance of a union seizing on a phrase to try to add support to their case.

   D   Local authorities are not in business to make a profit. The money they use is ratepayers' money. Any surplus would have to be directed towards assisting the community. No suggestion of this here.

Read the following passages and answer the questions that follow. Choose A, B, C or D for your answer.

First Passage

     Harrington Wilson's selling technique was simplicity itself. It was nothing more than a subtle manipulation of human vanity. He was aware that there were a number of people who professed to know a great deal about antiques, and even more who would rather not confess that they did not and who accordingly

5   practised little tricks and subterfuges to conceal their ignorance or impress their neighbours.

     The women – they were mainly women – jostling round his stall, picking over his shoddy wares, would sometimes run a finger round the rim of a cup or hold it

10 knowingly up to the light as if to test its lustre, and plates were invariably turned
upside down in search of china marks. To such a customer, Harrington would lean
forward, benevolent and confidential, and in a conspiratorial whisper would
murmur: 'No, madam, I'm afraid it's not genuine (Wedgwood, Sevres – whatever
it might be) but it is a superb copy – no one would ever suspect that it was not real,
unless, of course, you told them. I can let you have it for £2 – I could sell it for
15 much more, but it would be unethical of me to try to pass it off as genuine. ...'

The customer, overwhelmed by such honesty and privately determined not to be
quite so honest about the article to her friends, would then willingly pay £2 for
something that had cost Harrington a few pence. The profit margin on these
transactions was obviously so great that he was soon able to set up another stall and
20 another and then a shop and yet another and so on. He enlarged his specialities,
dealing in spurious Victoriana, Georgian silver, trinkets and bric-a-brac, eventually
branching out into reproduction furniture and paintings. Without any deliberate
intention of doing so, he acquired an extensive knowledge of the antique business
and as time went on, was accounted one of the greatest experts of his time.

1   It seems that Harrington Wilson's initial success owed a great deal to
    A   his apparent ingenuousness
    B   the good bargains he offered
    C   his air of gullibility
    D   the honesty of his methods

2   Among the people who patronised Harrington Wilson's stall, there were some who
    A   had more knowledge than they appeared to have
    B   were less knowledgeable than they appeared
    C   did not trouble to conceal their ignorance
    D   disliked being thought intellectual snobs

3   When a woman customer held an article 'knowingly up to the light' (line 9) she
    was trying to
    A   demonstrate her expertise
    B   make sure she was not being cheated
    C   compare it with another article she had bought
    D   show her appreciation of its charm

4   As Harrington Wilson became increasingly successful, it seems that he
    A   acquired a rather dubious reputation
    B   made no conscious effort to improve his prospects
    C   was not regarded as an expert
    D   acquired an unexpected prestige

Second Passage

As more and more people become redundant, now is perhaps the time to consider the
experience of unemployment. What are the first feelings? Well, losing a job, or not
being able to find one, almost always brings unwelcome changes. If you've lost a job,
the first feeling is often one of shock. As well as the loss of income, many people find
the whole routine of their life is shattered, their contact with other people reduced,
their ambitions halted and their identity as a worker removed.

At first there may be good feelings too – a new and better job is just around the corner – it's nice to be able to lie in bed in the morning or spend more time with the children; have more time to think. But, unless a better job does turn up, the chances are the days start getting longer and time becomes harder to fill. Many people pass through periods of difficulty in sleeping and eating, they feel irritable and depressed, often isolated and lonely, and perhaps worst of all, a feeling of lethargy, of being dull and run down sweeps over them.

Despite all these problems though, unemployment can be a chance for a fresh start. You can discover that it provides an opportunity to sort out or rethink what you want from life and how best you can get it. You can use the time to plan how to find a new job, learn a new skill, develop your hobbies, see if you can run your own business, do some voluntary work in your community or meet new people. It's up to you.

1   The writer considers that being made redundant

    A   causes people to lose touch with reality
    B   completely destroys people's lives
    C   lessens interaction between people
    D   stops people's chances of promotion

2   According to the passage, initial hope in the unemployed is replaced by disillusionment when they

    A   can no longer get up late in the morning
    B   get tired of playing with their children
    C   are unable to improve their position
    D   have nothing left to think about

3   One of the disadvantages of continuing unemployment is

    A   having time on your hands
    B   the lengthening of the days
    C   the feeling of being continually ill
    D   being ignored by most people

4   The writer's mention of a fresh start suggests that

    A   everyone should change their job sometimes
    B   unemployed people are capable of helping themselves
    C   unemployment can be of benefit to people
    D   the community can help unemployed people

5   What is the writer's aim in this passage?

    A   To bring home the facts of unemployment
    B   To bully unemployed people into improving themselves
    C   To make the unemployed face the facts of life
    D   To offer encouragement to unemployed people

Third Passage

PARTICULARS OF TERMS OF EMPLOYMENT
(Given pursuant to the Contracts of Employment Act 1972, s.4)

Date: 13th March 198–

To: MR GORDON BROWN

From: BETTS & BENSON LTD, 39 ST ANDREW STREET, LONDON W1A 3BS (the company)

Your employment began on MARCH 13TH 198–
The following particulars of the terms of your employment applied on MARCH 13TH 198–

1. Job Title   POSTAL CLERK

2. Remuneration

Your salary is at the rate of £5,000 p.a. payable monthly on the 15th of each month for the whole of that month. (Overtime, where applicable, is payable by arrangement with your head of department.) You are entitled to receive one 55p Luncheon Voucher for each day worked.

3. Hours of Work

Monday–Friday 9 a.m.–5.30 p.m.
You are entitled to one hour for lunch on each of these days and in addition two quarter-hour breaks, one in the morning and one in the afternoon. These breaks cannot be used to extend your normal lunch hour.

4. Holidays and Holiday pay

Your annual holiday entitlement in the year in which you join the Company is two weeks, but thereafter you are entitled to three weeks' holiday per year with full pay. Such holiday shall be taken at a time or times convenient to the Company and may not be carried forward from one year to another. You are also entitled to the usual Statutory Holidays with full pay. There is no right to unpaid holiday. For the purposes of calculating entitlement to accrued holiday pay on the termination of employment, you will be treated as becoming entitled to one week's holiday on completion of each period of four months in each year.

5. Sickness or Injury

A doctor's certificate must be sent to the Secretary by the third consecutive working day of absence due to sickness or injury and thereafter at weekly intervals. No pay will be given for absence during the first three months' service; thereafter full pay will continue during any period of absence due to sickness or injury up to a maximum of six weeks in any one calendar year.
You are required to keep the Secretary informed of any National Health Insurance benefits you receive for any period of absence and a deduction of like amount will be made by the Company from your next pay.

1. According to the terms of the contract, salaries are paid
   A every fifteen days
   B monthly in advance
   C monthly in arrears
   D in the middle of a month

2. During the working day, the time allowed for breaks is
   A an hour for lunch and two half-hour breaks
   B an hour and a half daily
   C an hour in the morning and half an hour in the afternoon
   D an hour including two fifteen minute breaks

3. The following holiday arrangements apply during the first six months of employment:
   A three weeks on full pay
   B one week paid and one unpaid
   C two weeks to include public holidays
   D two weeks as well as public holidays

4. In case of sickness a doctor's certificate must be obtained for
   A each day of absence
   B absence of three days or more
   C absence of three separate days
   D periods of not less than a week

5. If the employee receives sickness benefit from National Health Insurance
   A his pay will be adjusted accordingly
   B he will be asked to remit this to the Company
   C his pay will include an equivalent amount
   D he will receive half-pay for six weeks

Fourth Passage

Extract 1

The Home Office and Education Department Committees have just issued their report for 1901. It was the late Mr Hogg who two or three years ago drew attention to the fact that hundreds of thousands of children under eleven or twelve years of age are not protected either by the Factory Acts or the Prevention of Cruelty to Children Act from being put to and kept at work for appallingly long hours.

The Committee finds that 300,000 is the lowest figure at which it can put the number, and nearly half of these children have to work for over 20 hours a week in addition to their school hours, while in many instances the hours were found to be as much as 43, 52 or even 73 hours a week.

Extract 2

The training policies put forward by various agencies, notably the Manpower Services Commission, all contain certain elements. For example, the Youth Training Scheme seeks to provide some form of training for all young people.

The same ambition may well be applied to adult training, now in the discussion stage. There could be a 'universal right' to retraining for work or re-entry to education.

But, will it work? The changes will affect and involve the whole system – educators, commerce and industry, local authorities, trade unions, vocational institutions, small businesses and others besides. There will, predictably, be problems; conflict and confusion over policies and objectives, difficulties of gaining co-operation, the sheer complexity of communication among local and national agencies and, as always, the matching of resources and demands. We can only wait and see how the abstract objectives are interpreted by the many kinds of agency who have to make practical sense of the new ideas.

Extract 3

The aim of the series is to show how almost anyone can make some kind of money from working at home. Different programmes will deal with working within the home using existing skills and interests, as well as possibilities for the unskilled and unqualified; operating from home but going outside it to earn money; using a room at home as an office or workshop; using the home itself and inviting the public in. There will also be basic information about legislation, income tax and practical problems that arise. Case histories will be featured throughout the series.

1   What is the importance of Mr Hogg in extract 1?

    A   He was a member of the Education Department Committee
    B   He wrote the Home Office Report of 1901
    C   He triggered off the investigation into working conditions for children
    D   He was instrumental in changing the Prevention of Cruelty to Children Act

2   If the 'universal right' referred to in extract 2 were applied, then all adults would

    A   be included in the discussions about training
    B   be entitled to further education or training
    C   have to accept retraining or further education
    D   be provided with some form of work or education

3   Extract 3 is probably taken from

    A   an educational booklet
    B   a broadcasting journal
    C   a television magazine
    D   an information leaflet

4   Extracts 2 and 3 deal with

    A   retraining schemes
    B   unemployment strategies
    C   self-employment
    D   changing work patterns

5   Compared with extract 1, young people in extract 2 will

    A   be better off
    B   remain about the same
    C   have more work opportunities
    D   have less to do

REMINDER **2**

Punctuation

Don't hesitate to punctuate

A little punctuation is better than none at all

Fourteen points to remember

1   Start every sentence with a **Capital Letter.**
2   End every sentence with a **full stop.**
3   Put **commas** between lists of things, between two or more adjectives, but not
    before 'and':
    It was an ill-lit, stuffy office.
    Books, papers, unopened letters and catalogues lay on the desk.
4   Use **commas** to divide clauses:
    After he had read it carefully, he signed the contract.
5   Use **commas** to show difference in meaning, i.e. in relative clauses:
    The workers who were on strike picketed the factory gates.
    (only the ones who were on strike)
    The workers, who were on strike, picketed the factory gates.
    (all the workers were on strike)
6   End every direct question with a **question mark.**
7   Put an **exclamation mark** after exclamations: *How awful!*
8   **Semi-colon** to show a pause longer than a comma, but not so complete as a full
    stop:
    *The application form was extremely complicated and full of small print; it took me an
    hour to fill it in.*
9   **Colon** to introduce a list or explanation or dramatic dialogue:
    Candidates are asked to bring with them : a notebook, pen, pencil and slide rule.
    Manager : How old are you, Mr Brown?
    Brown : I'm just twenty-three, sir.
10 **Brackets** ( ) to separate or to clarify a statement:
    At retirement age (60 women, 65 men) you will be entitled to a pension.
11 **Dash** – to extend an idea:
    Nothing disturbed him – noise, bright lights, blaring radio, shrilling telephones.
    to round off an idea:
    He was polite, courteous, ready to help – a gentleman, in fact.
    to show interruption of speech:
    'I'm just going to –'
    'I don't care where you're going.'
12 **Quotation marks** ' ' for quotations from speeches or literature; also titles of
    books, plays, etc.
    'To be or not to be, that is the question' is one of the best-known quotations from
    Shakespeare.
    N.B. In printed speech, quotation marks are normally used in place of inverted
    commas (see below).
13 **Inverted Commas** " " for Direct Speech; or any part of Direct Speech.
    If the speech is broken by *he said* or a similar expression, then a comma is put
    before the closing inverted commas.

N.B. In English opening and closing **inverted commas** are put at the top of the line:

"It is impossible to discuss this now," Jones said, "we shall have to wait till we get home."

14 Apostrophe ' For Possessive case, normally of Persons

's for singular   s' for plural:
The worker's pay packet. The workers' pay packets.

For missing letters in short form expressions:
He doesn't approve of strikes.
There's too much time wasted in this office.

These fourteen points are intended as a guide and do not cover all the complexities of punctuation. In practice, however, the student can usually punctuate his work quite adequately with the use of the Full Stop, the Comma, the Question Mark and Inverted Commas. The greatest confusion arises from the student who ignores punctuation altogether or who just puts in a full stop or a comma when he feels like it.

N.B.

a   In English it is not good practice to divide short words like *very* (ve - ry), *table* (ta - ble) from one line to another. It is only words of several syllables that should be divided, e.g. *con - frontation*, and even then it is usually far better to put the whole word on the next line even if it does leave a little gap.

b   Candidates for examination are also reminded that even good punctuation won't help if their writing is:
too small, too large and curly, too thin and spidery,
or any other variation of almost illegible handwriting.
Graphologists may be interested but examiners aren't.

Exercise

Punctuate the following passage.

good afternoon mr brown do sit down now tell me what made you apply for this job well mr hopkins ive been wanting to improve my position for some time and it seemed to me that the job you advertised would give me an opportunity to learn more about marketing and sales techniques in general where are you working at present mr brown well actually i havent got a job at the moment i had a job as chief clerk in the buying department of a retail store johnson and king i expect youve heard of them but to tell the truth i didnt quite hit it off with the sales manager oh why was that mr brown well he was rather old fashioned in his methods and the sales policy of the firm seemed to me too slow im a great believer in the personal approach to selling i took a course in business management at the london commercial college and im afraid i found johnson and kings methods very out of date they first opened in 1880 you know and i dont think theyve changed their ideas since then really mr brown in that case you may be interested to know that our firm first started business in 1870 and we believe that the old slogan the customer is always right still holds good today im afraid our chairman samuel jackson great-great-grandson of the original founder of the firm josiah jackson does not approve of highpowered modern selling techniques and with some justification as our export figures show we base all our sales technique on petersons theory of salesmanship published in 1900 I presume youve read it well actually no mr hopkins but ill make a point of getting one from my local library without delay do that mr brown and then come and see me again

Unit three Ecology

ORAL SKILLS A
Intensive Listening

ANIMALS IN DANGER

Richard Murray, a zoologist and popular TV personality, has been giving a talk on 'Endangered Species of Wildlife' to members of the Young Conservationists Association in a small town in the South of England.
Listen to the extract from the discussion he had with two of the young people after his talk.

Now answer these questions. For questions 1–5, tick the box A, B, C or D for the answer you choose. For questions 6 and 7, tick the boxes which apply.

1 Whatever the motive for destroying wildlife, Richard Murray believes that

A	
B	
C	
D	

A Nature will correct the balance
B the end result is the same
C we shall be extinct in 20 years
D wildlife will continue to survive

2 What kind of people gain from the slaughter of seals and crocodiles?

A	
B	
C	
D	

A Food manufacturers
B Fashion editors
C Profiteers
D Conservationists

3 How can the risk to wildlife be reduced?

A	Natural wastage
B	Improved pesticides
C	Law enforcement
D	Public opinion

A
B
C
D

4 In certain areas the dolphin is killed because it

A	provides a source of food
B	threatens a source of income
C	endangers human life
D	pollutes fishing grounds

A
B
C
D

5 What does Jenny mean by the expression 'a caring society'? People who

A	suffer from anxiety
B	are concerned about others
C	need help and advice
D	are conscientious workers

A
B
C
D

6 Which of the following may result from the use of pesticides?

A	sterility of beneficial wildlife	
B	contamination of natural foods	
C	death from natural causes	
D	immunisation against disease	
E	pollution of the environment	
F	disease in infancy	

7 In what ways do Tony and Jenny question Richard Murray's argument? They suggest that

A	animals provide certain necessities	
B	most pesticides are harmless	
C	insecticides provide valuable protection	
D	conservation can affect people's livelihood	
E	crops must be protected against pests	
F	conservation ignores human needs	

Listen to the discussion again. Match these expressions used to the following meanings. Put the letter of your choice in the box.

	1	much of our wildlife *will have died out*
	2	we can't of course *rule out*
	3	it's going *to turn out*
	4	it's hard *to make out*
	5	well-intentioned people who *start out*
	6	danger to other forms of life, including humans, *comes out*
	7	not to say, *leaks out*
	8	our time *is running out*

A to distinguish, to understand
B to become gradually and unintentionally known
C to disregard
D to prove to be
E to come to an end
F to become generally known
G to become extinct
H to begin

Exercise 1

Using one of the above expressions with 'out', re-phrase the following sentences.

Example

The indiscriminate use of insecticides may prove to be one of Man's worst mistakes.
The indiscriminate use of insecticides may turn out to be one of Man's worst mistakes.

1 The gorilla will have become extinct in a few decades.

2 The two biologists will begin by examining the effects of DDT on the common cockroach.

3 They hope the experiment will prove to be worthwhile.

4 As far as the whale is concerned, there is little time left.

5 The side effects of this germicide will gradually become known even if we try to conceal them.

6 I can't understand why this crocodile handbag cost so much.

7 The danger of an outbreak of typhoid from this polluted water cannot be ignored.

8 The dangers of this insecticide became generally known when dead birds were found littering the countryside.

ORAL SKILLS **B**

Listening Comprehension

Listen to the dialogue and complete the form with the information you hear.

PESTAWAY   Questionnaire

Name (Block letters please) _____

Address _____ **Age** _____

_____

_____

Occupation _____

Why did you buy Pestaway? (Tick where appropriate)
cockroaches ☐   fleas ☐   ants ☐   woodworm ☐

How long have you been using Pestaway? _____
How often do you use it? _____
Where do you use it? _____

Where did you buy it? (Tick where appropriate)
supermarket ☐   chemist ☐   department store ☐
corner shop ☐

How did you first hear about Pestaway? (Tick where appropriate)
friend ☐   advertisement ☐   supermarket ☐
newspaper ☐   radio advertisement ☐

Are you (Tick where appropriate) **with Pestaway?**
very satisfied ☐   satisfied ☐
fairly satisfied ☐   dissatisfied ☐

ORAL SKILLS **C**
Picture for Discussion

Questions

1 What does the picture show?
2 Which continent seems to have most animals at risk?
3 Which type of animal seems most vulnerable?
4 Why do you think there are so few endangered animals in South America?

Topics

Man versus wildlife.
Endangered species should be protected.
The dangers of over-population.

ORAL SKILLS **D**
Dialogue

Read or listen to the following dialogue between two women in a department store.

	Helena	Do look at those fur coats! They're rather lovely, aren't they?
	Laura	Well, I suppose they are – quite.
	Helena	Quite? Just feel this one, it's all soft and silky and it's got a fabulous sheen. It must be sealskin.
5	**Laura**	It's not sealskin, it's squirrel.
	Helena	Sealskin or squirrel – I'm terrible about furs, I never know the difference. I think I'll try it on. Oh no, perhaps not, it's pretty expensive. It is beautiful, though.
	Laura	Of course it is. Squirrels are beautiful creatures.
10	**Helena**	Now, how about this one? It's fairly reasonable compared to the others, and it's got one of those huge collars that frame the face. I always think they're very flattering. What sort of fur is it, do you think?
	Laura	If it's fairly cheap, it's probably coney.
	Helena	What's that?
15	**Laura**	It's a sort of rabbit – used to be pretty common before myxomatosis.
	Helena	Well, anyway, I'll try it on. Here, hold my handbag a moment, will you? I'm terrified of losing it. It's the crocodile one John gave me for my birthday. It cost the absolute earth. The trouble is, it's rather heavy, so I don't use it very often.
20	**Laura**	Quite.
	Helena	Are you all right?
	Laura	Quite all right, thank you. Why?
	Helena	Oh, nothing. I thought you sounded a bit annoyed or something. There! Now, how does that look? It's rather on the long side, of course, but then that's the in-length this year, isn't it? I think it looks gorgeous, just like something out of a thirties film, all sophisticated and glamorous. What do you think?
25		
	Laura	I think it's horrible. I can hardly bear to look at it, let alone touch it. Honestly, Helena, if you must waste your money, why don't you buy a fake fur?
30		
	Helena	But I never buy synthetics, you know that. They're horrible, if you like.
	Laura	You don't care, do you? You're quite happy to ignore the suffering those poor creatures have gone through to provide you with a fur coat, a crocodile handbag –
35	**Helena**	Really, Laura, you're quite impossible! I'm pretty sure you wouldn't refuse a fur coat if someone offered you one. And anyway, what about those shoes you're wearing? The leather for those must have come from some animal or other.
	Laura	They're not leather. They're plastic.

Notice how Helena and Laura use the words: **quite, fairly, rather, pretty** in the dialogue.

(line 2)   I suppose they are – *quite*

(line 7)   It's *pretty* expensive

66

(line 10) It's *fairly* reasonable
(line 13) If it's *fairly* cheap …
(line 15) … used to be *pretty* common
(line 18) it's *rather* heavy
(line 20) *Quite*
(line 22) *Quite* all right, thank you
(line 24) It's *rather* on the long side
(line 32) You're *quite* happy to ignore the suffering …
(line 35) You're *quite* impossible!
           I'm *pretty* sure you wouldn't refuse a fur coat …

'Quite', 'fairly', 'rather', 'pretty' are really strong or weak forms of 'very'. In speech, however, it is often only the stress placed on the word that shows what the speaker really means. This applies particularly to 'quite' which can also be used to signify agreement. In general, 'fairly' is used in a slightly negative sense and 'rather' in a more positive sense. 'Pretty' is a strong form of 'very'.

Study or listen to these examples.

Quite 1	weak form of 'very'	*They're quite expensive* (not unreasonably expensive)
2	perfectly, completely	*You're quite impossible!* (completely impossible)
3	agreement, usually indicating the speaker has no more to say on the matter	*I've always wanted a fur coat* *Quite* (agreed but no comment follows)
Fairly	weak form of 'very'	*The experiments have been fairly successful* (moderately successful – not as good as expected)
Rather	stronger form of 'very'	*The experiments have been rather successful* (very successful – better than expected)
Pretty	a strong form of 'very'	*Be careful! That insecticide is pretty strong* (very, extremely strong)

Exercise 1

Using expressions with *quite/fairly/rather/pretty*, ask or tell someone the following.

1   You didn't hear exactly what the lecturer was saying about whales. *tell us*
    ....

2   Donations to the Wildlife Fund were not as generous as expected. *ride a ml*
    ....

3   Explain to someone that an aerosol he has bought is not particularly strong. *a flirt Jon*
    ....

4   Ask someone if he/she is completely satisfied with modern forms of pest control.
    Are you quite satisfied with modern forms control

5   Explain that you are very interested in conservation and would like to know more about it.
    You are rather in conservation

6   Ask someone if the information he has given you is entirely correct.
    you a the information he has given you is

7 Say how angry you feel about the killing of dolphins.

....

8 Suggest to someone that it would not be very difficult to organise a Wildlife Appeal.

.... would be easy ....

N.B. Alternatives are possible here, much will depend on the stress.

Exercise 2

Study the following passage. Answer the questions that follow and then read it aloud.

All the exhibits in this section have been presented by the Arctic Wildlife Association. This is a rather fine specimen of a fairly large male polar bear. As you see, his white fur is tinged with yellow and notice how it even grows between the thick, black pads on the bottom of his feet. Polar bears are carnivorous and live mainly on seals. They are pretty strong swimmers and can stay under water for as long as a minute.

Where is the speaker?
What part of the world does the animal come from?
What does he say about the animal's appearance?

ORAL SKILLS **E**

Group Discussion

Progress and Pollution

damage to the environment   crop-spraying   endangered species

USE OF ENGLISH **A**

Revision of Future Tenses

N.B. These are Active forms; for Passive forms, see Unit five.

1 Simple Future Shall/Will do

a	Simple statements of future fact	*The water board will test the water tomorrow.*
b	Opinions, assumptions, speculations, beliefs, doubts, hopes, fears about the future	*I don't think they'll spray that field till next week.*
c	Habitual actions in the future	*Fertilising will start again in the spring.*
d	Often with verbs of perception or emotion	*They'll be sorry they didn't investigate the side effects of that insecticide.*
e	As the main clause of a likely condition with 'if' (see Conditionals, Unit four, page 106)	*If they test that water, they will find it is polluted.*
f	Assumptions about present facts	*Mary : 'Who's that at the door?'* *John : 'That'll be the dustman.'*

2   **Future Continuous**   Shall/Will be doing

a   For an arranged action that will be   *Dr Hall will be appealing on behalf of the*
    taking place at a certain time in   *Wildlife Fund on TV next Friday.*
    the future
    (Alternative with Present Continuous; see Unit one, page 21)

3   **Future Perfect**   Shall/Will have done   *seen needed.*

a   For an action that will have taken   *They will have sprayed the whole of that*
    place by a certain time in the future   *area with insecticide by Friday.*
b   For assumptions based on known facts   *The chemical waste from the factory*
    will have polluted that water.

4   **Future Perfect Continuous**   Shall/Will have been doing

    For an action which began before a   *By next February, he will have been*
    certain future time but will not have   *researching into the causes of air*
    been completed by then   *pollution for two years.*

5   **'Going to' + Infinitive**

a   Firm intention   *They are going to decontaminate that lake.*
b   Extreme probability   *The whale is soon going to be extinct.*

Exercise 1

Using one of the five Future Tenses, complete the following sentences.

1   I (not watch) that documentary about seals; I know it (give) me nightmares.
2   Don't disturb Dr Paul when you come in; he (listen) to a radio talk on de-
    infestation.
3   We (hold) a protest meeting about Clean Air outside the Town Hall next Thursday
    and hope there (be) plenty of supporters there.
4   Does Professor Beamish usually come to the meeting?
    Yes, but he (not come) this week, as he (be) in Edinburgh.
5   By the end of next week I think we (raise) £500 for the Wildlife Fund.
6   If I see Dr Morris next week, I (tell) him you (give) a talk on River Pollution at
    the Educational Institute next month?
7   Scientists predict that by the year 2050, world population (increase) to almost
    double its present size.
8   If they dispose of all that chemical waste into the river, the water (not be) fit to
    fish in less than a week, and all the fish (die) by the end of the month.
9   Do you think they really (exterminate) those cockroaches with that
    insecticide?
10 If we continue to pollute the atmosphere, the Earth no longer (be able) to support
    life as we know it.
11 The Pest Control Committee would like to know if Dr White (arrive) on the
    6 o'clock or the 7.15 train.
12 How long it (be) before we realise that our grandchildren probably (never see) a
    tiger or a gorilla except in a picture?

USE OF ENGLISH B

Other Common Future Forms

1 Simple Present Do/Does   (see Unit one, page 23)
Firm statement of future fact   *The nuclear test starts at 6 a.m.*

2 'To be' + infinitive Am/Are/Is to do   (see Unit one, page 23)
Orders, Instructions, etc.   *All personnel are to report to Research Headquarters in half an hour.*

3 Present Continuous Am/Is/Are doing   (see Unit one, page 21)
Certain future   *They are exploding another atom bomb in the Pacific next week.*

Exercise 1

Using the tense forms given, write a short paragraph for each of the following.

1 'To be' + Infinitive

Give instructions to a group of children who are to visit a private Game Reserve. Include the following points.

Time and place of meeting
Type of clothing, footwear needed
No cameras
No feeding of animals

2 Simple Present

Your boss, who is an eminent ecologist, has been asked to give a talk at a meeting of the Harford Conservation Society in Sussex. He lives in London and will have to travel by train from Victoria Station. Explain to him the arrangements that have been made. Include the following points.

Time and place of departure
Time of arrival
Where the talk takes place
Duration of talk and lunch breaks
Period set aside for questions and discussion
Time of return to London

3 Present Continuous

Write an extract from a letter to a friend who is interested in a visit you are planning to make to a Bird Sanctuary at Hilldown. Include the following points.

Where and how you are going
Where you are staying and for how long
When you are returning and how

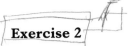

Exercise 2

Read the following passage and answer the questions that follow it, using one of the future forms.

'It'll be all right,' said the man. 'If we tie this bit of shirt to the mast, it'll show which way the wind is blowing.'

'It's a dead calm,' said his companion. 'By sundown, we shall have been drifting for four hours.'

5 'It'll be all right,' repeated the man. 'You sleep for a bit, I'll keep a look-out.'

'They'll be sending a helicopter to look for us soon,' said the other. 'They'll find us – they always do.'

'They won't bother,' said the first man, trying to conceal his doubts. 'They'll reckon we'll have drowned in that storm two days ago. What's it to them? Two

10 jailbirds on a working party steal a boat, get away –'

'Political jailbirds,' corrected his friend. 'They won't give up that easy.'

'It'll be all right,' the first man said again – it was his favourite phrase and it covered all the nagging anxieties and doubts that beset him. 'It'll be all right.'

The boat drifted on, the rag of shirt barely moving in the breeze. The men

15 slept, their bodies blistered, their hair and beards already caked with sea salt. Presently the first man woke. He opened his eyes painfully and then, suddenly alert, shook his companion. 'Look,' he cried, 'land! That'll be the island.'

'What do you mean "island"?' murmured his companion sleepily. 'Milo Island', said the man, cupping his hands round his eyes to get a better view. 'It's not

20 marked on the map. They'll look everywhere, but they'll never find this. Land there and we'll have fooled them.'

'Will there be water there – food?' asked the other man. He leaned over the side of the boat, peering at the small mound of land towards which the boat was gently drifting.

25 'Course there will.' The first man was exultant. 'Look at all that green. That means there'll be water and fish and birdlife.'

'Looks pretty,' said the other man, 'but what's going to happen to us? Shall we have to stay there for ever?'

'Who knows?' said the first man. 'Governments come and governments go. We

30 aren't that important. They'll have forgotten all about us in five years' time.'

'Five years' time?' His companion considered this. 'We'll probably have gone mad by then.'

'Well, who cares?' The first man was impatient now. 'There aren't any notices there, saying we're to be arrested or shot or brought to trial. We'll be running

35 aground in a minute. Give us a hand. We don't want to scrape the bottom off the boat. After that, you do as you please. I'm staying.'

After a few moments, the two men scrambled ashore on to an island, fringed with tall palms weighted with coconuts, and brilliant with patches of scarlet hibiscus and purple bougainvillaea. For a short while they lay exhausted on the

40 sand. It was soft and silver, enfolding their tired bodies like a blanket. 'It'll be all right,' the first man repeated to himself with more assurance. 'We're going to be all right here.'

In a control room many miles from Milo Island, two men reviewed the plans for the following day.

45   'It's all set for tomorrow then,' one of them said proudly. 'It'll be the biggest bang yet.'

'Will there be much risk of fall-out?' the other inquired. It was an idle question. He was not greatly concerned about the answer.

'Well, there's always fall-out,' the man who had spoken first liked to air his
50   knowledge, 'but that island's about as remote as you can get. There won't be any ships in the area, that's for sure. A few birds'll be killed, a good many fish – and no one'll be able to go near there for a very long time. But what's it matter, no one goes there anyway. ...' He hesitated, looking a little doubtfully at his friend. 'Don't you worry. No one's going to get hurt. It'll be all right, you'll see.'

1   What do you think will happen if you tie a piece of rag to the mast of a small boat?
....

2   What does the first man mean when he says he will 'keep a look-out'?
....

3   Why does the second man sound so pessimistic?
....

4   How does the first man reassure him?
....

5   What does the first man mean by the phrase 'it'll be all right'?
....

6   How do we guess that the first man was not surprised to see Milo Island?
....

7   What doubts did the other man express about the island?
....

8   Why does the first man ask his companion to 'give him a hand'?
....

9   What phrase does the first man use to express his determination to remain on the island?
....

10 'It'll be the biggest bang yet' (line 45). What do you think is going to happen?
....

11 State briefly what the first man in the control room thinks is likely to happen.
....
....

12 What restrictions do you think will be placed on the area surrounding Milo Island and why will this cause no particular inconvenience?
....
....

13 Summarise in 50–100 words the reasons why the two men in the boat were seeking refuge on Milo Island.
....
....

Exercise 3

Look at the diagrams on the right and, given the following facts, state which lake you think will be most polluted in two years' time. Give your reasons and the possible result of such pollution.

1   All three lakes provide a source of water supply to neighbouring villages.

2   All three lakes are surrounded by farmland which is regularly treated with insecticide and fertiliser.

3   The factory and the sewage works discharge waste into Lakes A and C respectively. The power station returns hot water to Lake B.

4   Deposits of clay and gravel seeping into water cause pollution.

5   Chemical waste, discharged into the water, is highly toxic and may be lethal.

6   Properly treated sewage is a low pollution risk unless the water is very shallow, when salts may produce sewage fungus or 'blanket weed'.

7   Fertiliser and insecticide may also find their way into the water from the land surrounding it.

8   Partly or wholly untreated sewage entering the water provides a breeding ground for bacteria which remove the oxygen from the water and spread disease.

9   Leaves and dead branches which fall into water may cause pollution as they rot.

10 Lake A is deeper than Lake C but not so deep as Lake B.

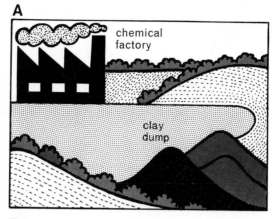

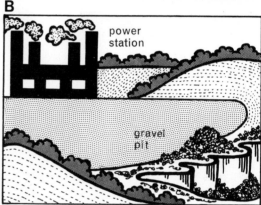

'The earth we abuse and the living things we kill will, in the end, take their revenge'
(*More in Anger* Marya Mannes)

Smog in Los Angeles, USA

WRITTEN SKILLS **A**

Exposition: Giving an Opinion

Comment

In Paper 2 of the Cambridge Certificate of Proficiency examination you may be asked
to write a composition which involves commenting on a given statement or quotation.
To comment really means to say what you think about the subject – in other words, to
give your opinion. But to give an opinion alone is not enough; you must back it up
with some facts or evidence or, perhaps, details of your own personal experience.
Then, after developing your theme, you should finish by drawing all your main points
together and restating your position. So the framework of your composition could look
something like this:

1 Statement

State your position and say what you think about the situation. Try not to start your composition with 'In my opinion ...' or 'I think ...'

2 Development

Substantiate your position with facts and evidence – which could be something you had heard or seen on radio or television or read in the newspapers or a magazine. You could also describe some event or make an observation from your personal experience; relevant anecdotes add interest to your composition, but be very careful if you use humour as what appears hilarious to you will often appear banal to your reader. Similarly, limit your imagination to making reasoned hypotheses based on present evidence; don't get carried away on flights of fancy.

3 Conclusion

Draw all the strands together and round off the composition with a brief summary of your main points and a reaffirmation of your position.

Bearing this framework in mind, it is generally advisable also to make a plan before writing your composition.

The following is a suggested plan for a composition which is commenting on the statement: 'If atmospheric pollution continues at the present rate, in fifty years' time the air will be impossible to breathe.'

1 Statement

Growing concern about air pollution – stronger measures of control should be taken. Increasing hazard in industrial countries – detrimental to health. Planes, cars, factories main culprits.

2 Development

Clean Air History Gt Britain – 1875 Public Health Act – air pollution section – controlled fumes from furnaces. 1952 smog disaster (smoke + fog = smog) 4,000 deaths – 1956 Clean Air Act (CAA) – limit on amount of smoke from fires and factories – smokeless zones.

Effects on Health – Birmingham City Public Health Dept report – rising levels of lead in blood of people living near motorways. MOH Southwark report – tests on children showed 'excessive exposure to lead'. Lead accumulative – high concentrations cause headaches, confusion and forgetfulness, brain damage in children. Carbon monoxide concentrated in atmosphere contributes to chronic respiratory disease. Sulphur dioxide plays major role in bronchitis. Air pollutants significant factor in lung cancer.

Main Culprits space and aircraft – vapour trails – oil sprays from liquid fuel jet emissions – Concorde banned in New York – environmental pressure groups. Cars – exhaust fumes – lead, sulphur dioxide, carbon monoxide – all injurious to health. Japan police on point duty – oxygen masks. Oxygen sold on streets – Tokyo. Move towards developing non-pollutant electric cars – USA, Japan, W. Germany. Factories – give off poisonous gases – some control CAA – fines too low. Flixborough disaster & Italy. Brickworks – fluoride poisoning of cattle 1972.

Unit three

1978 mysterious death farm animals in England. Aerosols – destroy ozone layer in ionosphere which filters ultra violet rays – harmful to man. Insecticides/pesticides – DDT largely banned in developed countries – used extensively in Third World.

Pollutant effects – Carbon dioxide – 'greenhouse' effect reflects/absorbs infra-red rays – heats up atmosphere – possible climatic effects – melting ice caps, flooding. Photochemical fogs of Los Angeles (car exhaust pollution).

3 Conclusion

Air becoming more polluted – increasing amounts of toxic chemicals entering atmosphere – affecting people's health. Web of life upset. Air non-renewable – amount available limited – comparatively thin layer blankets the Earth – should be protected – pollution strictly controlled. Hopeful signs – formation of ecological/conservation groups. USA declared Sun Day (3 May) importance of sun to life – rays can't penetrate atmosphere if too polluted – keep air clean. Solar energy.

Exercise 1

Having made a plan you are now ready to tackle the actual composition. The opening paragraph is given here. Continue for about 200 words, being careful to develop the theme and come to a logical conclusion. Not all the facts in the plan have to be used necessarily – they were jotted down only to remind you of the general direction your essay would take.

If atmospheric pollution continues at the present rate, in fifty years' time the air will be impossible to breathe.

Nowadays there is a growing concern about air pollution and it is widely agreed that stronger measures of control should be taken. In the industrialised countries particularly, pollution is recognised as an increasing hazard and experts and the general public alike acknowledge that it is detrimental to health. It should not be forgotten that the amount of air available to our planet is finite, so the main culprits of pollution – aircraft, cars and factories – must be more strictly controlled, if we do not want to damage our atmosphere beyond redemption.

Exercise 2

The Amazon forests have been called 'the lungs of the world' – comment.

The following notes may help you. Trees/plants breathe out oxygen – oxygen necessary for life. Industrial countries increasingly pollute air – Brazil becoming industrialised – Amazon forests being cut down for roads, industrial development, etc. Shallow layer of air round Earth – non-renewable.

Exercise 3

Write a composition of not more than 350 words on
either
Everything man touches he spoils
or
Pollution goes hand in hand with modern life

Exercise 4

On the right is a reproduction of the Ringelmann Smoke Chart which is used to assess the colour of smoke emitted from factory chimneys.

Taking the following information into consideration, comment on 'How effective would this chart be in helping to control pollution?'

1 Shade 0 indicates completely clean air.
2 Shade 2 smoke is illegal if emitted for more than 10 minutes in any 8-hour period.
3 Shade 4 smoke is strictly forbidden in any circumstances.
4 Some poisonous gases are colourless.
5 This chart cannot be used at night.

Ringelmann Smoke Chart

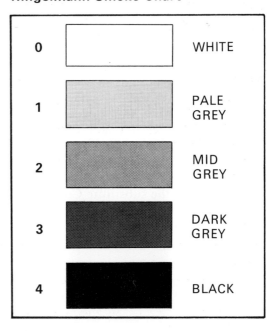

0		WHITE
1		PALE GREY
2		MID GREY
3		DARK GREY
4		BLACK

WRITTEN SKILLS **B**

Intensive Reading

The following passage from Charles Dickens' 'Hard Times' conveys superbly the effect of industrial pollution on a northern town in England in the nineteenth century.
Read the passage and then answer the questions that follow.

Coketown. It was a town of red brick, or of brick that would have been red if the smoke and the ashes had allowed it; but as matters stood it was a town of unnatural red and black like the painted face of a savage. It was a town of machinery and tall chimneys, out of which interminable serpents of smoke trailed
5   themselves for ever and ever, and never got uncoiled. It had a black canal in it, and a river that ran purple with ill-smelling dye, and vast piles of buildings full of windows where there was a rattling and a trembling all day long, and where the piston of the steam-engine worked monotonously up and down like the head of an elephant in a state of melancholy madness. It contained several large streets all
10 very like one another, and many small streets still more like one another, inhabited by people equally like one another, who all went in and out at the same hours, with the same sound upon the same pavements, to do the same work, and to whom every day was the same as yesterday and tomorrow, and every year the counterpart of the last and the next.
15   A sunny midsummer day. There was such a thing sometimes, even in Coketown. Seen from a distance in such weather, Coketown lay shrouded in a haze of its own, which seemed impervious to the sun's rays. You only knew the town was there, because you knew there could have been no such sulky blotch upon the view without a town. A blur of soot and smoke, now confusedly tending this way, now
20 that way, now aspiring to the vault of heaven, now murkily creeping along the earth, as the wind rose or fell, or changed its quarter: a dense formless jungle, with sheets of cross light in it, that showed nothing but masses of darkness.
    The streets were hot and dusty on the summer day, and the sun was so bright that it even shone through the heavy vapour drooping over Coketown, and could
25 not be looked at steadily. Stokers emerged from low underground doorways into factory yards, and sat on posts, and steps, and palings, wiping their swarthy faces, and contemplating coals. The whole town seemed to be frying in oil. There was a stifling smell of hot oil everywhere. The steam-engines shone with it, the dresses of the hands were soiled with it, the mills throughout their many storeys oozed and
30 trickled it. The atmosphere of those places was like the breath of hell: and their inhabitants wasting with heat, toiled languidly in the desert. But no temperature made the melancholy mad elephants more mad or more sane. Their wearisome heads went up and down at the same rate, in hot weather and in cold, wet weather and dry, fair weather and foul. The measured motion of their shadows on the
35 walls, was the substitute Coketown had to show for the shadows of rustling woods; while for the summer hum of insects, it could offer all the year round, from the dawn of Monday to the night of Saturday, the whirr of shafts and wheels.

1   What do you think was the author's opinion of Coketown?
2   Give three reasons why life in Coketown would be unpleasant.
3   What was Dickens' purpose in comparing the steam-engines to 'melancholy mad elephants'?

4 Normally in northern European countries the sun is welcomed, but how do you think the people of Coketown viewed it?

5 What took the place of nature in Coketown?

6 In what ways were the town and the people alike?

7 Comment on the author's way of portraying Coketown, with particular reference to: **a** industrial pollution; **b** the life of the people.

WRITTEN SKILLS **C**

Fact and Comment

N.B. In the following exercises, the student is expected to draw his own conclusions and support them by facts taken from the information given.

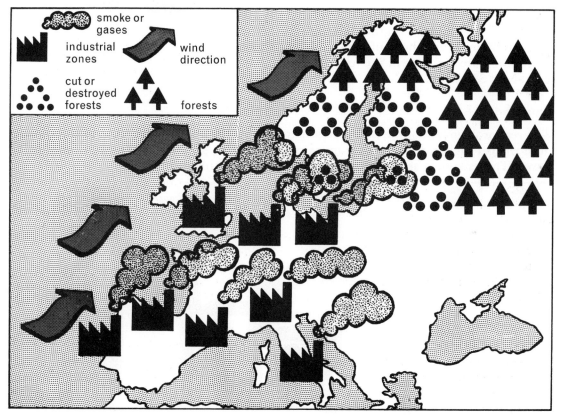

Exercise 1

1 Study the map of industrial Europe carefully.

2 Consider these points:

   a Most of the winds blow from a westerly direction

   b Scandinavia is the biggest producer of timber in the world

   c Sulphur dioxide causes extensive damage to forests

   d One of the gases emitted by factories is sulphur dioxide

   e Gases are airborne

3 Write not more than 150 words on how you would expect air pollution to affect Scandinavia.

Unit three

Exercise 2

The Population Explosion

At the moment the world population is over 4,000 million and the overall growth rate is 1·9%; experts therefore predict that the population will have doubled by the year 2014. Unfortunately the highest growth rate is in the developing countries which are the least able to support rapidly growing populations. Air, sea and land pollution is increasing and natural resources are running out.

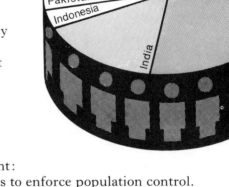

Taking all the above facts into consideration, comment on the statement:
either Mankind's only hope of survival is to enforce population control.
or Children are the hope of the future.
Use about 350 words.

Exercise 3

The real problem about the population increase is, of course, the fact that as the numbers get higher, the growth is more rapid even though the actual percentage rate is lower. This is known as exponential growth and works like this.

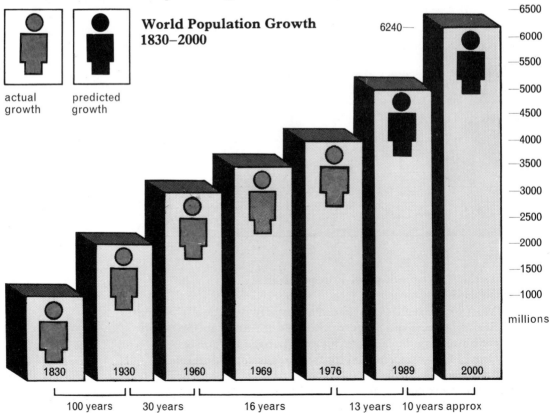

actual growth

predicted growth

World Population Growth 1830–2000

1830 | 1930 | 1960 | 1969 | 1976 | 1989 | 2000

100 years | 30 years | 16 years | 13 years | 10 years approx

From the histogram (bar chart) on the previous page you can see that less and less time is required to produce 1,000 million people. It took many thousands of years to produce the first 1,000 million people but only 30 years to produce the next 1,000 million, and experts predict that it will take only 10 years or less to produce 1,000 million in the future, even though the actual growth rate is dropping.

1 When would you expect the population to reach 7,000 million?

2 Why do you think the first 1,000 million was reached so slowly?

3 Comment on the statement, 'The World Population has increased in leaps and bounds since 1930'. Take the following points into account.
Increased industrialisation – better medical facilities – control of disease – lower death rate – growth of technology – better communications – improved farming methods – increased food production – more balanced diet.

Exercise 4

Unfortunately as the population rises, so does pollution. More waste material has to be disposed of, which causes pollution of the land, sea and air. Also, the increasing population demands more and more energy supplies and the production of this energy causes some of the worst pollution of all. Until the natural resources run out, one of the most difficult pollutants to control is oil. Millions of tons of oil are poured into the sea each year; some deliberately as tankers wash out their tanks, but much of it is spilled accidentally as tankers go aground or collide with other ships. Although oil companies are held responsible for the spillage and have to pay compensation, it is left to the local authorities to clean up the mess.

Fighting Oil Pollution

Oil pollution can be tackled in several ways and different countries use different methods. Consider the pros and cons of these methods of fighting oil pollution.

	Method	Pros	Cons
1	Dispersal with detergents	Breaks up oil slicks fast; easy to spray on sea from tugs	Damage to marine life
2	Restriction with a boom	Stops oil reaching land, beaches; easy to operate	Can only stop modest leakages reaching shore; oil remains on sea behind boom
3	Use of absorbent materials to soak up oil	Cheap, safe method	Lengthy procedure – material must be collected and burnt or buried
4	Sinking by rubber granules or specially treated sand	Easy to apply	Expensive; takes long time to sink oil
5	Burning at sea	Fast and effective if done as soon as oil leaks	Dangerous as could set tanker alight

Now consider the following situations and discuss the most appropriate method to combat oil pollution for each one.

Unit three

Situation 1
A large oil tanker has gone aground on sandbanks just off the coast of eastern Britain. Oil is slowly seeping from the hull of the tanker but there is a danger that the tanker could become tilted by the rough seas and winds and then the seepage would become a flood. Action must be taken quickly.

Situation 2
A slick of oil several miles long is floating in the channel a few miles off the Channel Islands – sea currents could sweep the slick on to the islands. The islands' economy depends on tourism – they cannot risk the beaches becoming polluted – the authorities haven't got much money to spend on fighting pollution.

Situation 3
There has been a blow-out at an oil rig and tonnes of oil have spouted into the sea – the flow has been stopped but the oil company concerned is now faced with a huge mopping-up operation – they have plenty of money to spend and a lot of equipment.

Situation 4
An oil tanker has been sliced in half by another ship and tonnes of oil are being pumped into the sea. The tanker is lying about one mile out from a bay – the villagers depend on fishing for their livelihood.

Situation 5
The captain of an oil tanker is unloading oil at sea by washing out his tanks, when he is spotted by the navy patrolling those waters. He is instructed to clear up the pollution – if necessary he can get help from the country he's registered under.

Exercise 5

Comment on the statement, 'More oil is wasted than used as energy'.

Exercise 6

'We must cease degrading our environment and start to improve it'
– Dr Samuel Lehner, Vice-President, Du Pont Chemical Company
Make brief notes and then write 200 words commenting on this statement.

WRITTEN SKILLS D
Vocabulary

One of the main difficulties encountered when writing a composition is not having enough vocabulary for the specialised topics you may have to tackle. Although the Proficiency candidate will not be expected to know specialist vocabulary, he should be able to use general words and expressions which are connected with specialist topics. For example, when dealing with ecology the student would be expected to be familiar with the meaning and use of such general terms as: pollution, environment, balance of nature, the population explosion, wildlife, conservation, survival. The next question is how to acquire a good general vocabulary? Well, perhaps the best way is by reading as much and as many different kinds of material as possible. To memorise some of the new vocabulary, you might find it helpful to make vocabulary lists, especially on specialised subjects.

Consider the following lists on ecology. See how many of the words you know and add any more in this field that you may come across.

Ecology

Wildlife	Population	Pollution		
endangered species	population explosion	pollutants	(air)	(land)
extinct	over-populated	poisons	fumes/smog	rubbish tips
survival	growth	toxic	pall	slag heaps
	birth/death rate	lethal	blotted out	dumping
words connected with destruction:	birth control/ family planning	contaminate	haze	refuse
		deteriorate	emission	soil erosion
	contraceptives		spew out	dustbowl
	stability	(water)	water vapour	barren land
bludgeoned to death	decline	sewage	lead particles	insecticides
slaughtered	fertility drugs	pumping	exhaust pipe	pesticides
harpooned		purifying	smokeless zones	fungicides
battered		discharge	aerosol sprays	defoliants
exterminate	_General ecology_	clean-up	ozone	fertilisers
annihilate		waterlogged	smoke stacks	detergents
	eco-systems	fluorides	filter	recycle
	conservation	effluents		
words connected with preservation:	interbalance	sludge	(oil)	(nuclear)
	web of life	decompose	spillage/leakage	fall-out
	balance of nature	slime	slick	radioactive
bird sanctuary	environment	ooze	tanker	waste processing plant
game reserve	lungs of the world	outlets	tug	quick breeder reactor
safari park	preservation		gush/pour out	plutonium
zoos (breeding)	destruction		patches	
			skim	
			boom	

Organisations

Oxfam	Family Planning Association	The National Trust
War on Want	The Nature Conservancy	The Royal Society for the Protection of Birds
Friends of the Earth		

Unit three

Exercise 1

In each of the following sentences fill the blank space with the most appropriate word or phrase from the selection given.

1 It seems inevitable that some species of wildlife will become .... as countries become industrialised.
   A extinguished   *B* extinct   *C* extricated   *D* exfoliated

2 The .... of life is in serious danger of being broken because of Man's pollution of the Earth.
   A net   *B* thread   *C* web   *D* cord

3 .... detergents on to the surface of the sea is one of the usual methods of dispersing oil.
   A strewing   *B* scattering   *C* spattering   *D* spraying

4 Local councils are obliged to designate certain areas of land as rubbish ....
   A tips   *B* piles   *C* heaps   *D* mounds

5 Sometimes oil spillage in the sea can form a .... several miles long.
   A streak   *B* slick   *C* strip   *D* smear

6 The blue whale has practically died out as so many have been .... and dragged back to land for their oil and blubber.
   A clubbed   *B* battered   *C* harpooned   *D* speared

7 .... believe that the exploitation of natural resources should always be less than the maximum possible.
   A industrialists   *B* conservationists   *C* custodians   *D* protectors

8 The waste materials from Man's industries have now begun to poison his ....
   A locality   *B* situation   *C* settlement   *D* environment

9 Burning is one method of combating oil pollution but is only effective if done immediately the oil begins to ....
   A leak   *B* pour   *C* dribble   *D* drip

10 One of the methods of producing alternative energy is by using a plant which takes in organic .... and produces methane gas.
   A rubbish   *B* sewage   *C* pollution   *D* waste

11 Atmospheric pollution in Los Angeles is .... the sun; on some days no rays penetrate this smog.
   A rubbing out   *B* striking out   *C* wiping out   *D* blotting out

12 The Minemata disease in Japan was caused by people eating fish which had been .... by mercury poisoning.
   A contaminated   *B* corrupted   *C* desecrated   *D* defiled

13 Techniques such as .... raw materials relieve the drain on natural resources.
   A re-using   *B* recycling   *C* restoring   *D* re-assembling

14 The indiscriminate use of .... to control insects is having a detrimental effect on the land and atmosphere.
   A detergents   *B* fungicides   *C* defoliants   *D* pesticides

15 Technological research has resulted in machinery which purifies .... from factories.
A expulsions   *B* ejections   *C* emissions   *D* evictions

16 In 1956 Great Britain started to tackle the problem of air pollution by creating smokeless ....
A areas   *B* regions   *C* districts   *D* zones

17 Ecologists and conservationists in America originally succeeded in getting Concorde banned in New York as they thought the quality of their life would be ....
A abated   *B* diminished   *C* mitigated   *D* blunted

18 Some of the pollutants in the .... fumes emitted from cars can cause asthma and bronchial diseases.
A effluent   *B* exhaust   *C* explosive   *D* erupting

19 The survival .... of some wild animals is not very high as they are ruthlessly hunted for their skins.
A rate   *B* degree   *C* ratio   *D* scale

20 There is growing opposition to the building of nuclear power stations as people realise the devastation that would result from nuclear .... if there were an accident.
A blow-out   *B* fall-out   *C* drop-out   *D* knock-out

21 A bird .... has been established on an island off the west coast of Scotland.
A haven   *B* refuge   *C* sanctuary   *D* asylum

22 Recent research indicates that the use of asbestos can be .... to factory workers.
A deadening   *B* lethal   *C* annihilating   *D* intoxicating

23 Pesticides sprayed on crops .... the environment.
A infiltrate   *B* influence   *C* permeate   *D* adulterate

24 Water must be kept clear of leaves and branches as pollution may result if they ....
A dissolve   *B* liquefy   *C* rust   *D* rot

25 By the end of the century many species of wildlife will have become ....
A defunct   *B* extinct   *C* obsolete   *D* void

Exercise 2

Look at the vocabulary lists again and consider the names of these organisations.

Greenpeace (for the protection of whales)	Family Planning Association
Oxfam	The Nature Conservancy
War on Want	The National Trust
Friends of the Earth	The Royal Society for
The Soil Association	the Protection of Birds
World Wildlife Fund	World Health Organization
	Watch (for young conservationists)

1 Make three lists, placing each organisation under one of the headings:
Conservation of the Earth   Preservation of Wildlife   Protection of People
N.B. Some will go under more than one heading.

2   The names of some of these organisations do not immediately indicate their aim – which ones are they? Why do you think these names were chosen – is there an emotional connection? Could you think of better names?

3   Think of names for organisations connected with: **a** the responsible use of technology, **b** the countryside, **c** children, **d** the environment, **e** rivers and canals.

Exercise 3

These are the titles of recent publications concerned with different aspects of ecology. Look at the titles and then for each one write down the first three words that come into your mind.

Guilty	Nature's Network
Breakthrough	The Good Earth
Crisis	Help
Undercurrents	At Risk

Study your replies and then for each group of words write a sentence showing how your words link up with the themes as indicated by the titles.

REMINDER 3

Uses of Shall/Shan't and Will/Won't

Shall and **Shan't** and **Will** and **Won't**
How you use them, how you don't.

Students are sometimes confused by the differences in stress and meaning that can occur in the use of Shall/Shall not (Shan't) and Will/Will not (Won't) in future tenses. Following is a brief revision of their uses.

Shall/Shan't is used for:

1   1st person sing./plural: 'I/We', but in practice 'Will/Won't' are often substituted. No particular emphasis is understood as both are usually expressed in the short form ''ll' in affirmative speech

I'll check the rain gauge tonight.
We will start the lecture promptly at 2 o'clock.
We shan't leave before ten.
I won't see him today.

2   2nd/3rd persons sing./plural: You/He/She/It/They. Orders and obligations

The children shall paint some posters for the Wildlife Show.
They shan't spray my garden with that insecticide.

Promises

You shall certainly have the information by first post tomorrow.

3   Offers, suggestions, enquiries. Rarely used except in the 1st person

Shall I help you prune that tree?
Shall we go blackberrying this afternoon?
Shall John bring his camera?
Shall you visit the bird sanctuary, do you think?

Will/Won't is used for:

1 2nd/3rd persons sing./plural
   No particular emphasis
   Short form affirmative speech ''ll'

   They'll be distributing the Anti-Pollution leaflets this afternoon.
   He'll have finished his report by four o'clock.

2 All persons: Inflexible determination
   Short form ''ll' not used as stress is placed on 'will/won't'

   I will sign the petition; I don't care what you say.
   He won't take advice from anyone.
   She will keep interrupting during the lecture.

3 All persons: offers in response to questions

   'Who'll help me mow the lawn?'
   'I will, but I know John won't.'

Exercise

Complete the following paragraph using suitable forms of 'shall/will' with the verbs given.

The Government have decided that they (build) a nuclear waste processing plant in North Wales. The local residents are determined that this (not take place). They say they (cause) every kind of obstruction to prevent it. The only question is, they (start) to cause trouble now or they (wait) till the construction company arrive? 'I (go) to prison rather than allow this processing plant to endanger our district,' said Mr Billings, one of the local farmers. 'No one (desecrate) our beautiful countryside with this eyesore, to say nothing of the pollution that it (cause).' The local Conservation Society say they are sure they (be able) to obtain at least 5,000 signatures to their petition and they have promised that a copy of the petition with the names of those who have signed (be displayed) in every shop window and public place in the neighbourhood. 'We (not let) the matter rest,' said Mrs Johnson, mother of five. 'Our children (not be put) at risk in this way. We (fight) them to the bitter end. We are determined that they (understand) the lengths to which we are prepared to go to prevent this thing happening. We realise that they probably (not take) any serious notice of us at first, but I promise you it (not be) long before they do.'

Unit four Health and Fitness

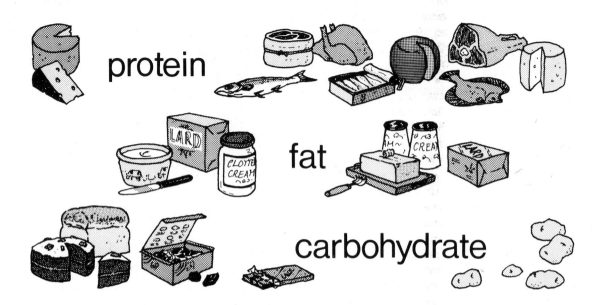

protein

fat

carbohydrate

ORAL SKILLS A

Intensive Listening

Listen to this extract from a lecture by Dr Taylor to a group of first-year student dieticians.

The primary consideration in achieving a balanced diet is not how much or how little we eat, but what we eat. The body is a highly complex self-generator, that is to say, provided it is given the right fuel, it is capable of both curing and warding off disease. Like any other machine, however, if it is inexpertly cared for, over-
5   taxed or insufficiently used, it will become rusty, sluggish or clogged and parts of its mechanism may even grind to a halt. The proper care of the body requires an understanding of its needs, allowing for variations resulting from climate, age or occupation. To keep in good running order, the body requires the raw materials for growth and the replacement of tissues when necessary. Our bodies burn food like
10 fuel to produce the energy we need. Basically we need carbohydrates, protein, fat, vitamins and minerals, together with regular but not excessive exercise. Carbohydrates are found in foods such as bread, potatoes and sugar. They are excellent energy producers, but if eaten to excess may be largely converted to fat and a reduction in the amount of carbohydrates or 'starchy' foods is one of the
15 obvious ways to reduce weight, since most of us eat too much of them anyway. Protein, found in meat and cheese, is used for tissue building and in the developed countries most people eat about 110 g daily, which is a good deal more than the recommended minimum of 70 g a day. In underdeveloped countries where food is scarce and periodical famine may occur, children in particular suffer from protein
20 deficiency, since this is the material most needed for growth. Animal fats, e.g. butter, are also good sources of energy, but are sometimes held to cause increased cholesterol levels in the blood (which may lead to fatty deposits in the arteries) and

are therefore best avoided by people suffering from certain forms of heart disease, vegetable fats being recommended as a substitute.

25   Vitamins are another essential requirement for health. There are about forty known vitamins, but the most generally referred to are A, B, C, D and E. Deficiency of Vitamin A, found in carrots, rose-hips, liver, etc., is alleged to affect the vision and the skin and reduce resistance to infection. Vitamin C, present in nearly all fruit, particularly oranges and other citrus fruit, has come to be regarded

30   as particularly effective in the prevention of colds and low energy states and claims have recently been put forward regarding the efficacy of large doses of Vitamin C in the treatment of certain mental illnesses.

Among the minerals we need, the most important are calcium, iron and iodine. Milk is one of the richest sources of calcium, which helps to build our bones and

35   our teeth. Lack of iron in the blood produces anaemia and children and others suffering from anaemic conditions are generally advised to increase their intake of iron, which may be found in liver, lentils, molasses and dates among other foods.

In any diet, natural foods are best. In the Western world, at least, we have become increasingly dependent on 'convenience foods': frozen peas, tinned meat

40   and fish, ready-to-eat meals from the supermarket, anything which is quick to prepare, looks more or less appetising and satisfies our immediate hunger. We have ceased to care that most of what we eat has had the goodness processed out of it. We rely on pills to supply what our food lacks. We ignore the preservatives, artificial colouring and additives in the packaged foods we buy. In the kind of

45   world we live in, however, there is, of course, no quick, easy answer.

Climate and work play an important part in diet. People in hot climates require fewer carbohydrates than those in colder regions, and those engaged in heavy manual labour or physical exertion, such as dockers or athletes, require more protein to keep them fit for their work. We are all individuals and a balanced diet

50   must take into account genetics, environment, employment and, last but not least, emotional stress. Tension and anxiety are often the underlying causes of over- and underweight and even dietary deficiency since our nervous system needs to be fed as much as any other part of our body.

Exercise

Read or listen to the talk again – you may make notes if you wish – and then answer the following questions.

1   Why is the body described as 'a highly complex self-generator'?
2   What will happen if the body is not properly looked after?
3   What basic materials does the body need to function adequately?
4   Why should an excessive intake of carbohydrates be avoided?
5   Why do we need protein and what is the minimum amount the average person needs daily?
6   State the reason why people suffering from heart complaints should not eat butter.
7   Give examples of foods in which Vitamin A and Vitamin C are found.
8   In what way has attention recently been drawn to the use of Vitamin C?
9   Why do we need calcium and iron and in what kinds of food can these minerals be found?
10   What is the speaker's chief objection to 'convenience foods'?
11   Why do you think a weight-lifter needs more protein than a clerk in an office?
12   What four important points should be considered in planning a balanced diet?

ORAL SKILLS **B**

Look and Choose

You have invited two friends, Harry and Christine, to lunch with you at a small restaurant. Study the following menu and choose the most suitable lunch for each person, including yourself, taking into account that:

1 you cannot afford to spend more than £6.50 altogether,
2 Harry is a physical training instructor,
3 Christine is rather anaemic after a bad bout of 'flu,
4 you, yourself, are trying to lose weight.

Orange, grapefruit or tomato juice   *30p*

Potato soup   *30p*

Prawn cocktail   *50p*

Sausage, egg and chips   *55p*

Liver and bacon   *65p*

Fried fillet of plaice and chips   *75p*

Grilled herrings in mustard sauce   *70p*

Steak and kidney pie   *75p*

Roast beef and Yorkshire pudding   *£1.30*

Chicken casserole with mushrooms   *£1.25*

Assorted cold meats and salad   *85p*

Egg mayonnaise   *75p*

Cheese, apple and date salad   *75p*

Vegetables

Roast, baked or boiled potatoes   *25p*

Grilled tomatoes   *25p*

Creamed cauliflower   *30p*

Runner beans   *20p*

Garden peas   *20p*

Buttered carrots   *25p*

Sweet Course

Apple pie and cream   *35p*

Steamed chocolate pudding   *30p*

Caramel custard   *30p*

Trifle   *35p*

Fruit salad and cream   *35p*

Assorted ice cream   *30p*

Cheese and biscuits   *30p*

Coffee   *25p*

Service charge included

ORAL SKILLS C
Listening Comprehension

Two businessmen have met in the park before breakfast. One is exercising his dog, the other is trying to keep fit by running twice round the park every morning.

Listen to the dialogue and then for each of the questions 1–5 put a tick (✓) in one of the boxes A, B, C or D.

1 How often does Charles Evans go jogging?

A	Once a day
B	Twice each morning
C	Every month
D	Before and after breakfast

2 George Barker's dog

A	is too thin
B	doesn't weigh enough
C	only eats cream cakes
D	is very fat

3 To 'overstrain' yourself means to

		A	
		B	
		C	
		D	

A be exhausted by too much exertion

B do something to excess

C work excessively hard and long hours

D do more than you are physically fit to do

5 Which of these expressions would best express a heightened feeling of stimulation?

		A	
		B	
		C	
		D	

A To have overeaten

B To be overexcited

C To have overdone it

D To be overweight

4 Charles Evans sat down because he

		A	
		B	
		C	
		D	

A was exhausted by jogging

B needed to have a short rest

C was too tired to continue running

D found it an effort to keep awake

Note the expressions with 'over' used in the dialogue:

so long as you don't *overdo it*

she gets a bit *overexcited*

she's terribly *overweight*

the trouble is she *overeats*

you don't want to *overstrain* yourself

been *overworking*, have you?

a man who's *overtired* doesn't do his work well

To overdo it	to do something to excess
To be overexcited	to be too excited
To be overweight	to be too fat
To overeat	to eat more than is good for you
To overstrain yourself	to do more than you are physically fit to do
To overwork	to work excessively hard and long hours
To be overtired	to be exhausted by too much exertion

Exercise

Using one of the expressions with 'over', respond to the following situations.

1 One of your close friends is always eating chocolates and cream cakes and is putting on weight. Advise him/her what will happen if he/she continues to eat like this.

2 A colleague at work has been staying late at the office every day and taking home work every evening. He looks very tired. What do you say to him?

3 You have recently recovered from an internal operation and now a friend has suggested that it would do you good to come on a climbing holiday in Austria. Your doctor does not think this advisable. Refuse your friend's offer politely and explain why.

4 Your little niece, aged five, is going on holiday tomorrow and will be travelling by plane for the first time. She is looking forward to it all so much that she cannot get to sleep. How would you describe her state of mind?

5 You are supposed to be slimming, but when you spent a holiday with your aunt in the country, you couldn't resist her good cooking. Explain why you are now on a strict diet.

ORAL SKILLS **D**
Comparative Idioms

Note the following comparative idioms which are often used when referring to physical fitness.

As fit as a fiddle
As strong as a horse
As thin as a rake
As fat as a pig
As stiff as a poker
As light as a feather
As heavy as lead
As hungry as a hunter

Exercise

The children at Barford School have to attend a Physical Training class twice a week. Most of them enjoy it, but one doesn't.
Read or listen to the following.

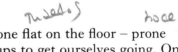

Teacher	Now children, are we all ready? Everyone flat on the floor – prone position – right? Now for a few press-ups to get ourselves going. One and two – and one and two and – Johnny, you shouldn't bend your legs like that, you should try and keep them straight – one and two and –
5	one and two and –
Johnny	I wish we didn't have to do this. I bet I'll be stiff as a poker tomorrow. I hate P.T.
Jenny	I don't. I'd much rather do P.T. than sit through some boring old lesson. Doing P.T. makes you fit as a fiddle, that's what my Dad says.
10 **Johnny**	He would. He's nuts about keeping fit, your Dad. He'd better watch out or he'll have a fit or something, jogging round the park every morning like he does.
Jenny	No, he won't. He's as strong as a horse, so there!
Teacher	Now, children, all together – roll over, arms flat by your sides –
15	tummies in – that's right, tighten those tummy muscles. We don't want a lot of flabby tummies, do we?
Johnny	I wish she wouldn't keep talking about flabby tummies. I'm starving. I wonder what's for dinner?
Jenny	Oh, you – you're always thinking about food. You're as fat as a pig as
20	it is.
Johnny	No, I'm not. Anyway, I'd rather be fat than skinny like you. Thin as a rake, that's what my Mum says you are.
Teacher	Now, come along, children. On your feet. Time for skipping. Have you all got your ropes?
25 **Johnny**	I wish I hadn't got mine. I hate skipping. It's stupid. If only I'd sprained my ankle or something.
Teacher	Are we all ready? Right. Light as a feather, everyone. One and two and three and four – try not to thump, Johnny. Jenny, don't stand so near to Johnny, you'll hit him with your rope. No, Johnny, you're not really
30	skipping, you're hopping. Come out to the front and let me show you.

Read or listen to the dialogue again and repeat what Johnny says.

ORAL SKILLS **E**
Wishes and Regrets

Notice these expressions in the dialogue.

I wish we didn't have to … (line 6)
I'd much rather … (line 8)
I wish she wouldn't … (line 17)
I'd rather be … (line 21)
I wish I hadn't … (line 25)
If only I'd … (line 25)

Repeat these phrases.

Exercise 1

Using one of these expressions of wishes or regret, what would you say if:

1   Someone invited you to a judo display, but you would prefer to watch TV

    ....

2   You'd overeaten and now you'd got indigestion

    ....

3   You'd been persuaded to take up jogging, but you didn't realise how tired you would get

    ....

4   Your friend was always telling you that you ought to give up smoking

    ....

5   Someone suggested you went to Keep Fit classes to lose weight, but you would prefer to be on a diet

    ....

6   You attended a Keep Fit class but you were very bad at doing press-ups

    ....

Exercise 2

Note that 'had better' and 'hadn't you better?' give *advice* here.

Example
My eyes are troubling me.
Hadn't you better see an oculist?

Give advice in these situations.

1   Mary has been overworking.   .... ?
2   John has toothache.   .... ?
3   Your friend has 'flu.   .... ?
4   The girls don't get enough exercise. .... ?
5   Mr Brown is very irritable.   .... ?
6   Sally wants to go riding before breakfast tomorrow.

    .... ?
7   Your friend wants to slim.   .... ?
8   Mrs Brown wishes she could relax more.

    .... ?

ORAL SKILLS **F**
Photograph for Discussion

Look at this picture and be prepared to talk about it.

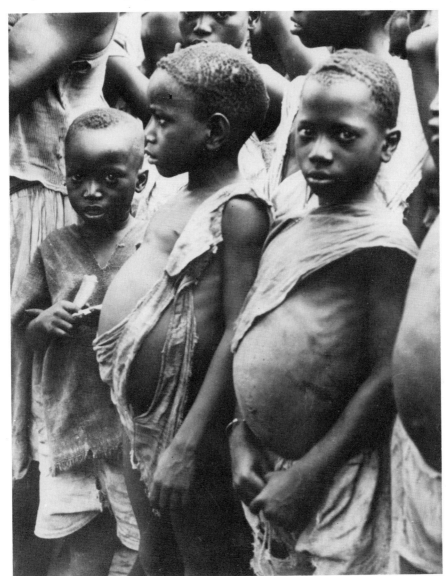

There

wait

Questions

1 Describe the children in the picture.
2 Which part of the world do you think they come from?
3 Why do you think their stomachs are swollen?
4 How are they dressed?

Topics

Malnutrition in developing countries.
Uneven distribution of food resources.
Developed countries' aid to the Third World.

ORAL SKILLS **G**

Reading Aloud

Look at this passage and be prepared to answer some questions about it and then to read it aloud.

> Now, just listen to the beat and follow me. Stretch and pull, turn, turn, up, up and flop. And again – stretch up and twist, right, left, right and flop. Fine. Now for the neck: up and down, right then left and drop. With the beat, up, down, side right, side left and centre – now drop. And the shoulders, forward and centre and back and centre and forward and relax. Right again, forward and centre and back and centre and forward. Good, now let's go for the burn: forward, centre, back, centre, forward – that's fantastic!

Who might be speaking here?   What is happening?   Where might it be taking place?

ORAL SKILLS **H**

Group Discussion

Fitness and Health

the importance of diet   the effects of exercise   'convenience foods'

USE OF ENGLISH **A**

Revision of Conditional Tenses with If/If not/Unless

OP: FUTURO
OC: PRESI

1   Very probable   If/If not/Unless + Present Tense + Simple Future
If she takes the trouble to diet, she'll lose weight.
If he doesn't take more exercise, he'll soon be ill again.
Those children will have trouble with their teeth, unless they drink more milk.
Will he have to go to hospital if he overstrains his heart?

N.B. **a**   'Not' is not used in a clause with 'unless'.
   b   The position of the 'if' and the main clauses are interchangeable, but it is usual for questions to begin with the main clause.
   c   A comma is needed when the 'if' clause comes first, but is not necessary when the main clause comes first.

OC: ... OP: Condicial

2   Possible but unlikely   If/If not/Unless + Simple Past/Past Continuous + Present Conditional/Present Conditional Continuous

If Peter ate less, he would be in better condition.
They would be practising now, if they were taking part in the gymnastics display tomorrow.
He wouldn't give up smoking, unless the doctor insisted.

N.B. If not/Unless can also be used to express the *reason* why something is being done:
He wouldn't run round the park every morning, unless he wanted to be in good condition for the athletics meeting.

96

3   **Impossible**   Refers to an action which, if done, would affect a Present or Past
situation

a   **Present situation:** If/If not/Unless + Past Perfect + Present Conditional
If he had taken the doctor's advice, he wouldn't be in hospital now.
If she hadn't worked so hard, she wouldn't be so tired today.

b   **Past situation:** If/If not/Unless + Past Perfect + Perfect Conditional
If you hadn't taken part in the race, you wouldn't have broken your leg.
If she had learnt to swim, she wouldn't have drowned.

4   **Wishes and Advice**   The Subjunctive of the verb 'to be' + Present Conditional is
often used to express wishes and advice.

N.B. 'Were' is used for all persons singular and plural
If I were rich, I'd buy a swimming pool.
If I were him, I wouldn't work so hard.
If you were me, what would you do to put on weight?

N.B. Unfulfilled wishes or Advice can also be expressed with:
Past Perfect 'to be' + Perfect Conditional
If I'd been him, I'd have given up smoking.
If only I'd been rich, I'd have taken up motor racing.

5   **Assumptions, natural laws and scientific facts**   If/If not/Unless + Present
Tense + Present Tense
If you don't have enough iron in your diet, you become anaemic.
If your mother feels dizzy, she hasn't taken her tablets.
If the water bubbles, it's boiling.

Exercise 1

Put the correct form of the verb in the following sentences.

1   If he (train) as an athlete, I am sure he would have been world famous.
2   What you (do) if there isn't a Keep Fit class in your district?
3   If they had expected such a poor harvest, they (lay in) emergency stores.
4   If you (be) me, (take) you more vitamin C?
5   If the doctor told him to take more exercise, do you think he (take up) jogging?
6   Most business men (be) healthier if they (not eat) so many expensive lunches.
7   I shan't see Mrs Brown today unless she (come) to see the judo class.
8   If you (give) the children more calcium, they wouldn't have had so much trouble
with their teeth.
9   I wouldn't drink quite so much alcohol, if I (be) you.
10   If I'd been their father, I (not allow) them to go skateboarding.
11   If he hadn't insisted on doing those strenuous exercises, he (not suffer) from
backache now.
12   If the light doesn't come on, the kidney machine (not work).
13   I wish I (be) better at skipping; then the other children (not laugh) at me.
14   He will never be any good at gymnastics unless he (practise) more.
15   If they (be) my children, I'd have made them drink a glass of milk every day.
16   What you (do) about the old lady's diet, if you'd been me?
17   You (diet) if I promised to diet too?

18 If he had had the opportunity to train more regularly, I think he (win) the race.

19 If I (not get) enough sleep, I (feel) very irritable.

20 You're looking very tired; I (go) to bed early if I (be) you.

21 Mr Brown (not be) so short of breath if he (not smoke) so much.

22 If you had time, you (take up) yoga?

23 I'm sure you (feel) much better if you didn't work so hard.

24 If those children had had more protein, they (not be) so weak and emaciated as they look now.

25 If only he'd had a good doctor, he (not die).

Exercise 2

You are a trainee social worker and have been asked to study the following information and make a report of 100–150 words to your Senior Tutor, making suggestions that you think would be helpful in improving the general condition of Mrs Bowater and her family; i.e., diet – planned routine – assistance with care of children – holidays, etc.

CASE REF: BOW/4568: Mrs Hilda Bowater
15 Park Buildings, NW2

Husband	*Albert Bowater* – labourer – aged 45 – unemployed – suffering from slipped disc
Wife	*Hilda Bowater* – aged 35 – recovering from mild nervous breakdown following birth of 3rd child – anaemic – overtired – below average intelligence – suffers from feelings of inadequacy – unable to cope with temporarily disabled husband, new baby and two school-age children
Children	*Bobbie* – aged 11 – undersized – listless – frequent colds – poor attendance at school
	Janice – aged 9½ – compulsive eater – grossly overweight – attends school regularly but not yet literate
	Barbara – aged 2 months – clean and well cared for but seriously underweight. Cries incessantly – sleeps for short periods only. Mrs Bowater is breast feeding her.
Accommodation	Two rooms, kitchen, shared bathroom and toilet. The two elder children sleep in one room, mother and father and the baby in the other, which also serves as living room. Both rooms are dark and insufficiently heated. The kitchen is small and inconvenient, containing only a sink and cooker, and two small cupboards.
Income	The family are at present subsisting on Unemployment Benefit, Child Benefit and Supplementary Benefit and are finding it a struggle to make ends meet.

Having carefully considered the circumstances of this family, it seems that there would be a marked improvement if ....

....

....

....

....

USE OF ENGLISH **B**
Degrees of Opportunity, Advice and Obligation

Can/Could May/Might Should/Ought to Must/Have to
are also used in the main clauses of Conditional sentences.

Can	good opportunity	*If you come to our college, you can learn judo.*
Could	suggestion relating to opportunity	*If you came to our college, you could learn judo.*
May	fairly likely	*If he has time, he may take up yoga.*
Might	remote possibility	*If he had time, he might take up yoga.*
Should	recommendation or advice	*If you're tired, you should go to bed early.*
Ought to	stronger recommendation or advice	*If you're so tired every morning you ought to go to bed earlier.*
Must	obligation made by the speaker	*If you want to become a ballet dancer, you must practise every day.*
Have to	obligation not made by the speaker	*If I want to become a ballet dancer, the teacher says I shall have to practise for three hours every day.*

Exercise 1

Re-phrase the following sentences using the words given.

1 I understand there is a possibility of the Mayor being able to attend the Swimming Gala.
   MAY
   ....

2 The doctor advised her to eat plenty of fresh fruit if she wanted to improve her complexion.
   SHOULD
   ....

3 Even if the children are hungry, I don't think it is right for them to eat so many cream cakes.
   OUGHT
   ....

4 If they came a little earlier, they would have a chance to watch the winter Olympics on TV.
   COULD
   ....

5 If you haven't got a bicycle of your own, there's a shop in the village that hires them.
   CAN
   ....

6 I don't think it's very likely that John will win the race, but it's just possible, I suppose.
   MIGHT
   ....

7 If you want to keep fit, you would be well advised to take more exercise.
OUGHT TO

....

8 If you care to stay after the lecture, there will be an opportunity to discuss vitamin deficiency with Dr Harrington.
CAN

....

9 If Peter goes to that school, they will insist on him learning to swim.
HAVE TO

....

10 Do you think there is any possibility of John being persuaded to give up smoking if he reads this article?
MIGHT

....

USE OF ENGLISH **C**
Special Uses: Will/Would/Should

1 **Will**
   a **Will + If + Will/Do**   Parallel offers and promises
      I'll diet, if you will.
      Will you give up smoking if I do?
   b **Will**   for a regular, expected event
      'Is that the phone?'
      'Yes, that'll be my brother, he always rings about this time.'

2 **Would**
   Past Habit – a substitute for 'used to' (not necessarily a Conditional form; more often used with 'when')
   When they lived at the seaside, the children would bathe three times a day.

3 **Should/Would**
   Assumption (not necessarily a Conditional form)
   Mr Brown should have arrived by now.
   'Who were you talking to?'
   'Oh, that would have been our team manager, John White.'

4 **Should/Would + If + Would**
   Formal polite form usually used in letters
   I should be glad if you would let me have an answer by return.

5 **Should**
   a Possibility: literary alternative to 'if' clause
      Should the match be cancelled, the ticket money will be refunded.
   b Remoter possibility with 'if' clause
      If it should rain, the match will be cancelled.
   Note the use of the Simple Future in the main clause.

Exercise

Complete the following sentences using **Will/Would/Should** in a suitable form.

1   When he was staying with us, he .... early every morning to go jogging in the park.   *would get up*
2   'Do you think the team will be late?'
     'Oh no, they .... in their dressing room by now.'
3   Mary says she will join the Keep Fit class if I ...... *I will — I do*
4   I .... grateful if you .... me know how many students will be taking part in the gymnastics display.
5   .... delayed, I will telephone you from the airport.
6   'Who is that man you were talking to in the gym?'
     'Oh, that .... Alan Smith, our team leader.'
7   It's gone three o'clock. The match .... by now.
8   'I think there's someone at the door.'
     'Oh, that *will be* the postman.'
9   If the diet *should* disagree with her, she will discontinue it.
10 Please write to Mr Brown and tell him I .... obliged if he .... to see me tomorrow at 11 o'clock.
11 .... the ground be too muddy, the match *will be* postponed.
12 When we lived in the country, we .... our Saturday afternoons fishing in the river.

USE OF ENGLISH **D**

Expressions of Certainty

When we feel *certain* that a person is, or is not, the one referred to, or that an action did or did not take place we often use:

Positive   Must + Infinitive or Perfect Infinitive
      That man in the blue track suit *must be* the referee.
      He *must have lost* at least ten pounds since he went on that diet.
Negative   Can't/Couldn't + Infinitive or Perfect Infinitive
      That *can't be* our PT instructor, he's too old.
      You *couldn't have taken* two hours to cycle round the park! It's only two miles.

Exercise

Rewrite the following sentences, using Must/Can't/Couldn't to express your certainty.

1   Peter did not take part in the weight-lifting contest. He was in hospital.
     ....
2   The man judging the boxing is Simon James, a well-known sports commentator. You recognise his face.
     ....
3   John brought his camera. You saw him put it in his case.
     ....
4   Mary is not trying to slim. You saw her eating roast potatoes.
     ....
5   Andrew didn't go on the mountaineering expedition. He sprained his ankle.
     ....

6 There was probably some trouble at the football match. The crash barriers had been broken down.

....

7 Learning judo is very difficult.

....

8 You know John didn't pay £25 to join the yoga class. The fee is £15.

....

9 You are sure they haven't sold all the tickets for the Cup Final.

....

10 That's not the college sports ground. It's much too small.

....

'What is more important in life than our bodies?' (George Santayana)

WRITTEN SKILLS **A**
Reading for Information

When you read a piece of writing you may be looking for, or expecting, a number of different things. Perhaps you are looking for information or studying the language used or using the writing as a process of discovery – an insight into experience – as you emotionally respond to the author's words. Possibly you are doing all of these things without being aware of the fact; you only realise that you are receiving pleasure or satisfaction from your reading. In this unit we will be looking at reading for information. Do you read efficiently? Do you use books effectively when you are looking for information? How much can you deduce from the information given? We will be trying to answer these questions during our reading. Another kind of reading – as a study of language – will be covered in Unit six.

Look at the two following advertisements and then consider how much information is given in each one.

A

BOOMPH YOUR WAY TO HEALTH

Does this course work! We have thousands of satisfied customers. Mrs X of East Cheam says, 'It really does work.' Mr Y of Balham states, 'It made a new man of me.' It could work for you too. So don't delay – phone today: 001 1101.

Get trim and stay slim

the

B O O M ! B O O M ! B O O M ! W A Y

B

UNFIT?   OVERWEIGHT?   DEPRESSED?

The Overhill Health Farm has a team of experts who will devise a personal slimming course for you, including a carefully controlled diet, exercise under medical supervision, saunas, massage and yoga classes for relaxation. All the staff are medically trained and qualified dieticians are in charge of the kitchens. You will be assured of complete privacy as the **Overhill Health Farm** is in a beautiful 18th century country house set in 20 acres of secluded grounds. A private swimming pool, tennis courts, a croquet lawn and an 18-hole golf course are available for the use of our clients. Accommodation is either in the house itself or in extremely comfortable chalets in the grounds. Meals are taken together in the house dining room. Come for 1 month, 2 weeks, 10 days, 1 week, or a special long weekend course. Maximum number of clients 35 per course. For prices and further details send for our illustrated brochure:

The Secretary, The Overhill Health Farm, Iving, Berkshire.

Unit four

Advertisement A

How much information does it give? What in fact is it advertising? How does it achieve its effect? What kind of language is used? If you answer these questions I think you will agree that very little information is actually given about the course advertised. The language is emotive and designed to persuade the gullible that they are in good company when they take the course (after all Mrs X and Mr Y are perfectly satisfied and give glowing testimonials). This type of advertisement has been heavily criticised for not providing information and for using the language of persuasion for commercial gain only.

Advertisement B

What information is given here? Is it clear what is being advertised? Is the language used appropriate? What effect does it have? These questions should show you that quite a lot of information is given both about the course available and about the club and its staffing and situation. The language is more controlled and factual, but manages to have a very reassuring effect with its references to 'experts', 'medical supervision', 'medically trained and qualified staff', 'complete privacy' and 'seclusion'. Less criticism can be levelled at this type of advertisement, I think, as it does the job of providing information even if a fair amount of reassuring language is used which might lure the unwary into an uncritical acceptance of the prices.

Exercise 1

1   Which of these advertisements would appeal to people with a modest amount of money to spend? Why? Would they be justified in choosing that kind of course, do you think?
2   Collect some advertisements and divide them into two groups according to whether you think they give information or not. Notice the kind of language used.
3   Write two advertisements recommending a special shampoo. One should use emotive language and give very little factual information, the other should give much more information but may use reassuring or explicit language.

Exercise 2

Consider the following definitions of 'obesity' and decide which gives the most information and which is the easiest to understand.

a   an excess of adipose tissue

b   condition of corpulence

c   being very fat

Your answer will depend upon certain factors. If you choose **a** it is probable that you have some medical knowledge and understand 'adipose tissue'. If you choose **b** then you probably have a wide vocabulary and understand 'corpulence' and if you choose **c** then you understand good basic English and have acquired all the information you need from three simple words. Therefore the information you can get from reading sometimes depends on your own particular skills.

1   Give definitions of 'protein' using three different kinds of language if possible. If you get stuck use a dictionary, but try to make at least one of the definitions in your own words. Give as much information as possible.

2   What do you think the following definition is referring to? 'Rhythmical thrust felt over the artery as it expands in time with the heart beat.' When you think you know the answer, write down the word and then define it in your own words.

3   If you saw a quotation such as, 'Exercise is bunk. If you are healthy you don't need it; if you are ailing you shouldn't take it!' how much information would you get from it? Could you guess any unusual word from its context? Write the quotation in your own words, showing what the author means and using an alternative for 'bunk'.

Exercise 3

You may want to get information, or be asked for it, from a chart, so the ability to pick out facts quickly and correlate them is important. Consider the following chart which is based on information from the Michigan Heart Association.

DO YOUR OWN HEART DIAGNOSIS

*SEX/AGE/ BUILD	FAT% IN DIET	EXERCISE	TOBACCO SMOKING	WEIGHT	HEREDITY	AGE NOW
female under 40	no animal fat	intensive work/play exertion	non-smoker	2·25 kg below normal	no history of heart disease	10–20
1	1	2	0	0	1	1
female 40–50	10% animal fat	moderate work/play exertion	cigar or pipe	2·25 kg above normal	1 relative over 60 with heart disease	21–30
2	2	2	1	1	2	2
female over 50	20% animal fat	sedentary work; intense play exertion	10 cigarettes a day or less	2·75– 9·0 kg overweight	2 relatives over 60 with heart disease	31–40
3	3	3	2	2	3	3
male	30% animal fat	sedentary work; moderate play exertion	20 cigarettes a day	9·5– 15·5 kg overweight	1 relative under 60 with heart disease	41–50
5	4	5	4	3	4	4
stocky male	40% animal fat	sedentary work; light play exertion	30 cigarettes a day	16·0– 22·5 kg overweight	2 relatives under 60 with heart disease	51–60
6	5	6	6	5	6	5
bald stocky male	50% animal fat	complete lack of exercise	40 cigarettes a day or more	23·5– 29·5 kg overweight	3 relatives under 60 with heart disease	61–70 and over
7	7	8	10	7	7	8

*For women, the most important factor is age; for men, it is build.

Unit four

How to calculate the chances of suffering from heart disease

a Study the seven columns, mark the appropriate box in each and then add up your score.

b Add 1 point if you are a smoker who inhales deeply and smokes a cigarette to a short butt.

c Remember that cream, butter and eggs are high in animal fat.

d When calculating the heredity factor, only count parents, grandparents, brothers and sisters as relatives.

e If you are an aggressive personality or live under a lot of stress, add 2 points to your total.

Scoring		Scores	
		Sex	
6 – 11	well below average risk	Fat in diet	
12 – 17	below average risk	Exercise	
18 – 24	average risk	Smoking	
25 – 31	moderate risk	Weight	
32 – 40	dangerous risk	Heredity	
40 – 54	imminent danger,	Age	
	see your doctor immediately	Extra points	
		Total	

1 Calculate the risk run by a short man aged 31 who smokes 20 cigarettes a day, does not inhale deeply, has a diet containing 10% animal fat, is 5·5 kg overweight, works as a clerk, plays tennis and golf and has a father of 62 with heart disease.

2 Work out your own chances of suffering from heart disease.

3 A woman of 55 has a dangerous risk score of 35 points. Which of the following factors do you think would contribute to this score? Tick all the factors relevant to risk.

Smokes 5 cigarettes a day	
High fat diet	
Obesity	
No known history of heart disease	
Takes no exercise	
Anxious personality	
Doesn't eat eggs	
Works as a shop assistant	

Exercise 4

Sometimes the information you require is not presented as clearly as in the chart but has to be deduced from the facts given. Read the following text, which presents an extreme view, and then answer the questions on it.

How the Government can help people conserve their health

Most of the ill health we suffer could be prevented if people made more effort to change their life styles. Instead many people continue to smoke, to drink excessively and to eat unbalanced diets. How can governments help people conserve their health and avoid premature death?

5   Well, many of the measures which need to be taken are primarily a matter of new legislation and need not be expensive. One of the first preventive health measures should be an increase in taxes on tobacco to the point at which consumption falls off. The aim should be to raise the same amount of revenue from a decreasing number of people. In the short term such a policy could even
10   raise extra money which should then be spent on subsidising sport so that advertising tobacco through sports sponsorship could be banned.

      Legislation is badly needed to ban all advertising of tobacco products as it persuades people to smoke more and so is in a large part responsible for the ill health and thousands of premature deaths caused by cancer of the lung. Other
15   measures should be enforced, such as a much tougher health warning on cigarette packets, and tobacco companies should be made to contribute to research into a cure for lung cancer.

      Alcoholism could be prevented by making wines, spirits and strong beers more expensive and the revenue raised could be used to set up clinics to help the people
20   who already have a drink problem and want to give up. Similarly all advertising of alcohol should be banned and compensation paid to families of alcoholics who die of cirrhosis of the liver.

      In Great Britain the national diet was recently blamed by the Royal College of Physicians as a major cause of heart disease. It may also be a cause of breast and
25   bowel cancer. However, a report published by the Department of Health and Social Security does not agree with the findings. In fact the United Kingdom seems to stand alone among some 14 developed countries as the only one whose Department of Health does not recognise the importance of animal fats in diet as a cause of heart disease. The DHSS should now re-assess its position and take the
30   advice of a broader spectrum of experts.

      A country's food and agricultural policy should also be based on a coherent health policy. For political reasons it is considered important to have a relatively cheap supply of eggs, cheese and milk, the very foods which are blamed as the cause of heart disease when eaten in excess. And even if it is disputed that excess
35   animal fat is detrimental to health, foods could be labelled with the average percentage of different fats so that consumers who wanted to reduce their saturated fat intake would be able to do so easily. Food labels should clearly state the sugar content of the food, since excess sugar in the diet is the major cause of dental decay and tooth loss and may also be a factor in heart disease. The
40   Government in Britain has put most of its resources into backing fluoridation instead of financing health warnings on sweets and sweet foods. More severe measures such as restrictions on TV advertising of sweets to children could also be enforced.

      Much more could be done to improve people's diet in Britain and everyone
45   should be encouraged to eat the types of food which are good for health. Current research on the nutritional value of foods should be freely available and the Government should control the advertising of 'rubbish' food. A programme of health education and lessons on sensible eating could be started in the schools with the Government's backing.
50   Finally, the Government should invest in the nation's health by funding more clinics for health screening; the early detection of disease could save many lives, and eventually would prove less costly than the provision of hospital beds, drugs, doctors' services, etc. which become necessary if the disease is not caught at an early stage. Governments should certainly rethink their policy towards people's health and emphasis should be put upon prevention rather than cure.

Unit four

Choose the correct statements from those given and tick the appropriate boxes.

1 The suggested Government legislation on tobacco would have the following effects.

Cigarette prices would rise
Fewer people would pay more
More people would pay less
Tobacco companies would sponsor sports
Revenue would be raised for advertising
Tobacco advertisements would be banned
Compensation to families would come from revenue
There would be fewer deaths from lung cancer

2 In the text a total ban on tobacco advertising is suggested.
   Is this so that:

The money saved can be spent on subsidising sport
The tougher health warnings on the packets will have more effect
There would be less temptation to tobacco users
There would be more money to pay in compensation to families

3 What do you consider to be the main pieces of information contained in this text? How many important points are there?

4 In not more than 100 words, and using your own words, rewrite the text including all the points that you consider important. Remember you are writing to convey information to other people. Keep your language fairly factual and try not to be too emotive.

....

....

....

....

....

Exercise 5

Read the following passage from 'Some Thoughts Concerning Education' by the seventeenth-century writer, John Locke. It is similar to the kind of passage that you may find in Section B of Paper 3 in the Cambridge Certificate of Proficiency examination. Study it carefully and remember that you are reading for information.

Fruit makes one of the most difficult chapters in the government of health, especially that of children. The regulation of this cannot come under any general rule. I am, however, by no means of their mind who would keep children almost wholly from fruit, as a thing totally unwholesome for them; by which strict way,
5 they make them but the more ravenous after it, and to eat good or bad, ripe or unripe, all that they can get, whenever they come at it. Melons, peaches, most sorts of plums, and all sorts of grapes in England, I think children should be kept wholly from, as having a very tempting taste in a very unwholesome juice; so that, if it were possible, they should never so much as see them, or know there were
10 any such thing. But strawberries, cherries, gooseberries or currants, when thoroughly ripe, I think may be pretty safely allowed them, and that with a very liberal hand, if they be eaten with these cautions: 1. Not after meals, as we usually do, when the stomach is already full of other food. But I think they should be eaten rather before or between meals, and children should have them for
15 their breakfasts. 2. Bread eaten with them. 3. Perfectly ripe. If they are thus eaten, I imagine them rather conducing than hurtful to our health. Summer fruits, being suited to the hot season of the year they come in, refresh our stomachs and therefore I should not be altogether so strict in this point, as some are to their children who, being kept so very short, instead of a moderate quantity of well-chosen
20 fruit, which being allowed them, would content them, whenever they can get loose, or bribe a servant to supply them, satisfy their longing with any trash they can get, and eat to a surfeit.

Apples and pears, too, which are thoroughly ripe and have been gathered some time, I think may be safely eaten at any time and in pretty large quantities;
25 especially apples, which never did anybody hurt that I have heard, after October.

Fruits, also dried without sugar, I think very wholesome. But sweetmeats of all kinds are to be avoided.... This I am sure, is one of the most inconvenient ways of expense that vanity has yet found out; and so I leave them to the ladies.

1 Why would some parents forbid their children to eat fruit?
2 What happened if the children were not allowed to eat fruit?
3 What fruits does the writer consider particularly bad for children and how would he prevent them from eating them?
4 What fruits does the writer consider beneficial for children and what provisos does he make about them?
5 Give the meaning of (a) 'them' (line 11), (b) 'them' (line 14).
6 What do you understand by the phrase 'refresh our stomachs' (line 17)?
7 To what does 'some' (line 18) refer?
8 Explain the meaning of the phrase 'being kept so very short' (line 19).
9 How did the children react if they were denied sufficient fruit in the summer season?
10 What views does the writer express about apples?
11 Explain the use of the expression 'some time' (lines 23–24).
12 Give another word for 'pretty' (line 24).
13 The writer believes that sweetmeats should never be eaten because....
14 In a paragraph of not more than 100 words comment on the writer's views and those of his contemporaries regarding fruit and compare them with those generally held today.

WRITTEN SKILLS **B**
Vocabulary

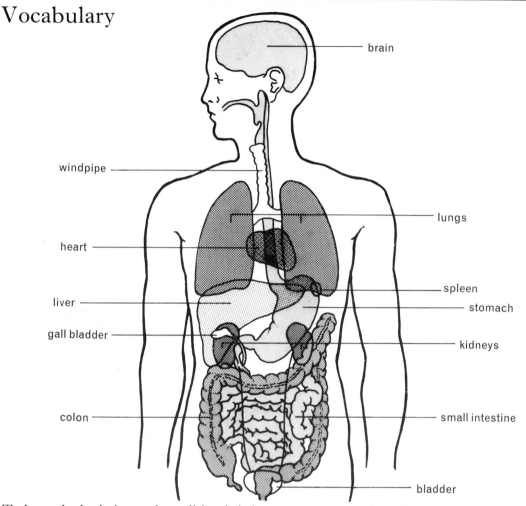

brain

windpipe

lungs

heart

spleen

liver — stomach

gall bladder

kidneys

colon — small intestine

bladder

To keep the body in good condition it is important not to misuse it. It should be kept healthy by exercise, eating and drinking the right things, relaxation and sleep and avoiding over-fatigue. Let's take the vocabulary connected with each area separately.

1 Vocabulary connected with exercising

Exercise helps to: firm sagging flesh
improve body shape
tone up flabby muscles
break down fat
trim the figure
make the joints supple

increase {
physical fitness
mental alertness
pulse rate
}

improve {
appetite
circulation (of blood)
posture
}

Many methods of exercising are possible:

Keep Fit classes	jogging	gymnastics
body building	walking	all active sports
weight lifting	cycling	exercise machines
yoga	swimming	isometrics

110

- demasiado

2 Vocabulary connected with eating and drinking

diet/go on a diet	obese	emaciated	overeat/drink
slim/a slimming diet	overweight	underweight	eat/drink the
give up/cut out	fat	skinny	wrong things
reduce/limit/cut down	stout	bony	gulp/gobble/bolt down
lose/take off weight	plump	thin	feel full/full up
calorie controlled	to bulge _Michelines_ to stick out		to be greedy/a glutton _caprichoso_
fat/salt free	fat as a pig/butter	thin as a rake _espantapájaros_	to be fussy/faddy _protestón_
balanced diet	pudding-like	like a scarecrow	nibble/peck at
deficiency	to have a paunch/	to be all skin	to feel empty/starving
gain/put on weight	pot belly	and bones	dying of thirst
build up	a roll of fat/spare	to look half _medio_	sip/swallow _masticar_
nourishing/nutritional	tyre/double chin	starved _hambriento_	chew/bite
nutrients	broad/spreading	slim/lean/slight	digest/indigestion
	obesity	anorexia	
	flácido flabby/sagging	firm/taut	

3 Vocabulary connected with fatigue, relaxation and sleep
amodorrado _aborrise de una tensión_

to feel drowsy/sleepy	to get rid of tension	ways of relaxing:
to be weary _fatigado_	slow down	saunas/Turkish baths
to be dead tired/beat	take it easy	have a warm bath/shower
overtired	unwind	massage
worn out/exhausted/done up	put your feet up	yoga/transcendental
more dead than alive	take a breather	meditation
physical/mental fatigue	lull to sleep	deep breathing
to look tired/heavy-eyed	_adormecido_	health farms/clubs (also
haggard _trasnochado_		for slimming)

Vocabulary practice/Reading comprehension

In Paper 1, Section A, of the Cambridge Proficiency, you will be asked to answer 25 vocabulary/structure questions. In each question a choice of four words is given and you are required to choose the most appropriate in context. The other three words given are very close in meaning, so careful consideration should be given to your choice.

Exercise

1 A lack of certain vitamins often results in .... and depression.
   A staleness   *B* tension   *C* prostration   *D* dilapidation

2 .... your food will give you indigestion.
   A bolting   *B* gorging   *C* munching   *D* cramming

3 There's an old saying, 'it's the double gins that cause the ....'
   A flat feet   *B* crossed eyes   *C* double chins   *D* knock knees

4 A diet high in carbohydrates contains little of the .... material needed to build up tissue.
   A calorific   *B* nourishing   *C* digestible   *D* sustaining

5 A popular way of keeping fit is to go .... which is a kind of slow to medium paced running.
   A trotting   *B* jogging   *C* cantering   *D* ambling

6 The acrobat was so amazingly .... that she was able to bend over backwards and put her head between her knees.
   A supple   *B* malleable   *C* stretchable   *D* pliable

7 After twelve hours continuous work the labourer was ....
A dead slow   *B* dead quiet   *C* dead-beat   *D* dead-on

8 When there is excessive obesity patients are sometimes put on a .... diet which enables them to lose weight extremely quickly.
A slim   *B* crash   *C* balanced   *D* light

9 When dieting, eat only to satisfy your hunger .... not to gratify your desire to eat.
A aches   *B* twinges   *C* pangs   *D* spasms

10 Heavy smokers are twenty times more likely to be .... by lung cancer than non-smokers.
A attacked   *B* gripped   *C* ravaged   *D* stricken

11 The main function of the heart is to .... blood round the body.
A pump   *B* push   *C* propel   *D* shove

12 Exercising generally begins with standing up straight, ... slowly and then letting your breath out evenly.
A exhaling   *B* inhaling   *C* ingesting   *D* exuding

13 As people get older their bodies begin to .... and they have less immunity to disease.
A run out   *B* run off   *C* run down   *D* run low

14 In the stomach, the protein in food is .... into simpler substances by the action of acids and enzymes.
A melted down   *B* broken down   *C* knocked down   *D* rendered down

15 If people are deprived of dreaming during sleep they begin to show signs of mental ....
A deficiency   *B* derangement   *C* decay   *D* subnormality

16 The recent study of .... has produced some interesting results showing that humans have a built-in 24-hour biological clock.
A biorhythms   *B* biographs   *C* bioscopes   *D* biotypes

17 Yoga is very beneficial for people who suffer from emotional .... as it helps them gain an inner peace.
A havoc   *B* violence   *C* carnage   *D* stress

18 After any hard or prolonged exercise it is advisable to check your ....
A pulse rate   *B* mental balance   *C* brain waves   *D* eyesight

19 The .... is the main air passage of the body.
A bladder   *B* intestine   *C* spleen   *D* windpipe

20 Very fat men sometimes have a .... at the back of the neck.
A spare tyre   *B* roll of fat   *C* ton of flesh   *D* double chin

21 He had a terrible cold and found it difficult to breathe as his nose was ....
A shut up   *B* closed up   *C* filled up   *D* stuffed up

22 Jane Fonda, the American actress, has made .... exercises popular by demonstrating them on video.
A acrobatic   *B* aerobic   *C* aerobatic   *D* exotic

23 Sometimes people feel not exactly ill but just slightly ....
A off colour   *B* off form   *C* off key   *D* off hand

24 She remained depressingly fat .... all her efforts to slim.
A against   *B* although   *C* contrary   *D* despite

25 Many Asian people are of .... build while Europeans often have a heavier frame.
A slim   *B* slight   *C* lean   *D* thin

REMINDER **4**
Can and Could

And now if you would be so good
Another look at **can** and **could**

There are three distinct meanings for **can** and **could**:

1	Possibility or opportunity	You can learn judo here.
		You could see the lake from the pavilion.
2	Ability	He can swim very well.
		He could swim when he was six.
3	Permission	You can go at six o'clock.
		She said I could borrow her skis.

N.B. 'To be able' can be substituted for *Possibility* and *Ability* but not for *Permission*.

Exercise

Using 'can' or 'could' and making any other additions that are necessary, complete the following dialogue.

Bobbie .... boxing at school now, Mum.
Mother Can you, dear? That's nice.
Bobbie .... boxing lessons next term?
Mother I don't know, dear. You'll have to ask your father.
Bobbie All right, I will. He's sure to say 'yes'. Mum, do you think if I learnt to box I .... as Mohammed Ali?
Mother As good a boxer as Mohammed Ali? Well, I suppose you ....
You'd have to do a lot of training and I don't know where you'd do it in this small house.
Bobbie I .... a punch ball in the bathroom.
Mother Oh no, you .... Your father would never allow it.
Bobbie Well, I .... one in the garden then.
Mother I suppose that would be all right as long as it didn't annoy the neighbours.
Bobbie .... my pocket money now?
Mother No, dear, you .... it till Saturday; that's pocket money day. Why do you want it now?
Bobbie I thought if I had it now I .... and buy some boxing gloves and then I .... on my old football till I had enough to buy a punch ball.
Mother I'm sorry, dear. You .... on your old football. I gave it to the dustman this morning.

Unit five Money

ORAL SKILLS A
Intensive Listening

Presenter   Good evening, this is Radio Nine and here is Adrian More, our Parliamentary Correspondent, to give you his report on the Budget proposals.

Adrian More   Good evening. Many of you will have listened to the Chancellor's
5   speech, which was broadcast live from the House this afternoon. Inevitably, some of you will have been disappointed and others relieved, perhaps, that the tax on tobacco and wines has not gone up again. I think everyone was hoping that the tax on petrol would not be increased, but the Chancellor had other ideas and it
10   goes up by 5p a gallon from midnight tonight. But first, let's look

114

at what concerns us all most – Income Tax. On the face of it some fairly hefty reductions have been made in the hope, no doubt, that the economy will be stimulated and unemployment figures be substantially reduced in the coming year. So, how does it all
15 affect you and me?

The Personal Allowance has been increased from £945 for a single person to £985 and from £1,345 to £1,500 for a married man. At the same time the Child Benefit is to be raised by 75p a week for the first child and 40p for subsequent children, with the
20 proviso that Child Benefit is now to be paid direct to the mother if she has care of the children.

There is no overall reduction in tax, but the first £750 of taxable income is now to be taxed at 25% and thereafter at 33% as at present. The better-off will benefit, however, from the
25 proposal that the higher income band should be raised from £7,000 to £8,000 a year, which means that you can now earn £8,000 after allowances before you start paying at the higher rate of 40%. Pensions will be increased by £2 to £17.50 a week, but not till November and the Age Allowance for pensioners over 65
30 goes up to £1,200, but any income over that will continue to be charged at the standard rate.

So far so good. More money in the pay packet for the majority of earners, apart from those whose incomes are below the tax threshold. But is it so good?
35 National Insurance contributions by employers are increased by 10% which, in its turn, may result in staff being cut down. The increased tax on petrol will mean higher costs of transport, freight and commuter services, all of which will be passed on to the consumer, and inflation, which has been kept steady over the last
40 few months, may very well soar into double figures once more. Consideration is also being given to increasing Company Tax and Stamp Duty on house purchase, but it was stated that no firm decision on this would be taken before July.

Not surprisingly the Opposition are prepared to challenge a
45 number of these proposals, particularly the increased tax on petrol, so we may look forward to some fireworks in the House when it comes to the Budget Debate next Thursday....

N.B. The figures given in Adrian More's report and the following exercises are notional and do not correspond to the current rates of tax in Great Britain.

Vocabulary Notes

the budget:	annual estimate of revenue and expenditure by the Chancellor of the Exchequer in the House of Commons
taxable income:	that part of income which is liable to tax after the deduction of allowances.
Allowances: (Single Person's, Married Man's, Age Allowances, etc.)	that part of income on which tax is not paid according to personal circumstances; i.e. married, over 65, supporting mother or children etc.

Unit five

Child Benefit:	a tax-free state benefit payable to families with children
higher income brackets:	those liable to higher rates of taxation
tax threshold:	level of earnings below which no tax is payable
Company Tax:	tax payable by a company on its profits
Stamp Duty:	registration fee payable on transfer of property
National Insurance contributions:	payments made by employer and employee, in proportion to earnings, towards Social Security Benefits, sickness, state pensions etc.
direct taxation:	tax levied on income
indirect taxation:	tax levied on consumer goods, i.e. petrol, tobacco
VAT:	Value Added Tax
PAYE:	tax deducted from income before it is received by the employee: Pay As You Earn
Income Tax Code: (to be coded)	reference number showing how much tax a person has to pay
rebate:	money returned to the earner, if tax has been overpaid

Exercise 1

Read or listen to the report again and then answer the following questions.

1 Why were people able to hear the Budget speech at the time it was actually made?
2 By how much has the Petrol Tax been increased and when does this take effect?
3 What are the Budget proposals mainly designed to achieve?
4 What changes have been made in the Personal Allowance?
5 By how much has the Child Benefit been raised and to whom is it to be paid?
6 At what rate is tax paid after the first £750 of taxable income?
7 How will people in the higher income brackets be affected?
8 What new provisions are proposed for the old?
9 What is likely to be the result of increased National Insurance contributions by employers?
10 How and when may house purchasers be affected by the proposed changes in the Budget?

Exercise 2

1 Mr Stanley is a pensioner of 85. He has a State pension of £892.50 p.a. and an additional pension from his previous employers of £500 p.a. How much tax will he have to pay?
2 Bob Harrison is married with two children. What increased child allowances can he claim?
3 Elsie Jarvis is an unmarried shop assistant earning £2,500 p.a. How much tax will she have to pay?
4 Mr Ellis is a Managing Director earning £20,000 a year. He is married but has no children. On how much of his income will he have to pay 40% tax?

ORAL SKILLS **B**

Dialogue

Listen to the following dialogue.

Anne	Philip, I've been sent this form from the Income Tax people. Can you help me fill it up? I've never had one before.
Philip	Well, you'd better do it, or you won't get properly coded. It's quite simple, really; just a question of getting down to it.
Anne	It's all very well for you to talk. I can't make head or tail of it. Look, my name isn't even spelt correctly.
Philip	Oh, really, as if the Inland Revenue cared about a trifle like that! It's the system that matters. You're sent a form, you put down any additional earnings and anything you can claim for – disablement benefit, mortgage, insurance payments, that sort of thing – and then when the assessor receives it, it's all gone into very thoroughly and after a suitable lapse of time, you get a slip of paper saying how you've been coded and what allowances you've been given.
Anne	Do stop being so pompous. You know perfectly well I don't earn anything except my salary. I'm not disabled and I haven't even got a mortgage.
Philip	I was only trying to help. I thought you wanted to go over it with me. Not that it's really necessary. It's all set out perfectly clearly on the form. You just give your employer's name and address and your tax is deducted at source.
Anne	What do you mean 'at source'?
Philip	PAYE, of course – the tax is deducted by the employer and sent to the Inland Revenue. But, of course, as I said, if you don't get your right code, you'll be put on Emergency Code and that sometimes takes a bit of sorting out, though you do get a rebate eventually. Still, as far as you're concerned, it looks as though all you have to do is sign the form and get it off as soon as possible.
Anne	Why didn't you say so in the first place? You always go on about things so. Anyone would think you thought I was stupid or something.

Listen to the dialogue again and then practise reading it aloud with someone.

117

Unit five

These expressions here mean:

Can you help me *fill it up*?	complete a form
… just a question of *getting down to it*	start some work that has been postponed
… it's all *gone into* very thoroughly	discuss in detail
I thought you wanted to *go over* it with me	check fairly briefly
it's all *set out* perfectly clearly	present in clear form
… you'll be *put on* Emergency Code	included in a list
… *get it off* as soon as possible	post
You always *go on about* things so	talk continually about something

Exercise 1

Using one of the above expressions in *a suitable form* ask the following questions.

1 When the accountant is going to make a start on the sales figures.

2 Why Mr Brown hasn't completed his Income Tax Return.

3 Whether the rent ought to be sent off by first post tomorrow.

4 Where you can find the Budget proposals clearly listed.

5 If the cashier has had time to check the figures.

6 Why the Managing Director is always talking about the Government pay policy.

7 If you have to state how old you are on an Income Tax Return.

8 When the cost of the new pension scheme will be discussed.

Exercise 2

Work in pairs.
Old Mrs Brown is in the Post Office. She wants to send a cardigan as a present to a friend abroad, but she doesn't understand the customs form. One of you is Mrs Brown. Have the conversation with the Post Office clerk and complete the form.

CUSTOMS/DOUANE CI
(May be opened officially) (Peut être ouvert d'office)

Detach this part if the packet is accompanied by a Customs declaration **Otherwise it must be completed**
See instructions on the back
Detailed Description of Contents
(Désignation détaillée du contenu)

....
....
....
....
....

Insert 'x' if the contents are:
(Faire 'x' s'il s'agit:)
a gift (d'un cadeau) .... ☐
a sample of merchandise
(d'un échantillon de marchandises) .... ☐

Value (Valeur) (Specify the currency)	Net Weight (Poids-net)

INSTRUCTIONS

If the value of the contents exceeds £40, only the upper part of this label should be affixed to the packet and a non-adhesive Customs declaration C2/CP3 must be completed.

Describe the contents of the packet fully and correctly overleaf (**even if they are a gift or a sample**). *Failure to do so is likely to delay the packet and inconvenience the addressee, or even result in the seizure of the packet by the Customs authorities abroad.*

ORAL SKILLS **C**
Listening Comprehension

Exercise 1

Listen to this extract from a popular radio programme and answer the following
questions. Tick the box A, B, C or D for the answer you choose.

1 What is the purpose of the Prinknash Abbey project?

    A To attract visitors to Prinknash Abbey

    B To solve industrial problems

    C To promote local craftsmanship

    D To draw attention to British technology

A	
B	
C	
D	

2 Which of these statements about the Yorkshire company is true?

    A The contract is for $7\frac{1}{2}$ tons of bubblegum

    B A consignment is on its way to Egypt

    C The bubblegum is being shipped from Alexandria to Sheffield

    D The bubblegum stretches across the Suez Canal

A	
B	
C	
D	

3 The American Bank is profiting from the public's

    A sentimental associations

    B infantile behaviour

    C animal worship

    D business acumen

A	
B	
C	
D	

4 Daniel Ludwig's floating factories

    A have made a transoceanic voyage from Brazil

    B are more than halfway to their destination

    C were commissioned in Japan

    D are now nearing structural completion

A	
B	
C	
D	

Exercise 2

Work in pairs.

Listen to the extract from the radio programme again. Which of the four extracts
would you give the first, second and third prizes to, and why? Compare your decision
with other members of your class.

ORAL SKILLS D

Reading Aloud

Study the following passages. Answer the questions and then read them aloud.

1 Well of course a legacy of £2,000 is not a great deal of money these days. I think the best thing you can do is to put it on deposit with us – I see your current account is in credit – until you decide what you want to do with it. It will earn 8% before tax, and of course if you don't draw the interest the amount will increase proportionately. If, on the other hand, you decide you want to put the money towards a car or the down-payment on a mortgage, then, of course, as you are one of our customers, you can have immediate access.

Who do you think the speaker is?
Who is he advising?
Why is he giving this advice?

2 Excuse me, my name is Mrs Blake. I'd like to query my account. I think there's been some mistake. I've been away for six months and my flat has been unoccupied, so I haven't used any electricity. Nor do I owe any arrears. I settled all my accounts before I went away. I can't possibly owe you £45. Would you please check your records. It's perfectly obvious you must have muddled my account with someone else's.

Where is the speaker?
What is she complaining about?
Why is she convinced she doesn't owe any money?

ORAL SKILLS E

Group Discussion

Inflation

investment v. spending
cost of living
unemployment

USE OF ENGLISH **A**
Revision of Passive Forms

1   The Passive is formed with:

a   'To be' + Past Participle of the main verb: *to be done*

Changes in the Budget were announced by the Chancellor of the Exchequer.
If the goods are damaged in transit, they will be replaced without charge.

b   Auxiliaries (should, may, can, etc.) + Passive Infinitive + Past Participle:
should/may/can be done

Your Income Tax form should be returned without delay.
The price of petrol may be increased again this summer.

c   'To be' + Present Participle of 'to be' + Past Participle of main verb:
to be being done

Your hotel bill is being checked in the office.
The money was being counted when the burglar alarm sounded.

Use

The Passive with 'to be' or Auxiliaries is a common form in English:

a   Where the Agent is known or understood, so that there is no need to refer to it

The price of petrol may be increased (by the Government) again this summer.

b   When the object of the action assumes more importance in the speaker's mind than the Agent

Changes in the Budget were announced by the Chancellor of the Exchequer.

c   Where the Agent is unknown or vaguely referred to as 'they', 'someone', etc. in the active

Cheques of more than £5 are not accepted without a Banker's Card.
This electricity bill has been sent to the wrong address.

N.B. a   An Infinitive construction using the Passive is often preferred to the impersonal 'it'

Impersonal 'it':   *It is said that the cost of living rises every month.*
Infinitive: *The cost of living is said to rise every month.*

b   Verbs such as *say, think, know,* etc. normally take the Infinitive after a Passive verb and take a Perfect Infinitive if the idea refers to a previous action
That man is known to be a compulsive gambler.
The last cashier is said to have defrauded the company of more than £5,000.

2   'To have' + Object + Past Participle of main verb

(all tenses and Auxiliary forms): to have it done, can/may/might have it done, etc.

Use

This form is used when the action is done by someone other than the speaker; i.e. causes something to be done

I have had/this invoice/checked.
He may have/his house/put up for sale.

Unit five

3 Need + Gerund or Passive Infinitive

(the Gerund is more common): needs doing/needs to be done

Use

This form is used to express the idea that something requires attention. The Agent is not normally stated.

The sales figures need checking every month.
The sales figures need to be checked very carefully.

Exercise 1

Rewrite these sentences in the Passive using the words given.

Example

The firm will reimburse your expenses.
REFUNDED
Your expenses will be refunded.

1 They say the tax on tobacco is going up again in the next Budget.
   EXPECTED

   ....

2 There will be no meeting of the Finance Committee next Friday.
   CANCELLED

   ....

3 They give a 10% reduction of the purchase price on cash payments.
   REDUCED

   ....

4 Prices of consumer goods soon show the effects of inflation.
   REFLECTED

   ....

5 You should consult your solicitor about the sale of those shares.
   CONSULTED

   ....

6 The cost of our All-in-Holidays covers air fare, hotel accommodation and personal insurance.
   INCLUDED

   ....

7 The Management will certainly not agree to the workers' demand for an overall pay increase of 12%.
   REJECTED

   ....

8 There is no signature on this cheque.
   SIGNED

   ....

9 Excessive gambling frequently results in bankruptcy.
   CAUSED

   ....

10 The auditors check the accounts every six months.
    AUDITED

    ....

Exercise 2

Have/Need

Complete this dialogue using 'have' or 'need' as required.

Mr Barnes   These invoices ...*need*... checking. They're full of mistakes.

Mr Hall   Yes, of course, Mr Barnes, I .... checked right away.

Mr Barnes   But, surely, you ought to .... checked by a senior member of staff before you brought them to me.

Mr Hall   Well, actually, Mr Hobson, the Chief Clerk, is on holiday, so I had to .... done by young Roberts. He did his best, I'm sure, but if you ask me, the whole of that department .... re-organising. They're terribly short of staff.

Mr Barnes   That's no excuse for careless work. We have our reputation to consider. The whole matter of staff shortages .... looking into, not just in the Accounts Department. Remind me to .... put on the agenda for the next board meeting.

Mr Hall   I'll do that. In principle I agree that the question of staff shortages does .... looked at very closely, but there are problems.

Mr Barnes   Such as what? If more staff .... taken on, we must take the necessary steps to do so.

Mr Hall   I'm afraid Head Office .... convincing of that. They .... stringent economies enforced in every department, particularly where staff is concerned, and I don't think they'll be persuaded to regard the Accounts Department as a special case.

Exercise 3

Put the following passage into the Passive, using the verb forms underlined and making any other necessary changes.

They <u>say</u> that money <u>causes</u> most of the miseries of the world, but it also <u>encourages</u> a great deal of ingenuity and hard work. A sufficient income <u>fosters</u> an independent spirit. Friends and colleagues <u>admire</u> a man with money and <u>tolerate</u>, even <u>approve</u> eccentricities in him that they <u>would deplore</u> in a poorer man. The possession of money <u>confers</u> power and others <u>will frequently estimate</u> his intelligence and humanity precisely according to how much a man has in the bank. It is small wonder then that people <u>have come to regard</u> the acquisition of money as a thing worthy in itself. Yet what, after all, <u>can one do</u> with money except spend it and that quickly, before inflation <u>depreciates</u> its value? And how poor a thing it is! In earlier times, they <u>fashioned</u> coins from gold, silver and bronze, but what <u>do they make</u> our money of today? An alloy of cheap metal giving no cheerful jingle in the pocket, and flimsy bits of paper that we <u>might well mistake</u> for the toy money in a children's game. If we are honest with ourselves, we <u>need to answer</u> this question: do scraps of paper and worn bits of metal really <u>represent</u> our heart's desire? We <u>spend</u> our lives worrying about money. Some people <u>occupy</u> their entire working life in counting it. Why do we believe that money <u>can buy</u> happiness, when the reverse is so obviously the case?

USE OF ENGLISH **B**
Special Uses

Instructions and Information of a general nature, when not given in the Imperative, are often given in the Passive.

Examples
a How to fill up a form (Instruction)

Your name and address should be written in block capitals.
Your age, date and place of birth must be clearly entered in the spaces provided.
Your occupation and the name and address of your present employer should be entered under *d* and *c* on the form.
Any other relevant information should be written or typed on the sheet attached to the back of the form.
The form must be signed with your usual signature.

b Extract from an Income Tax Return Guide (Information)

Note the use of both Passive and Active forms in this extract.
Social Security Pensions and Benefits :
Retirement pension and Old Person's pension
If the pension is received weekly, enter the total amount received in the year including any age addition (payable to pensioners over 80).
If the pension is not received weekly, enter the total amount that would have been received if the pension had been received weekly.
If your wife's pension is paid to her by virtue of her own contributions enter 'X' in the box on the form and so obtain wife's earned income allowance.

Exercise 1
Using Passive forms wherever possible, write Instructions and/or Information for the following.
1 How to use a pocket calculator
2 How to complete a passport form
3 What steps are normally taken to open a bank account
4 General instructions on checking-in and weighing of luggage at an airport
5 How to make out a cheque

Exercise 2

Study the following facts and then answer the question below them. You should write about 100 words and may use Active or Passive forms as required.

N.B. There is no *right* or *wrong* answer to this exercise. You are being asked to read for information; form your own conclusion and give reasons to support it.

1 Harry Simpson has been left £10,000 on the death of his father and is anxious that the money should be invested to the best advantage.
2 Taking into account his circumstances, he has been advised that the money should be used in one of three ways:
    a in buying the flat he now rents in Central London
    b in opening an account with a building society
    c as the deposit for obtaining a mortgage on a larger property for himself and his family in a country area within commuting distance of London

3   Harry is aged 35. He has a wife and two school-age children, a boy and a girl.

4   The family live in a rather small three bedroomed flat in a block with a shared garden. It takes Harry half an hour door-to-door to reach his place of work.

5   Harry has an income of approximately £4,500 after tax. At present his rent is £1,000, rates are £300 and heating costs £200, but all these are subject to increases annually.

6   He has been offered the chance to buy his present flat for £16,000. Assuming he paid £10,000 of the purchase price, he would be left with a mortgage of £6,000, repayable over 20 years. This mortgage would cost him approximately £600 p.a. plus the rates and heating charges he pays at present. In addition there would be a service charge of £200 p.a. subject to annual increase.

7   To buy a larger house on similar mortgage terms, he would have to move outside the city. Travelling to work would probably cost him £500 p.a. instead of the £200 it costs at present, but there would be no service charge and rates would be considerably lower. The children would benefit from the fresh air.

8   If the money were invested in a building society, he would receive interest at the rate of approximately 8% p.a. after tax, i.e., his income would be increased by approximately £800 p.a.

Having considered all these facts, state in which way you think Harry's money should be best invested, and give your reasons.

WRITTEN SKILLS **A**

Register

All register really refers to is the type or variety of English used for a particular purpose, such as the English of public finance, scientific English, the English used in personal relationships, the English of advertising and journalism, etc. All these are different registers of English and they are both spoken and written. One of the difficulties at your level of English, now you have a grasp of the main structures, a reasonable vocabulary and a rough idea of how to pronounce most words that you come across, is choosing the right register to speak or write in. You can run the risk of offending someone, or produce an irrelevant piece of writing if you get the register wrong. Consider the following situations:

1 Spoken

A man calls on his bank manager to ask for a personal loan. They have never met before.

Here the bank manager looks taken aback, because the man has chosen the wrong register. Firstly, he uses the kind of English which would be more appropriate in a conversation where he knows the other person well, and secondly he doesn't use vocabulary specific to bank finance. Now look at what he says in picture B.

Notice that because he has moved out of a personal register his style of speaking has become more formal – the colloquial verb 'popped in' has been changed to 'called'; 'some money' has been changed to the more specific financial expression 'a personal loan' and the rather slangy phrase 'falling to bits' has changed to 'in a rather bad condition'.

2 Written

A short article is needed for a semi-official publication giving information about the
work of one of the people on the Stock Exchange – a Jobber. This is what someone
unaccustomed to the Stock Exchange register might write.

> A Jobber, or dealer, on the Stock Exchange buys articles from agents' customers
> at a low price and hopes to sell them at a higher price when the time is right.
> He always trades through an agent and each time bargains to get an adequate
> difference between the price he buys at and the price he gives to a possible
> 5   buyer. Unfortunately, he has to give the agent both the selling and the buying
> price before he knows whether the customer wants to buy or sell. The amount
> of articles he buys or sells is important to him because, naturally, he can make
> more money by selling a lot at a low price rather than by selling a few at a
> higher price; therefore he often makes the price cheaper if he sells a large
> 10   number of articles. Because a Jobber buys and sells a lot of articles he generally
> belongs to a company which gives him more money to use. Sometimes two or
> three Jobbers set up a company themselves to get some more money to buy
> some more goods.

This article is very unlikely to be accepted for a semi-official publication as the
writer has not used, or is not aware of, a register appropriate to the Stock Exchange.
Firstly, none of the specialised vocabulary relating to the Stock Exchange is
included and, secondly, the writer has allowed a personal bias to enter the article
which is not appropriate at a semi-official level. The article might have been
accepted if it had been written something like this:

> A Jobber, who acts as a dealer or trader on the Stock Exchange, buys stocks
> and shares from Brokers' clients and resells them at a profit when the market
> climate is favourable. The Jobber always deals through a Broker and every
> transaction is bargained for, with the Jobber attempting to get an adequate
> 5   margin between the price at which he buys the shares and the price he
> quotes a prospective buyer. Stock Exchange procedure requires the Jobber to
> quote both a buying and a selling price before he knows whether the Broker's
> client wishes to buy or sell. The quantity of shares involved in a transaction is
> important to the Jobber; a small margin on a large number of shares can yield a
> 10   better profit than a larger margin on a relatively small number of shares, so the
> Jobber will adjust his price accordingly. A Jobber generally belongs to a firm
> which provides him with greater financial security and enables him to stand the
> risk of buying and selling large quantities of shares. Sometimes several
> Jobbers form themselves into a company so that they can raise outside capital
> 15   to finance further transactions.

The writer has now moved away from a register which expressed his personal bias,
shown by the use of words such as 'unfortunately', 'what's more', 'naturally';
therefore his style has become more impersonal and more appropriate to the article
he is writing. Much of the language has been changed from general English to the
more specific vocabulary of the Stock Market register: 'articles' become 'stocks and
shares', 'agents' customers' become 'brokers' clients', 'when the time is right'
becomes 'when the market climate is favourable'.

Exercise 1

Study the two articles and continue to list the changes that have been made to achieve
the right register. Notice the kind of English that is used.

Unit five

Exercise 2

Study the following sentences, say what you think might be wrong and then rewrite them in the correct register.

1 Husband speaking to his wife in the kitchen
   'The performance of this gas-powered cooking apparatus falls far below expectation.'
2 Candidate saying goodbye to an examiner at the end of an oral examination
   'Cheerio, dear, and thanks a lot; it was great having the chance of a chat with you.'
3 A rather slovenly waitress in a workers' cafe talking to a customer
   'I really am most frightfully sorry but I'm afraid there's absolutely no stew left.'
4 A farmer addressing a meeting of the National Farmers' Union
   'Dearly beloved brethren, we are gathered here today to give thanks for an abundant harvest.'
5 A stockbroker advising a client on investment
   'Bung a few quid on Malperts, mate – you can't go wrong, they're a dead cert.'
6 One labourer is explaining to another why he thinks the other won't get part of his wages in advance
   'As your gross weekly income falls below the minimum allowable level you are not entitled to an advance on salary.'
7 The Managing Director of a company congratulating one of his marketing staff on good sales performance
   'Who's a clever boy, then!'
8 A man explaining to his bank manager why he needs to increase his overdraft
   'I'm drifting into economic chaos; last month I had a payments deficit of £300.'
9 A girl trying to convince her boyfriend that what she says is true
   'To the best of my knowledge and belief the particulars I have given you are correct and complete.'

Who do you think might have spoken these sentences before you changed them to correct registers?

From the examples of register given, it is possible to see that there is a variety of English for each particular purpose, and to get the register right you need to know some of the vocabulary identified with the register. For example, it would be almost impossible to speak or write about computers if you did not know any of the technical terms associated with computer science. Often to get the register right, it is also necessary to use distinctive grammatical patterns, such as are found in the English of newspaper headlines, telexes, telemessages or in the abbreviations of advertisements found in newspaper columns.

Headline

Bank rate up – Mortgages up – Tax down

Notice how all verbs have been omitted and there are no words connecting the three statements. The vocabulary has been pared down to the minimum necessary for intelligibility. The meaning is often implied rather than stated.

Telex

Send money urgent creditors pressing payment imperative

Here the grammatical items are reduced to verbs, nouns and adjectives. All prepositions, articles, pronouns, etc. have been omitted to keep length and so the cost down.

Advertisement (in newspaper)

Highly prof. business for sale. Turnover approx. £125,000 p.a. Offs. in regn. of £27,000 consd. Box DB 009.

Abbreviations are used to save space and money, but only easily recognisable words are shortened; where there might be confusion the words are written out in full.

Notice

False statements can result in prosecution

Notices often carry some kind of warning. They are generally in the Imperative or Passive tenses.

Instruction (filling paraffin can)

Place spout in can. Put coins in slot. Push red button and hold until reservoir is full. Pull red button and hold until reservoir is empty. Remove spout from can.

The Imperative tense is generally used and all articles are omitted. The instructions are kept as short and simple as possible so there is no misunderstanding.

Exercise 3

Rewrite the following information in the register suggested.

1 Telemessage

Dear John
Do you think you could possibly meet me at the station next Friday? The train will arrive at 2.30 unless it is late and I shall most certainly be on it. I'm really looking forward to seeing you again as it's been such a long time since we last met.
Love
Polly

2 Instruction

Of course everyone suffers from indigestion at some time or another. When you feel an attack coming on the best thing to do is to find your bottle of Muffets Indigestion Mixture and then proceed as follows: start by agitating the bottle thoroughly so that all the sediment at the bottom is dispersed. Then get a glass, carefully measure out the correct dose, using a spoon of the right dimension and slowly sip the mixture. Don't forget to do this two or three times a day, depending upon the severity of the attack. It is also advisable to take the medicine after rather than before meals as this is generally when the attacks occur. Care should also be taken that you do not take more of the medicine than is indicated on the label on the bottle. Muffets Indigestion Mixture will, of course, bring you instant and satisfying relief; do not be misled by rival companies' claims for their products – there is only one Muffets.

3 Headline

It was a beautiful day yesterday, and every railway station was packed with happy pensioners taking advantage of British Rail's offer of one day's unlimited free travel. Such an offer had never been made before and the pensioners were excitedly discussing the possibility of future offers if enough of the 750,000 holders of senior citizens' Railcards, who were entitled to the free travel, took advantage of it. Looking around the stations there seemed every possibility that such future offers would be made.

4   Notice

There are many problems involved in trying to keep the streets of big cities clean and tidy. Unfortunately, as populations grow and tourism expands, more and more people use the streets and dispose of their litter by throwing it down on the pavements. Prominently displayed notices do not seem to have had any effect, so regretfully the Council has decided to impose a fine of £100 on anyone found dropping litter in public places.

5   Newspaper Advertisement

Any person requiring a mortgage may lay himself open to exploitation by entering into dubious contracts. Care should be taken to consult a reliable private mortgage specialist; remember, prosecution may result from contracts entered into where the conditions cannot be fulfilled. Contact Malper, Canns and Associates before signing anything. Tel 109 0009.

Don't forget that many registers depend upon a combination of specialised vocabulary, specific grammatical features and a particular use of English. Consider the following registers.

Legal English

Legal English requires particular vocabulary such as 'hereunder', 'forthwith', 'heretofore', 'aforesaid', archaic words which are not found in other registers; complicated, formal, grammatical patterns, as in the following: 'The Seller will use his best endeavours to secure delivery of the vehicle on the desired date but shall be under no liability whatsoever for loss occasioned by delay in delivery arising out of any cause whatsoever'. This would be said much more simply in practically any other register; legal English also employs much repetition where the same words or phrases are used again and again: 'If the Retail Customer shall fail to take and pay for the vehicle within 7 days of notification as aforesaid the Seller shall be at liberty to treat the contract as repudiated by the Retail Customer and at his option to retain the said deposit without prejudice to the Seller's right to recover from the Retail Customer by way of damages any loss or expenses which the Seller may suffer or incur by reason of the Retail Customer's default.' This use of English, involving repetition, is not normally found in other registers.

Business English

Similarly, the business register carries its own vocabulary and grammatical structures, words such as 'turnover', 'profit and loss', 'subsidiaries', 'liquidity'; in fact some of these words have taken on a completely different meaning in a business context. The language used in business is generally pompous and formal; the passive tenses are often used to achieve a distancing effect: 'The continued recession in trade has resulted in the Group profit being well below expectations.' Recently a new jargon has emerged from America which has complicated the business register more than ever. In fact an American has coined the word 'gobbledygook', which expresses the idea of a lot of noise being made about nothing, to describe the business management register. This is something you might come across on a Business Management Training Programme: 'The cognitive continuum is concerned with objectives related to the knowledge and the intellectual abilities and skills, arising from comprehension to evaluation.' This might be described, quite rightly, as 'gobbledygook'.

English of Finance

1 Banking, Public Finance and Insurance

Restricted registers occur in the English of finance. The style is generally formal, the language ponderous, the vocabulary specialised and the grammatical structures often passive in mood. Here is an example of the English used when presenting the Accounts of a private Trust registered as a charity (Public Finance):

Accounting Policies ; Note 1
The accounts are prepared under the historical cost convention as amended by the revaluation of investment and administrative properties referred to in Note 1b and the annual revaluation of quoted investments to market value.

Banking

This is an example of an extract from a letter sent out from a bank to current account holders.

In the past, as long as you kept an average of £150 or more in your personal current account, no service charges were made. In future, your account will be free of charge, however much it is used, provided a minimum balance of £100 is maintained throughout the Bank's half-year charging period.

If the balance falls below £100 during this period your charge for each cheque, standing order or indirect debit will now be $12\frac{1}{2}p$ instead of 9p. All credit items are free.

Insurance

The preamble to a Document of Insurance

Whereas the Insured described in the Schedule has made to the Underwriters below mentioned a proposal of Insurance containing certain particulars and statements which shall be the basis of the contract and deemed to be incorporated therein as evidenced by this Document and has paid the premium stated in the said Schedule as consideration for the proposed insurance.

Notice that much of the language is similar to the legal register as it is a legal document and therefore the two registers overlap. Capital letters are used to give formality and importance.

2 Shopping, Gambling

These registers may overlap with entertainment, social relationships, etc., but there is specialised vocabulary and a use of English that identifies these categories.

Shopping (selling and buying)
Specialised vocabulary: sales, special offer, discount for cash, prices slashed, reductions, on display, in/out of stock, stock taking, sales assistants, department/chain stores, mark up, guarantee.
Here is an example of a guarantee supplied with a piece of electrical equipment.

Guarantee of Service
Should any fault develop in this merchandise, other than caused by accident, neglect or mishandling, return it to us and we will replace any defective part within the limits set out on the guarantee of service certificate.
If you have a claim to make, please return the purchase accompanied by this receipt. We regret that we are unable to accept any claim under the guarantee of service unless supported by this receipt. Please keep it carefully.

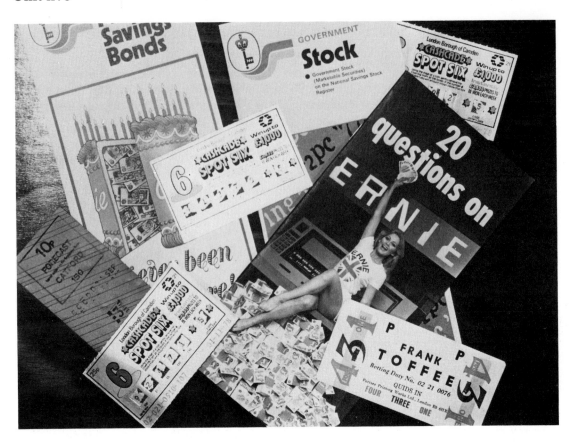

Gambling

Specialised vocabulary such as: betting, putting money on, to win, each way, accumulators, the Tote; football pools, treble chance, permutations, stakes, dividends; lottery tickets, prizes. Future passive tenses often used. Here are the rules printed on the back of a lottery ticket.

Rules for the Lottery
No ticket shall be sold by or to a person who has not attained the age of 16 years. No money can be refunded once a ticket has been sold. No correspondence will be entered into in the case of lost tickets. Ticket void if stolen, misprinted, torn, defaced or defective in any other manner.

Notice the rather formal style imposed by the use of passive tenses and the imperative voice. Compare with the English used for notices.

Exercise 4

Say what you think the following extracts mean; then rewrite using your own words. What register were they originally in?

1   Whatever computer control system is devised to increase production efficiency, it must ultimately control a piece of mechanical hardware. At present there are not sufficient funds within companies to invest in the necessary mechanical hardware to automate on a large scale, whether controlled by microprocessors or not. During the past two years, several automatic machines controlled by

microprocessor systems have been successfully developed. In every case the software writing and the design of the mechanical hardware of the machine posed the biggest problems and caused the largest portion of expenditure.

2 If the Publishers at any time by themselves or anyone acting on their behalf wilfully fail to fulfil or comply with any of the conditions accepted by them in this Agreement within two months after receipt of written notification from the Author of such failure, this Agreement shall thereupon determine and the Author shall be free to license any other person to print and publish the Work, notwithstanding anything to the contrary contained or implied in any part of this Agreement.

3 For every £100 of public revenue, £61 is in the form of taxes collected by central Government. Taxes on income come to £37 while VAT provides a further £24. National Insurance contributions bring in a further £15 but the Rates add a mere £9. The remaining £15 comes from other sources, mainly the surpluses of nationalised industries and rent from Government property.

4 No exchange or refund can be made on any sale merchandise. Bought in goods are clearly so marked and this store accepts no liability for the quality of 'seconds'.

5 Endorsement No. 2H. In consideration of driving being limited under Section 4 of this insurance to the insured and spouse only a discount in premium has been allowed.

WRITTEN SKILLS **B**

Style

Generally style is only considered in connection with literature – the literary style of the eighteenth century is compared and contrasted with the styles of the nineteenth and twentieth centuries, or the style of one author is contrasted with the style of another. This confines the study of style to within the literary register, which will be looked at in Unit six when the language of literature is considered. But in this unit the variety of styles, both spoken and written, that can be used within most given registers is our consideration.

Often a person will speak or write differently, on a given subject, to different people; to his wife and to his boss's wife, to his son and to his bank manager, to his window cleaner and his Member of Parliament. If the content of his speech or writing is the same, then what is changed? Possibly he changes from one dialect or accent to another or sometimes he may change registers, but often he changes his style or manner of speaking or writing. It depends very much on the social relationship which exists between the people involved, as to which style is chosen. Perhaps the changes that could be made are best illustrated by taking a sentence of extreme formality and impersonality and gradually altering it to become more informal and personal, thus showing the different styles that could be used. These are some suggested styles.

1 Spoken

Very formal style: Visitors to the Stock Exchange should make their way to the cinema on the first floor by way of the right hand staircase if they wish to see the final performance of 'My Word is My Bond'.

Unit five

Impersonal:	Visitors should go up the stairs on the right to the cinema if they want to see the film 'My Word is My Bond'.
Polite:	Would you mind going upstairs, please, as the film is about to begin.
Casual:	It's time you all went up to the cinema, the film's just starting.
Colloquial:	Get a move on, get up there quick – it's starting.
Slang/rude:	Don't hang about – move your bloody selves – Up!

Not all these styles can be used in every register; for example, in legal English only the formal and impersonal styles are generally used. At the other extreme the slang style would probably only be used in personal relationships, and is frequently accompanied by gestures, rude noises and swear words.

Exercise 1

Change the following sentences into the style indicated.

1 Casual: If you could possibly lend me £5 until the end of the week, I'd be extremely grateful.
2 Formal: You're not supposed to give the lions food.
3 Friendly: Passengers are advised to stand well back from the doors as injury could result from not doing so.
4 Polite: Bung the sugar over here.
5 Colloquial: If you would kindly seat yourselves at the table, dinner will be served directly.
6 Impersonal: There's not a hope in hell of getting your money back in this flea pit.

2 Written

As in spoken English, there are many styles of written English in each register. They range from the very formal to the colloquial; slang is not generally written, except in the literary register when it might be used in plays or novels, as it is predominately a spoken style of English. Consider the following styles within the register of journalism; the same event could be presented very differently depending upon the readership aimed at.

Formal/impersonal style: (quality newspaper)	Careful consideration was given by the Chancellor of the Exchequer to the possibility of reducing the rate of taxation in the forthcoming budget.
Polite (medium range newspaper)	The Chancellor considered cutting taxes in the next budget.
Casual: (evening newspaper)	It seems as though taxes will be coming down in the near future.
Intimate: (woman's magazine)	Ladies, that little bit extra is in sight – your tax and mine is to be cut.
Colloquial: (popular press)	He's given the go ahead – taxes to be slashed very soon.

It's interesting to notice that the rather cautious possibility expressed in the formal style has become a definite fact by the time the colloquial is reached; the language has also become more dramatic and exaggerated.

134

Exercise 2

Present the following pieces of information in an appropriate style for the suggested publications.

1 Popular press: bank robbery – £50,000 stolen – armed gang – policeman shot

2 Evening newspaper: diamond found – value £½ million – possible royal purchase

3 Quality paper: wage rise 15% – pay code broken – inflation feared
4 Women's magazine: shopping budget – meat up – fruit down – shop around
5 Medium range paper: escalation of crime – 50 break-ins a day – crack-down by police

WRITTEN SKILLS **C**

Writing in Different Styles

In the Cambridge Certificate of Proficiency examination, Paper 2, Composition, you may be required to produce a piece of writing in an appropriate style based on information given. For example you might be given information in the form of a telemessage and be asked to present it as a personal letter to a friend, or you could be asked to produce a written interpretation of a table of figures. An extract from a report, or newspaper headlines, or a list of notes, might be provided as a basis for an article or you could be asked to reply to a formal letter or write a dialogue based on given facts. In each case you should study the question carefully and decide which register and style is appropriate. Remember, you generally need different vocabulary and grammatical structures for different registers and degrees of formality and informality in different styles of English.

1 Below is part of a speech given by the Chairman of a large company to the Board of Directors at a half-yearly meeting. It is followed by the beginning of a conversation between two of the directors when they discuss the speech over a drink when the meeting is over. Using the information given, continue the dialogue for about 100 words.

And so, Gentlemen, it is with the greatest pleasure that I am able to tell you that our half-yearly profits are well up on last year's. We shall be able to pay our shareholders a substantially increased dividend and I think we should now give careful consideration to the possibility of placing further shares upon the market. It is with confidence that I view the steadily expanding market and I feel we should seize the opportunity of increasing our share of overseas trade.

Mr Hamley   Well, what did you think of the Chairman's speech? He sounded pretty optimistic, didn't he? The outlook certainly seems rosy.

Mr Donbros Umm. Well ... yes, I suppose the company's doing fairly well at the moment, but the market's still rather tricky. I didn't quite like the way the Old Man waxed so enthusiastic about half-yearly profits.

Mr Hamley   ....

2 The Ross Valley Bus Company, a privately owned company, prides itself on keeping its fares as low as possible while still providing an efficient service. Unfortunately, a rise in fares has become necessary. Using the following information and any other facts that you consider relevant, write the newspaper column that reported the company's explanation for the proposed fare increase.

    a Price of diesel fuel increased 2p per gallon

    b Drivers and conductors gain 10% wage rise

    c 10 buses taken out of service for repair

    d 5 new buses purchased

    e Increase in sales of private cars

You should write about 200 words. The beginning of the column is given below.

Bus Fares Up

Yesterday, Mr Robson, the Managing Director of the Ross Valley Bus Company, regretfully announced that there would be a 5% increase in bus fares to take effect from Monday next. He said the rise was necessitated by...

....

3 The following diagram shows the structure of a bank. Using the information given, write a letter to a friend telling him/her about your new job at the bank and something about the working of the bank.

The Structure of a Bank

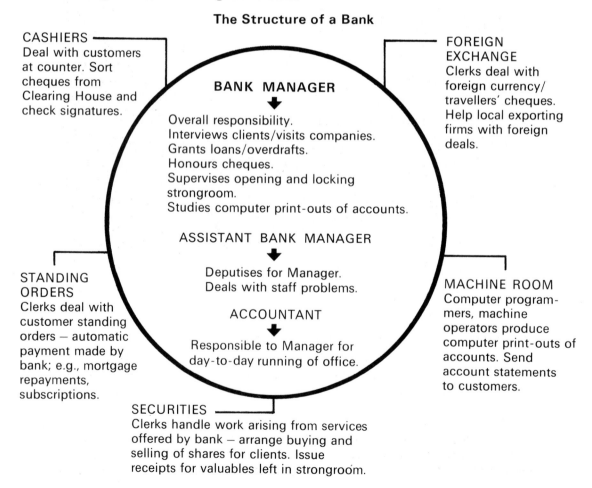

CASHIERS
Deal with customers at counter. Sort cheques from Clearing House and check signatures.

FOREIGN EXCHANGE
Clerks deal with foreign currency/ travellers' cheques. Help local exporting firms with foreign deals.

BANK MANAGER
Overall responsibility.
Interviews clients/visits companies.
Grants loans/overdrafts.
Honours cheques.
Supervises opening and locking strongroom.
Studies computer print-outs of accounts.

ASSISTANT BANK MANAGER
Deputises for Manager.
Deals with staff problems.

ACCOUNTANT
Responsible to Manager for day-to-day running of office.

STANDING ORDERS
Clerks deal with customer standing orders — automatic payment made by bank; e.g., mortgage repayments, subscriptions.

MACHINE ROOM
Computer program-mers, machine operators produce computer print-outs of accounts. Send account statements to customers.

SECURITIES
Clerks handle work arising from services offered by bank — arrange buying and selling of shares for clients. Issue receipts for valuables left in strongroom.

The beginning of the letter is given; you should write about another 200 words.

Dear ....,
    I started work today in the   ....
....

4   Study the graph below; it shows the fluctuating prices of soft fruit throughout the year. Then in approximately 200 words write an article for a magazine explaining the reason for the change in prices (weather, import cuts, dock strikes) and how it can be combatted (preserving, freezing, drying, bottling, buying only in season).

Soft fruit prices

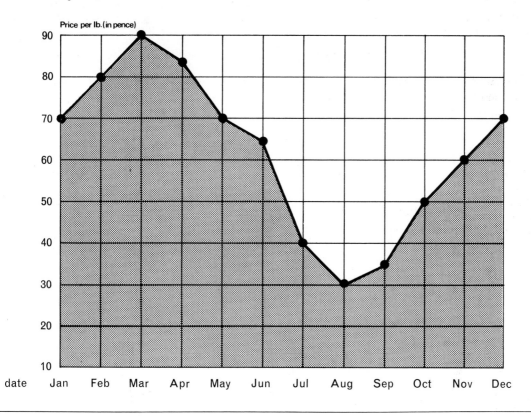

The article has been started for you.

Is the weather the only reason for high prices?

Recently it has been noticed that there is a very wide fluctuation in the price of soft fruit. Our consumer 'watchdog' thinks the peak reached in March may be due to..

5   The following notes on the next page are taken from a publication 'Business Guide to London'. Using the information from these notes, write a letter to the organiser of a tour who wishes to take a party of six businessmen to the Stock Exchange. Write your letter as if you are employed by the magazine and are replying to an inquiry.

137

The London Stock Exchange

The Stock Exchange

The Visitors' Gallery (entrance corner Threadneedle St and Old Broad St) open Mon – Fri 10.00 a.m. – 3.15 p.m. Admission free.

Guides in Gallery give commentary, answer questions. Visitors not allowed on Trading Floor. Leaflets in German, French, Spanish and English in Gallery. Bookstall in entrance hall sells many Stock Exchange publications.

Cinema (adjoining Gallery) shows film 'My Word is My Bond' at half-hour intervals – last showing 2.45 p.m. – advisable to book seats. Small exhibition and multi-panel presentation of Stock Exchange history in gallery behind cinema – telephone commentary in six languages.

Good pub/restaurant (for lunch) in Throgmorton St, behind Stock Exchange.

The beginning of the letter has been given below; continue for about 200 words.

Dear Sir,

     With reference to your inquiry ....

6 The passage below describes how to use a cashpoint card. Using only the appropriate material in the passage, write a set of short, clear and complete instructions for performing this operation.

It is always advisable to carry your cashpoint card with you; then, if you want to withdraw some money from your current account and the banks are crowded you do not have to wait in a queue at the counter but you can go straight to the cashpoint machine. Or at some banks you can withdraw money when the bank is
5 closed by inserting your cashpoint card into the machine on the wall outside the bank.

    Having decided to use your cashpoint card, what exactly do you have to do? Well, take your card, which is made of plastic and contains the branch number of your bank and an account number and place it in the slot of the cashpoint machine.
10 Almost immediately a metal cover below the slot will open to reveal two sets of

plastic buttons. On the left-hand side the buttons are numbered from 0 to 10 and on the right-hand side the buttons show amounts of money in multiples of £2 – £2, £4, £6, etc., up to a limit of £20 – or in multiples of £5 up to a limit of £50. At the same time a green strip on the right lights up showing the words 'enter your
15 personal number'. You should now press the appropriate numbered buttons on the left of the machine. After you have punched out your number another green strip will light up telling you to enter the amount you want; you should now press the buttons on the right indicating the amount of money you require. At this point a third green strip will light up showing the words 'remove card' and your
20 cashpoint card will slide back out of the slot ready for removal. Take it out and you will then hear a series of single tone pips followed by a whirring sound which indicates that your money is being delivered; when the whirring stops the cover will be automatically lowered over the rows of buttons and you will be able to remove the money.
25   If by any chance you should punch out the wrong number then a red strip will light up advising you to withdraw your cashpoint card and start the operation again. Also, in the event of your account being overdrawn another red strip will light up revealing the words 'refer to cashier' – you should then withdraw your card and go to the cashier's counter. Otherwise you should have no trouble in
30 using your cashpoint card and you should be able to get up to £20 or £50 cash any time you may need it.

The instructions have been started for you below; continue them for not more than 100 words. Number each instruction.

1 Insert the cashpoint card in the slot of the machine as indicated on card.
2 ....

REMINDER **5**

Articles

Articles **the** and **a** and **an**
Use them correctly if you can

Indefinite Article: A/An

1 A is used before nouns beginning with a consonant: *a ch*eque
An is used before nouns beginning with a vowel: *an o*verdraft
But A is used before words beginning with the sound /ju:/: *a E*uropean, *a u*nicorn
The same rules apply if the noun is preceded by an adjective: *a s*mall cheque; *an o*verdrawn account; *a u*seful service

2 **A/an** (plural: **some**) are used:
a before singular countable nouns   Have you got *a deposit account?*

b to refer to a generally understood
    occupation   He is *a doctor.*
c to introduce a new subject or   There is *a mistake* in this letter.
    unidentified person   *A man* called about the radio.

d to refer to an accepted shop/business etc.

There is *a bank* just up the road.

e to replace 'one'

I waited for over *an hour*.

unless this number is being emphasised

He has *only one* bank account.

3 **A/an** are **not** used before:

a uncountable nouns, i.e. substances/ indefinite quantities (money, gold, coffee, wood, etc.). In this case the plural **some** is used if required

I have *some money* in the bank.

There's *gold* in those hills.

b proper names, months, days of the week

John rang up this morning.

I have an appointment on Friday.

Unless

the name refers to someone completely unknown or to an established fact

A Mr Smith rang up this morning.

He is never at home on *a Saturday*.

Definite Article: The

1 **The** is used to define a *particular* object, state, group of persons or species, concept, etc.; but if these are referred to in a general sense, **the** is omitted.

We can't live without *money*.

The money that firm makes out of advertising is incredible.

2 **The** is used before:

rivers	the Ganges; the Thames
seas	the Atlantic; the Pacific
mountain ranges	the Alps; the Andes
groups of islands	the Channel Islands; the Hebrides
the Sun, the Moon, the Earth	the Sun; the Moon; the Earth
constellations and galaxies	the Milky Way; the Great Bear
points of the compass	the North; the East
deserts	the Sahara; the Gobi Desert

3 **The** is **not** used before:

a	lakes	Lake Windermere; Lake Ohio
	parks	Hyde Park; Windsor Safari Park
	streets, squares, etc.	Oxford Street; Trafalgar Square
	towns, cities, districts	London; Paris; West Kensington
	counties, states	Sussex; California
	countries	Austria; Brazil; China
	buildings and historic sites	Buckingham Palace; Windsor Castle
	churches, cathedrals	St Paul's Cathedral
	names of stars and planets	Mercury; Venus

Unless
'the' already forms part of the name
as in

the Tower of London; *the* Hague;
the United States

b first names

John; Mary; Andrew

surnames *unless* the person is unknown
or needs to be distinguished from
another

Mr Brown; Dr Jones;
Professor Hardy is coming to London
next week.

But

The Professor Hardy you were telling me
about is coming to London next week.

c Abstract conceptions, states and ideas

Illiteracy is a major problem in many
countries.

Unless defined

But

The illiteracy of this primitive tribe
is a major problem.

4 Students should hardly need reminding that **the** is also used before the superlatives
of adjectives.

This is one of *the most attractive* advertisements I have ever seen on television.
This is *the largest* dividend the firm have ever paid.

5 **The** is not always used for *the seasons* when referred to in a general sense, but may
be used when a particular season is being considered.

In England the crocus is usually the first sign *of spring*.
I am thinking of going to Norway *in the summer* (i.e., next summer).

Exercise

Insert 'a', 'an', 'the' or nothing in the following passage as required.

.........financier, wishing to get away from .... anxieties of .... business, decided
to go to .... remote island off .... north coast of .... Scotland, where he had
heard there was .... religious community which would offer him .... rest and
.... relaxation on .... payment of .... modest fee. He was so impressed by
.... beauty of .... surroundings and .... serenity of .... community, that
he decided to start .... new life there in which he would devote himself to ....
meditation and .... prayer. However, he soon discovered that there was .... lake
on .... island, ... water from which could be harnessed to provide ....
electricity for .... community, and it was not long before he realised that their
poverty was due to .... lack of .... organisation rather than .... means. All
.........island needed was .... good hotel offering facilities for businessmen like
himself to rest and meditate at .... prices that were suitably expensive. It was in
this way that .... chilly, mist-laden island of Cull became one of .... most
select and profitable tourist resorts in .... whole of .... Europe.

Unit six The Language of Literature

When the morning Stars sang together. & all the Sons of God shouted for joy

ORAL SKILLS **A**

Intensive Listening

Listening to poetry in a foreign language often seems hard at first, even discouraging, because the words and the forms used appear so different from those in everyday life. But poetry, which comes from the heart, was never meant to be a boring and difficult exercise. To enjoy it, you need to learn *how* to listen to it and in doing so, I would suggest the following.

1   Listen to the words, without troubling too much about what they mean, in the same way as you would listen to a new piece of music. If it's not possible to listen, then read them aloud to yourself, just enjoying the sound and rhythm they make.

142

2 Now, consider the theme of the poem and unless the theme is given as the title, ask yourself what it is about. Read or listen to it again. By now you should have caught the mood – angry, sad, despairing, comic or whatever.

3 Study the phrases the poet has used to express his feelings. Don't be afraid to criticise if you don't like them.

4 Try to find out a little about the poet, the age in which he lived, the problems he faced, so that you can understand better what moved him to write the poem.

5 The poetry will now begin to mean something to you, even if you don't understand all the words. Now is the time to check the vocabulary, but don't let your anxiety over the meaning of a particular word spoil your pleasure in a line.

6 Read or listen to it again. Repeat it. How does it make you feel – happy? bored? sad? excited?

Now read or listen to the following extract from an essay on learning to listen to poetry, which includes some short extracts from poetry and drama in English literature.

English seems to be a language peculiarly adapted to poetry, or perhaps the making of poetry is a kind of national characteristic. Our islands have produced comparatively few great musicians and artists, but across the centuries stride a veritable army of poets, dramatists and ballad makers, chronicling our history,
5 our hopes and fears on a rainbow bridge of words. Among these it is easy to see the giants – Chaucer, the father of English Literature busily writing his Canterbury Tales, Spenser, Milton, Pope and the gentle figure of William Shakespeare rising above them all. Yet, jostling for our attention are a host of others, romantic, tragic, patriotic, comic, all sorts and conditions of poets and
10 playwrights – if only we will take time to listen to them.
So, let us consider through their words the theme of Sleep. We sleep well or fitfully, we dream or not according to our imaginations or our digestions, we are insomniacs or somnambulists, but sleep is part of us from our life's beginning to its end. In fact the eighteenth-century poet William Wordsworth in his Ode
15 'Intimations of Immortality', suggests that birth itself is a kind of sleep:

        Our birth is but a sleep and a forgetting:
        The Soul that rises with us, our life's Star,
           Hath had elsewhere its setting
             And cometh from afar:
20   Not in entire forgetfulness,
           And not in utter nakedness,
        But trailing clouds of glory do we come
           From God, who is our home:
        Heaven lies about us in our infancy!
25   Shades of the prison-house begin to close
           Upon the growing Boy,
        But he beholds the light, and whence it flows,
           He sees it in his joy:
        The Youth, who daily farther from the east
30   Must travel, still is Nature's priest,
           And by the vision splendid
           Is on his way attended:
        At length the Man perceives it die away
        And fade into the light of common day.

35   Sleep, as we know it, begins in our cradle and from the earliest times gave rise to lullabies with which the mother rocked her baby to sleep. Here is one of the earliest nursery rhymes, familiar to most English children:

> Hush-a-bye baby, on the tree-top,
> When the wind blows the cradle will rock,

40

> When the bough breaks, the cradle will fall,
> Down will come baby, cradle and all.

And here are the words of a song written by Thomas Dekker in the sixteenth century and still sung today:

> Golden slumbers kiss your eyes,

45

> Smiles awake you when you rise,
> Sleep, pretty wantons, do not cry
> And I will sing a lullaby.

and the moving lines by Robert Herrick, seventeenth-century priest and poet, on the death of a little child:

50

> Here a pretty baby lies
> Sung asleep with lullabies.
> Pray be silent and not stir
> The easy earth that covers her.

Exercise 1

Read or listen to the first part of the essay on Poetry again and then answer the questions.

1   What is meant by the phrase, 'comparatively few great musicians and artists' (line 3)?
2   Why do you think the writer uses the expression 'a rainbow bridge of words' to describe the poets throughout the centuries?
3   Who are the 'giants' referred to in the extract?
4   Why do other poets and playwrights have to 'jostle for our attention'?
5   Why is it easy to take a subject like sleep when learning to listen to poetry?

Exercise 2

Read or listen again to the extract from 'Intimations of Immortality' by William Wordsworth and answer the following questions.

1   What do you think the poet means by, 'Our birth is but a sleep and a forgetting'?
2   Why does the poet describe the new-born child as 'trailing clouds of glory'?
3   How does the poet describe the limitations that life gradually imposes on the growing boy?
4   Why is the youth described as still being 'Nature's priest'?
5   What do you understand by the last two lines?

Exercise 3

1   Read or listen again to the nursery rhyme 'Hush-a-bye-Baby' and repeat it.
2   What does the rhythm of this rhyme suggest to you?
3   Read or listen again to the verse by Thomas Dekker and repeat it.
4   Give a brief paraphrase of this verse.
5   Read or listen again to the lines by Robert Herrick and repeat them.
6   What picture does your mind receive from these few lines?

ORAL SKILLS **B**
A Little from Shakespeare

This figure that thou here seest put
It was for gentle Shakespeare cut,
Wherein the graver had a strife
With Nature, to outdo the life.
5   Oh, could he but have drawn his wit
As well in brass, as he has hit
His face, the print would then surpass
All that was ever writ in brass.
    But, since he cannot, reader look
10 Not on his picture, but his book.
       (*On the Portrait of Shakespeare* Ben Jonson 1573–1637)

145

Unit six

The desire for untroubled sleep, often associated with death, constantly recurs in poetry. It is the great healer, the brief oblivion sought by all those whose worldly cares are too great to be borne. Some of the most moving lines on sleep were written by William Shakespeare. They are so familiar and so often quoted that their source is sometimes forgotten. Here, for instance, in 'Henry IV' Part 2 is King Henry, unable to sleep for the burden of responsibilities that weighs so heavily on him, envying his poorer subjects the sleep that comes so easily to them.

> How many thousand of my poorest subjects
> Are at this hour asleep! – O sleep, O gentle sleep,
> Nature's soft nurse, how have I frighted thee,
> That thou no more wilt weigh my eyelids down,
> 5   And steep my senses in forgetfulness?
> Why, rather, sleep, liest thou in smoky cribs,
> Upon uneasy pallets stretching thee,
> And hushed with buzzing night flies to thy slumber,
> Than in the perfumed chambers of the great,
> 10   Under high canopies of costly state,
> And lulled with sounds of sweetest melody?
> O thou dull god, why liest thou with the vile
> In loathsome beds, and leav'st the kingly couch
> A watch-case or a common 'larum bell?
> 15   Wilt thou upon the high and giddy mast
> Seal up the ship-boy's eyes, and rock his brains
> In the cradle of the rude imperious surge,
> And in the visitation of the winds,
> Who take the ruffian billows by the top,
> 20   Curling their monstrous heads, and hanging them
> With deafening clamour in the slippery shrouds,
> That, with the hurly, death itself awakes?
> Canst thou, O partial sleep, give thy repose
> To the wet sea-boy in an hour so rude;
> 25   And in the calmest and most stillest night,
> With all appliances and means to boot,
> Deny it to a king? Then, happy low, lie down!
> Uneasy lies the head that wears a crown.

Study the following vocabulary notes.

crib (line 6)	here means 'hovel or hut' (often means a child's cot)
pallet (line 7)	straw bed
lulled (line 11)	soothed or sent to sleep (noun: lullaby)
high and giddy mast (line 15)	the tall mast of a sailing ship
surge (line 17)	the swell of the sea
billows (line 19)	large waves
shrouds (line 21)	set of ropes supporting the mast or topmast of a sailing ship
hurly (line 22)	tumult of the waves
to boot (line 26)	as well

146

N.B. *Thou* is the familiar poetical and biblical form of 'you'. The verb form
is ....*t*, ...*st*, ...*est* :
Thou wilt, thou hast, thou liest, etc.
The form *thee* is used as the object of a sentence; *thy* means 'your'.

Exercise 1

Now listen to the speech from 'Henry IV' again and answer the following questions.

1   What do you understand by 'Nature's soft nurse' (line 3)?
....

2   What is the meaning of 'rather' (line 6)?
....

3   How are the sleeping rooms of the great compared with those of the poor?
....

4   Why is the word 'rock' (line 16) used to describe the ship-boy falling asleep up
the mast?
....

5   What lines describe the breaking of the waves and the sound they make?
....

6   Why are the shrouds described as 'slippery' (line 21)?
....

7   What is the meaning of the word 'partial' (line 23)?
....

8   Explain what is meant by the last line.
....

In all Shakespeare perhaps no speech is better known than the one in 'Hamlet'
beginning, 'To be or not to be ...' in which Hamlet, near to despair, muses on death.
Here is an extract from the speech in which the famous quotation 'To sleep –
perchance to dream ...' occurs.

> To be or not to be, – that is the question:
> Whether 'tis nobler in the mind to suffer
> The slings and arrows of outrageous fortune,
> Or to take arms against a sea of troubles,
> 5   And by opposing end them? – To die – to sleep
> No more; and by a sleep to say we end
> The heartache and the thousand natural shocks
> That flesh is heir to, – 'tis a consummation
> Devoutly to be wish'd. To die – to sleep;
> 10   To sleep! perchance to dream: ay, there's the rub;
> For in that sleep of death what dreams may come
> When we have shuffled off this mortal coil,
> Must give us pause....

'To sleep – perchance to dream' – this beautiful line expresses all the longing to escape
from a troubled world, all the uncertainty of what will happen to us when we die.

Unit six

Exercise 2

Read or listen to the extract again and then answer the following questions.

1 What verb could be used in place of 'be' in the phrase 'To be or not to be'?
2 To what does the line 'The slings and arrows of outrageous fortune' refer?
3 Why do you think the word 'sea' is used in the phrase 'a sea of troubles'?
4 Which phrase do you think best expresses the sadness and disappointment that comes to man?
5 Explain the meaning of the phrase 'ay, there's the rub'.
6 Which line refers directly to the act of dying?
7 What do you understand by the phrase 'must give us pause'?

 Some of the most familiar and tragic lines on sleep occur in 'Macbeth' in the scene where Macbeth enters with blood-stained hands, having just murdered Duncan in his chamber and in doing so disturbed the servants asleep outside his door.

	Macbeth	I have done the deed. Didst thou not hear a noise?
	Lady Macbeth	I heard the owl scream and the crickets cry.
		Did not you speak?
	Macbeth	When?
5	**Lady Macbeth**	Now.
	Macbeth	As I descended?
	Lady Macbeth	Ay.
	Macbeth	Hark! Who lies i' the second chamber?
	Lady Macbeth	Donalbain.
10	**Macbeth**	This is a sorry sight. [*looking at his hands*]
	Lady Macbeth	A foolish thought, to say a sorry sight.
	Macbeth	There's one did laugh in's sleep, and one cried *Murder!*
		That they did wake each other: I stood and heard them:
		But they did say their prayers, and address'd them
15		Again to sleep.
	Lady Macbeth	There are two lodg'd together.
	Macbeth	One cried *God bless us!* and *Amen* the other
		As they had seen me with these hangman's hands.
		Listening their fear, I could not say, *Amen,*
20		When they did say *God bless us.*
	Lady Macbeth	Consider it not so deeply.
	Macbeth	But wherefore could I not pronounce *Amen?*
		I had most need of blessing, and *Amen*
		Stuck in my throat.
25	**Lady Macbeth**	These deeds must not be thought
		After these ways; so, it will make us mad.
	Macbeth	Methought I heard a voice cry, *Sleep no more!*
		Macbeth does murder sleep, – the innocent sleep,
		Sleep that knits up the ravell'd sleeve of care,
30		The death of each day's life, sore labour's bath,
		Balm of hurt minds, great nature's second course,
		Chief nourisher in life's feast.
	Lady Macbeth	What do you mean?

Macbeth		Still it cried, *Sleep no more!* to all the house:
35		*Glamis hath murder'd sleep; and therefore Cawdor*
		Shall sleep no more, – Macbeth shall sleep no more!
Lady Macbeth		Who was it that thus cried? Why, worthy thane,
		You do unbend your noble strength to think
		So brainsickly of things. Go get some water
40		And wash this filthy witness from your hand.
		Why did you bring these daggers from the place?
		They must lie there; go carry them; and smear
		The sleepy grooms with blood.
Macbeth		I'll go no more.
45		I am afraid to think what I have done;
		Look on't again I dare not.
Lady Macbeth		Infirm of purpose!
		Give me the daggers: the sleeping and the dead
		Are but as pictures: 'tis the eye of childhood
50		That fears a painted devil. If he do bleed,
		I'll gild the faces of the grooms withal,
		For it must seem their guilt.

                [Exit, Knocking within]

Macbeth		Whence is that knocking?
55		How is't with me, when every noise appals me?
		What hands are here? Ha! they pluck out mine eyes!
		Will all great Neptune's ocean wash this blood
		Clean from my hand? No: this my hand will rather
		The multitudinous seas incarnadine,
60		Making the green one red.

Exercise 3

Read or listen to the scene again. Study it carefully and then discuss the following points.

1 What differences do you find in the immediate reactions of Macbeth and Lady Macbeth to the killing of Duncan?

2 Which is the more dominant character in the scene?

3 Towards the end of the play Lady Macbeth goes mad and walks nightly in her sleep, trying desperately to remove the imaginary stains of blood from her hands. What lines in the scene foreshadow this and how are the attitudes of the two characters shown here in reverse?

Sleep and death; death and sleep. But not always sad, not always offering a desperate remedy for life's misfortunes. Writing of actors, we find these lines in 'The Tempest', spoken by the magician Prospero.

 'We are such stuff
As dreams are made on, and our little life
Is rounded with a sleep.'

ORAL SKILLS **C**

Listening Comprehension

Listen to the text and then answer the following questions. Tick the appropriate boxes for the answers you choose.

1 Theatres in Shakespeare's time

    A   were either circular or square in design

    B   had some seats rising one above another

    C   were designed round a covered courtyard

    D   offered no protection against the weather

A	
B	
C	
D	

2 The main stage

    A   was surrounded by seats on all sides

    B   extended the full length of the courtyard

    C   was curtained off on three sides

    D   projected from the back of the theatre

A	
B	
C	
D	

3 Interior scenes could be shown by making use of a

    A   curtained recess below two doors at the back

    B   recess between two doors at the rear

    C   curtain to conceal the main part of the stage

    D   balcony stage overlooking two windows

A	
B	
C	
D	

4 Spectacular effects were often achieved by

    A   employing a simple mechanical device

    B   raising or lowering actors on a canopy

    C   displaying paintings of heaven or hell

    D   a machine designed to raise the platform

A	
B	
C	
D	

5 The Elizabethan theatre remained essentially intimate because

    A   the actor was not distanced from his audience

    B   eloquence was regarded as more important than spectacle

    C   the audience expected to participate in the play

    D   every actor commanded the attention of the audience

A	
B	
C	
D	

ORAL SKILLS **D**

Rhythm and Intonation

Now here are some old rhymes and verses, not about sleep this time, but about waking up. You will hear each one right through first, then line by line with pauses for you to repeat. It will then be repeated once through again, after which you should be able to repeat the whole verse yourself.

1. Dame, get up and bake your pies, Bake your pies, bake your pies; Dame, get up and bake your pies, On Christmas-day in the morning.

2. Dame, what makes your maidens lie, Maidens lie, maidens lie? Dame, what makes your maidens lie, On Christmas-day in the morning?

3. Dame, what makes your ducks to die,
Ducks to die, ducks to die?
Dame, what makes your ducks to die,
On Christmas-day in the morning?

4. Their wings are cut, they cannot fly,
Cannot fly, cannot fly;
Their wings are cut, they cannot fly,
On Christmas-day in the morning.

1 Early to bed and early to rise
Makes a man healthy, wealthy and wise.

2 He that would thrive
Must rise at five,
He that hath thriven
May lie till seven,
He that will never thrive
May lie till eleven.

3 'Tis the voice of the sluggard:
I heard him complain
You have waked me too soon,
I must slumber again!

4 Old Mother Slipper Slapper jumped out of bed
And out of the window she pops her head
Crying the house is on fire, the grey goose is gone
And the fox has gone to his den-O.

151

5   Elsie Marley has grown so fine
She won't get up to feed the swine
But lies in bed till eight or nine
And surely she does take her time.

6   Cock Robin got up early
At the break of day
And went to Jenny's window
To sing a roundelay.
He sang Cock Robin's love
To little Jenny Wren
And when he got unto the end
Then he began again.

7   Dame get up and bake your pies,
Bake your pies, bake your pies,
Dame get up and bake your pies
On Christmas Day in the morning.

Dame what makes your maidens lie,
Maidens lie, maidens lie,
Dame what makes your maidens lie
On Christmas Day in the morning?

8   Little Boy Blue come blow up your horn,
The cow's in the meadow, the sheep in the corn,
But where is the little boy tending the sheep?
He's under the haystack fast asleep.
Will you wake him? No, not I,
For if I do, he's sure to cry.

9   The year's at the spring
And day's at the morn;
   Morning's at seven;
The hill-side's dew-pearled;
The lark's on the wing;
   The snail's on the thorn;
   God's in his heaven –
All's right with the world!

ORAL SKILLS E

Group Discussion

Drama

plays should be performed not read
televised plays
ancient and modern

USE OF ENGLISH **A**
Revision of Gerund/Infinitive

The Gerund is a verbal noun, normally expressing an action, e.g. *swimming, painting*, and because it is used as a noun it can take the possessive case, e.g. *his swimming, his painting*.

1   Some verbs are always followed by the Gerund when a verbal expression is required;

e.g. *enjoy, finish, suggest*
I *enjoy listening* to classical music.
He *suggested going* to the opera that night.

2   Prepositions are normally followed by Gerunds when required. This may also include 'to' when it is not an Infinitive Particle (i.e. *to* read).

He ended his recital *by playing* Chopin's Polonaise in A.
I am *looking forward to seeing* the new ballet at the Coliseum.

3   Certain verbal expressions and phrasal verbs always take the Gerund, when a verbal expression is required, e.g. *give up, put off, can't help, it's no use, it's not worth, do you mind?/I don't mind*, etc.

Do you mind coming to the gallery again on Tuesday?
It's *no use turning on* the TV; it's out of order.

4   The Gerund can be used after adjectives, including those followed by certain prepositions, e.g. *busy, interested in, keen on*, etc.

He is *busy writing* his memoirs.
I am very *interested in learning* more about Shakespeare's early life.

5   The Perfect Gerund (**Having + Past Participle**) can be used to refer to *past* actions.

The young pianist was much encouraged by *having come* second in the competition.

6   The Passive Gerund (**Being/Having been + Past Participle**) often refers to an action before that of the main statement.

Being chosen to play Macbeth is the realisation of his greatest ambition.
The architect was delighted at *having been asked* to design the new Town Hall.

Exercise 1

Using one of the Gerund forms, complete the following sentences, making any necessary additions.

Example

I don't care for Pop music, but I always .... to classical music.
I don't care for Pop music, but I always *enjoy listening* to classical music.

1   Don't go to see the new play at the Palace Theatre, it's not ....
2   John doesn't know anything about painting, so it's .... him about the Impressionists.
3   There's no point in .... to play the piano, unless you practise every day.

153

4   My younger sister was delighted at .... first prize in the drawing competition at school.
5   Do you think Mary .... to the ballet on Tuesday instead of Thursday?
6   .... Professor of Literature at Barnes University was the culmination of all his hopes.
7   I can't .... sorry for people who don't enjoy classical music.
8   It was only after .... the poem several times, that I began to understand it.
9   Which do you enjoy more, ... to the opera or .... old films on television?
10 I don't object to your .... the flute when I'm out, but I can't bear .... when I'm doing my housework.

Exercise 2

Using the Gerund form, select the most suitable verbs from the list given to complete the blanks in the following passage.

admit	eliminate	look	reveal
bring	employ	paint	revolutionise
depart	exercise	record	see
depict	explore	reject	study
do	introduce	reproduce	substitute

It would probably not be an exaggeration to say that the nineteenth-century Impressionists were responsible for ....(1) European Art. By ....(2) the purely visual for the standardised composition forms, and ....(3) harsh or rigidly drawn lines, they succeeded in ....(4) a naturalism into ....(5) unlike anything that the patrons and critics of their time had been accustomed to ....(6).

   Much of their work was done in the open air by ....(7) the effects of light and colour, ...(8) nature as they saw it, and ....(9) colour to suggest varying tones of light and shade. Nevertheless, in spite of their concern with nature as in Claude Monet's 'Water-Lilies' or Cezanne's 'Chestnut Trees at the Jas de Bouffon', we are indebted to the Impressionists for ....(10) for us the vitality of café life in Paris in the nineteenth century. In ....(11) the scenes, the people who were part of their daily life, they found a way of ....(12) us to their circle as intimate friends in a way that not even the camera has succeeded in ....(13). No school of painters until then had ever been remarkable for ....(14) in such naturalistic form, their impressions of the society in which they were living. In ....(15) 'official art', it must not be assumed that they were uninfluenced by ....(16) the great masters; rather, they were painters of their own time who gave expression to tendencies that had for some time been lying dormant in European Art. On ....(17) at these pictures for the first time, it is not perhaps surprising that people who were unused to ....(18) their own judgment greeted them with hostility and criticism. By ....(19) from tradition, and ....(20) their own realism, the Impressionists were the precursors of all modern art today.

The Infinitive

The Infinitive, like the Gerund, is a verbal noun, but is used in a more personal or particular sense:

Learning to sing well requires at least an hour's practice a day. (general statement)
I should like *to learn* to sing well. (personal statement)

1   Verbs + Infinitive with 'to'
Most commonly those expressing some personal wish, decision or undertaking *by the subject* : want, decide, agree, promise, etc.
I want to visit the Louvre when I am in Paris.
They have decided to open the castle to the public on Sundays.

2   Verbs + Person Object + 'to' + Infinitive
Commonly those where the person object is required to carry out the wish, advice or instructions of the subject: advise, encourage, ask, tell, etc.

My teacher *advised me to study* Bernard Shaw's plays.
I *encouraged him to apply* for the post of Assistant Curator at the museum.
N.B. This is the normal Indirect Speech form for requests, orders and instructions.

Direct: 'You'd better make careful notes of Professor Brown's lecture,' said
             the teacher.
Indirect: The teacher *advised the students to make* careful notes of Professor
             Brown's lecture.
(See also Unit seven, page 187.)

3   Auxiliaries and Defective Verbs + Infinitive without 'to'
shall/will   should/would   can/could   may/might   must

You *must see* the new production of 'Hamlet' at the National Theatre.
We *could go* to the ballet tonight.

4   Auxiliaries and Defectives followed by 'to' + Infinitive
ought, have, used, need, dare, be

The art students *have to supply* all their own materials.
I *used to do* a lot of painting when I was at school.
(See also notes and exercise on Need and Dare with and without 'to', page 160.)

5   Verbs + Object + Infinitive without 'to'
see, watch, notice, hear, let, make
also help (with or without 'to')

I once *heard Yehudi Menuhin play* at a charity concert.
They *let us photograph* the medieval tombs in the cathedral.
This book *helped me understand*/*helped me to understand* more about the Renaissance painters.

6   Infinitive used to express Purpose
He went to Paris *to study Art*.
They organised the exhibition *to raise money for charity*.

The idea of purpose may be strengthened by the addition of *'so as to'*/*'in order to'*.
Dr Hobbs is taking a year's sabbatical leave *so as to*/*in order to* complete his research on the Mayan Civilisation.

N.B. Where the purpose refers to a subject different from that of the main sentence, the Infinitive cannot be used and a purpose clause with 'so that' is substituted:
Dr Hobbs brought some photographs of Mayan architecture to class *so that the students could study them.*

7 Infinitive of comparison with 'too/enough' + Adjective/Adverb

I find abstract art *too difficult to understand*.
This sculpture is *not interesting enough to exhibit*.
He speaks *too quickly for us to understand*.
The figurine was broken in transit because it was *not packed carefully enough to withstand* the journey.

Note the position of 'too' before the Adjective or Adverb and 'enough' after it.

8 Infinitive after 'To be' + Adjective forms to express emotion

happy, annoyed, glad, amazed, delighted, etc.

I *am delighted to hear* you passed your exam.
We *were amazed to see* how well the painting had been restored.

9 'To be' + Infinitive to express future intention/instructions

They *are to publish* a new novel by Adam Bain in the autumn.
(Passive) A new novel by Adam Bain *is to be published* in the autumn.
All candidates *are to bring* a photograph of themselves.

10 The Perfect Infinitive: 'Have' + Past Participle is used with auxiliary verbs to express Past ideas but frequently has a negative sense.

We *were to have visited* the museum, but we didn't have time.
He *ought to have gone* to Paris to study Art, but his father would not allow it.

Exercise 3

Using an Infinitive form, complete the following sentences.

1 His father recommended ....
2 When he was in Paris, he used ....
3 I think you ought ....
4 The critics did not consider Professor Morgan's new book on the Napoleonic Wars helped ....
5 The State Gallery is ....
6 The Art teacher made ....
7 When he saw the illustrations to the new edition of 'Grimms' Fairy Tales', he was disappointed..
8 A pageant is being organised in the city square in order to ....
9 Most of the poems in this book are too ....
10 When we visit the sculpture exhibition in the park, will they let ....?
11 I can't make up my mind whether ....
12 They were to have ....
13 Have you ever seen ....?
14 He practises the guitar for two hours every day so as..................................
15 All the children who visited the museum were told ....
16 How long did it take Beethoven ....?
17 Do you think he really wants ....?
18 When I was studying in Florence, I had ....
19 Visitors to the cathedral were advised ....
20 Do you always have ....?

Exercise 4

For each of the following sentences, write a new sentence *as similar as possible in meaning to the original sentence.*
Use the word given with or followed by one of the Infinitive forms.

Example
He is not sufficiently talented to get a place at Art school.
ENOUGH
He is not talented enough to get a place at Art school.

1   Have you come to any decision about applying for a university place?
    DECIDED
    ....

2   He only went to the concert because Mary wanted him to.
    PLEASE
    ....

3   The State Gallery will exhibit some of Turner's painting in the autumn.
    IS
    ....

4   The inscription on the stone was so worn that he couldn't decipher it.
    TOO
    ....

5   According to the records, Shakespeare left his second-best bed to his wife in his will.
    SAID
    ....

6   Why do you have such difficulty in understanding Wordsworth's poetry?
    SO
    ....

7   I did a lot of sketching at one time, but I was never any good at it.
    USED
    ....

8   The museum authorities refuse admittance to anyone with a camera.
    LET
    ....

9   Why are you so interested in visiting these old tombs?
    WANT
    ....

10 You had better make careful notes of the lecture.
    ADVISE
    ....

USE OF ENGLISH B

Special Uses

1 **'To remember/forget'** + **Gerund**
   = Past recollection

   + **Infinitive**
   = Past or Future reminder

I remember seeing that painting in the Louvre.

Did you *remember to bring* your camera?
I mustn't forget to bring my camera tomorrow.

2 **'To try'** + **Gerund** = test, experiment

   + **Infinitive** = attempt, make an effort

You may understand that poem better if you *try reading* it aloud.

He *tried to read* the poem aloud, but it was too difficult for him.

3 **'To like'** + **Gerund** = enjoy, take pleasure in
   + **Infinitive** = (a) want, wish, desire
   (b) think it's a good idea

I like watching horror films.

Would you *like to see* that new horror film?
I like to take plenty of exercise every day.

4 **'To mean'** + **Gerund** = to indicate, involve, result in

   + **Infinitive** = intend

Training to be a singer *means practising* at least two hours every day.

He says he *means to make* a special study of Renaissance Art.

5 **'To stop'** + **Gerund**
   = stop an action already begun/cease
   + **Infinitive**
   = stop one action in order to start another

I wish he would *stop pretending* to be an expert on Byzantine Art.

He was walking through the gallery, when he *stopped to look* at one of Gainsborough's portraits.

6 **'To regret'** + **Gerund** = past

   + **Infinitive** = present regret

I shall always *regret not seeing/not having seen the* Chinese Exhibition when it was in London.

I regret to say I don't like Pop music.

7 **'To go on'** + **Gerund**
   = continue an action already begun
   + **Infinitive**
   = introduce a new subject or extension of subject

The guide *went on talking* although most of the tourists had drifted away.

After telling us something about the Pre-Raphaelites the lecturer *went on to discuss* the influence of William Morris at that period.

Exercise 1

Complete the following sentences with the correct form of Gerund or Infinitive for the words given.

1   She says she means (take) a degree in Fine Arts, but this will mean (apply) not later than next month for a place at university.
2   I wish he would stop (tell) us about his experiences in the Antarctic. It's boring when someone goes on (talk) about somewhere you're never likely to go to.
3   He says he regrets never (read) more of Shakespeare's plays.
4   Do you like (listen) to classical music? If so, would you like (hear) my new record of Beethoven's Sixth Symphony?
5   I keep trying (understand) this poem by Wordsworth, but the meaning is quite beyond me.
6   Did you remember (tell) Mary to visit the Courtauld Institute when she was in London?
7   Now I am older, I regret (not pay) more attention to our Literature lessons at school.
8   I'd rather like (attend) evening classes on Archaeology. Do you think this would mean (get) home very late?
9   If you want to know more about life in Shakespeare's England, you could try (read) this book by Professor Tillotson.
10 I don't remember (see) that picture at the State Gallery, but I was in rather a hurry and I didn't stop (look) at the catalogue.

Exercise 2

Complete the following passage with the Gerund or Infinitive as required. This exercise includes a number of the forms discussed in this unit.

It would be interesting (discover) what instinct first prompted Man (make) music. Did it originate in a series of sounds designed (attract) the attention of other members of the tribe, (warn) them in the manner of the drum beats of Africa, or was it simply a succession of ferocious sounds made for the express purpose of (frighten) marauding enemies or dangerous wild beasts? (Demonstrate) fear possibly originated in the need (survive) and eventually evolved into (dance), warlike and sexual, which recorded the history and culture of the race long before Man mastered the arts of (read) or (write).

But on (look) back into the far distant ages, what evidence can we find (suggest) who sang the first song, who made the first tune? (Chew) a reed, (blow) an animal horn – some idle action must have given birth to the first musical instrument. And yet was it really so? Did Man mean (make) music or did it happen accidentally or by instinct? We are so used to (hear) music of all kinds, that we do not stop (ask) ourselves why it exists. No one taught the birds (sing), yet they sing from the sheer joy of (be) alive. Did Man, consciously or unconsciously, try (imitate) them? It is a curious fact that a very young baby who may never have heard a note of music in his short life will often start (sing) to himself when he is happy. Music, it seems, is part of us, whether we like (make) music or not. It is a means of (express) our emotions and perhaps it is no exaggeration (say) that music is as necessary to us as (breath), (sleep) or (eat). In the frightening and incomprehensible world in which primitive Man was obliged (live), perhaps music, weird and tuneless as it might seem to us today, was as natural a part of his life as it is of ours. The seventeenth-century writer, William Congreve, wrote, 'Music has charms (soothe) a savage breast ...'. Did primitive Man instinctively realise that by (produce) sweet sounds, he could calm or frighten away the terrors that surrounded him?

USE OF ENGLISH C
Need and Dare

Need and **Dare** can be formed in two ways:

A   With auxiliaries: **Do/Don't Will/Won't,** etc. for Negatives, Questions and Question tags in the same way as other verbs.
In this case they are followed by the Infinitive with 'to'.

I *need to buy* a new dictionary, don't I?
He *doesn't need to buy* a new dictionary, *does he?*
Do you need to buy a new dictionary?
He is the only student *who dares to argue* with Dr Brown.
They *don't dare to argue* with Professor Bartlett.
Do you dare to argue with Dr Brown?
N.B. **a**   'Need' can be used with a direct object without Infinitive:
I *need a new dictionary,* don't I?
b   'Dare' is sometimes followed by the Infinitive without 'to':
They don't *dare argue* with Professor Bartlett.
c   'Dare' is very seldom used in the Simple Present, 1st person affirmative.

B   By forming their own **Negative** and **Question forms** and **Question tags:**
'He daren't', 'Need I?' etc. with certain variations. In this case they are followed by the Infinitive without 'to'.

I *needn't buy* a new dictionary, need I?
He *daren't ask* Professor Bartlett, *dare he?*

N.B. 's' is not added for 3rd Person Singular in the Question form:

Need he buy a new dictionary?
Dare he ask Professor Bartlett for his opinion?

In common practice forms **A** or **B** can be used as preferred, but there is an important difference in the meaning of
'Didn't need to':   *didn't do it because it was unnecessary*
and 'Needn't have done':   *did it, but discovered later that it was*
                                                       unnecessary

I *didn't need to* buy a new dictionary because John gave me his.
We *needn't have got to* the concert so early. It didn't begin till 8.30 after all.

Expressions

Need

1   There's no need to   *There's no need to leave* so early, the
                                                  lecture doesn't start till 7.

    Is there any need to ...?   *Is there any need to leave* so early? The
                                                  lecture doesn't start till 7.

    (All tenses, negative and questions)

2   'To be in need of' + Noun – not   This house is *in need of renovation.*
    Infinitive
    (A fairly uncommon form)

Dare

1   How dare you!   *How dare you borrow* my typewriter
                                          without asking!

    (can be used with all persons, tenses)
    Meaning : What an impertinent or rude way to behave

2   I daresay   *I daresay* Wordsworth wrote a number of
                                          sonnets that were never published.

    (Cannot be used in any other person or tense)
    Meaning : It seems likely or possible to me

3   To dare someone to   *I dare you to ask* the pianist for his
                                          autograph.
                                          He dared me to touch the live electric
                                          wire.

    (Affirmative statements and questions only)
    Meaning : to challenge

Exercise 1

Complete the following sentences with a suitable form of 'need' or 'dare'.

1   I (not dare) disturb Professor Williams yesterday, because he was giving a violin
    lesson.

2   If you (need) look up any words in the dictionary, don't hesitate to borrow mine.

3   If I knew as little about Shakespeare as Arthur does, I (not dare) argue with
    Dr Brown.

4   If we'd known the cathedral was so near the station, we (not need take) a taxi.

5   He (dare) ask the Poetry Society to read one of his poems?

6   How you (dare) open a letter addressed to me!

7   When they go to university, they (need) buy all their own books?

8   Why didn't someone tell her she (not need bring) her cine-camera?

9   They (not need) translate the poem, as it had already been translated into four
    languages.

10 He (need) send his examination certificates with his application form?

Exercise 2

Using a suitable form of 'need' or 'dare', rewrite the following sentences, keeping as
closely as possible to the original meaning but using the word given.

1   It's unnecessary for you to write to Dr Brown personally.
    NEEDN'T

2 The students don't have the courage to tell Dr Brown they can't hear what he is saying.
DAREN'T

....

3 Is it really necessary for you to learn that poem by heart?
NEED

....

4 I think it very likely that Picasso did not sign all his early paintings.
DARESAY

....

5 I challenge you to recite one of your own poems at the meeting.
DARE

....

6 Did he have to be so rude to Dr Brown?
NEED

....

7 It wasn't necessary for us to pay a guide, because Professor Bartlett took us round the cathedral himself.
NEED

....

8 I don't know how he had the impertinence to speak to you like that!
DARED

....

9 There was no need for him to have gone to all that trouble to record that concerto.
NEEDN'T

....

10 I like playing the piano but I don't think I'd ever have the nerve to play in public.
DARE

....

Exercise 3

Using expressions with 'need' and 'dare' make sentences to express the following.

1 She spent several days rehearsing a speech from 'Romeo and Juliet', only to find she was being auditioned for the part of Lady Macbeth.
2 They might have had to make the costumes for the pageant, but luckily they were able to borrow them from the local Dramatic Society.
3 It would be as well to book early for the concert, as there is sure to be a big demand for tickets.
4 When they were at school, the boys were always trying to make each other ask the teacher silly questions.
5 I think it's quite probable the publishers never even read David's manuscript.
6 It's not necessary for you to bring your lecture notes.
7 I don't know how you had the impertinence to interrupt in the middle of Professor Bartlett's address.
8 We took a taxi to the museum, but by the time we got there it was closed.
9 I had never heard of Tennyson, but I didn't like to ask who he was because everyone else in the class seemed to know.
10 There was no necessity for us to take sandwiches, as lunch was provided by the tour organisers.

WRITTEN SKILLS **A**

Reading for Language

'Fine Art is that in which the hand, the head and the heart of man go together'
('The Two Paths', John Ruskin *1819–1900*)

In Unit four we considered reading for information and noted the kind of language used and in Unit five we saw how the register or style dictated its own language. Now let us consider the literary style of English and see what effects can be achieved by the use of certain devices of language.

Firstly we should remember that style is partly an expression of the writer's personality but is tempered by the historical influences of the period and the writer's education and background. Fundamentally the writer's style is formed by his choice of words, therefore it is important to examine the type and quality of the words used in any piece of writing. As Robert Bridges put it very succinctly, 'First, the right words: secondly, those words in the right order: thirdly, the agreeable sound of them in sequence.'

Figurative Language

All literature is an attempt to appeal to the imagination and the descriptive or evocative words which help to visualise or realise a scene are known as *Figures of Speech*. Through these literary devices an appeal to the imagination is made.

A Metaphor

Basic to language itself, and at its simplest a way of referring to or describing one thing in terms of another:

'Art is a jealous mistress.'

Sometimes the writer, with varying degrees of success, will extend the metaphor:

'Art is a jealous mistress, capriciously granting or withholding her favours.'

Unfortunately the imaginative inspiration of the writer will often cloud his literary judgment and then the images start to become confused, resulting in mixed metaphors:

'Art is a jealous mistress, alternately drowning or rescuing her servant.'

Here the writer continues the metaphor of 'mistress' with 'servant' but then destroys the whole effect by introducing words connected with the sea, 'drowning' and 'rescuing'. Mixed metaphors are rarely successful, even when used for a comic effect, although craftsmen such as Shakespeare can sometimes use them well:

'To take arms against a sea of troubles'

To be effective a metaphor must be vivid and fresh and it generally has far greater immediacy and precision than a simile.

B Simile

An imaginative comparison between two essentially different things, usually introduced by 'like' or 'as':

'Words are like leaves; and where they most abound,
Much fruit of sense beneath is rarely found.'

Alexander Pope here uses a simile effectively and metaphorically continues the image of trees, suggested by 'leaves', with 'fruit' and 'beneath'. Care should be taken when using similes that they are not too well known and therefore hackneyed:

'As pretty as a picture'

Any effect this simile may once have had has been lost through over-use. When using metaphors or similes it should be remembered that their effectiveness depends upon them being an intrinsic part of the passage in which they occur and not an end in themselves.

Exercise 1

Consider the use of metaphor or simile in the following extracts and say whether you think it has been effective; if you think not, say why not.

1 'All the World's a stage,
   And all the men and women merely players.'
2 'Concentration works like magic.'
3 'The eye is the painter and the ear the singer.'
4 'Art is like baby shoes. When you coat them with gold, they can no longer be worn.'
5 'Impervious to the attack of critics, the author swam through the storm and won success.'

Exercise 2

Think of a metaphor or a simile for each of the following.

1 Music
2 Abstract Art
3 Great Literature

Other figures of speech are used by writers which owe their effect to the force of contrast.

C Irony

The expression of a thought where one thing is said and another – often the opposite – implied:

> 'The Duke of Wellington's English despatches were well written in fine idiomatic English – and so were his French ones.'

Here the writer is implying that the Duke of Wellington did not write good French. Much English literature is ironic in tone and irony underlies satire, comedy, sarcasm and mockery. Often connected with irony is the epigram.

D Epigram

A clever, witty, concise, well-expressed saying:

> 'True ease in writing comes from art not chance'

If the writer wanted to be ironic he would probably change the epigram:

> 'True ease in writing comes from chance not art'

and so produce an ironical epigram. Contrast between what is said or written and what appears to be an underlying meaning is also shown by paradox.

E Paradox

The expression of an idea which at first sight appears absurd, but on closer examination turns out to have a serious meaning:

> 'He used poetry as a medium for writing in prose.'

Exercise 3

What type of figurative language is used in each of the following?

1 'I'm afraid there is no part in this play worthy of your talents.' – director speaking to failed actor seeking work.

2 'Art is long, Life is short'

3 'Less haste; more speed'

4 'All great truths begin as blasphemies'

5 'And to be sure, it is extremely pleasant to have one's house made the motley rendezvous of all the lackeys of literature!'

6 'A science is nothing but a well-made language'

Writers also use words as units of sound as well as sense. Much of the effect in poetry in particular is achieved by the sound of the words. According to Pope, 'It is not enough that nothing offends the ear, but a good poet will adapt the very sounds, as well as the words, to the thing he treats of. So that there is a style of sound.' The most powerful effects can often be achieved by alliteration.

F   Alliteration

The repetition of consonant sounds, often at the beginning of words:

'Music that brings swift sleep down from the blissful skies.'

Here the 's' sound used copiously at the beginning, end and middle of the words suggests the soft, dreamy link between 'music' and 'sleep'. The alliterative style was at its height in the Anglo-Saxon and Early English periods of English literature and in fact formed the basis of the earliest English poems; consider the effect of alliteration in this extract from 'The Ruin'.

Bright were the buildings, halls where the springs sprang,
high, hornbeamed, much music-noise;
these many meadhalls men filled
with loud cheerfulness: Fate changed that.

The alliterative element continued throughout the Middle Ages in both poetry and prose:

'In summer season, when soft was the sun'

'… withdraw and restrain the ravishing floods, and fasten and firm this Earth stable with thick bonds with which thou govern the heaven that is so large.'

After the Middle Ages alliteration became rarer in prose although it continued to ornament poetry. Here is Dryden using it to good effect in the seventeenth century:

'Birth-hour and death-hour meet,
Or, as great sages say,
Men dance on deathless feet.'

By the nineteenth century poets were using alliteration to achieve movement in their poetry; Coleridge, one of the poets of the Romantic movement expresses the sense of speed and urgency in 'The Ancient Mariner' alliteratively:

'The breezes blew, the white foam flew,
The furrow followed free.'

And there came a revival of the use of alliteration in prose by the writers of the Aesthetic movement at the end of the century:

'The Mona Lisa is older than the rocks among which she sits; like the vampire, she has been dead many times, and learned the secrets of the grave; and has been a diver in deep seas, and keeps their fallen day about her.'

Some of the writers of the twentieth century kept the alliterative form although the rhythm had changed:

'And she went to bed, leaving the door unlocked for him; but she lay listening until he came, often long after.'

Here D. H. Lawrence achieves a rather gentle, sad effect with the repetition of the liquid sound of 'l', while the poet Robert Graves suggests the comic/sinister with his recurring 's' in this extract from 'Welsh Incident' (notice the strong rhythm based on the sound of English spoken with a Welsh accent):

'... They came out on the sand,
Not keeping time to the band, moving seaward
Silently at a snail's pace.'

The use of alliteration has continued until the present day. Here the American poet Carl Sandburg has used it to capture the rhythm of a jazz band:

'Drum on your drums, batter on your banjos,
sob on the long cool winding saxophones.'

and John Fowles, the English novelist, by the insistent use of 'p' achieves the effect of a quick painting in words:

'Twice he stopped and noted down particularly pleasing conjunctions of tone and depth – parallel stripes of water-colour with pencilled notes of amplification in his neat hand.'

In its most extreme form, of course, alliteration is found in tongue-twisters where a comical effect is gained through using the same letter to start practically every word:

'The priest praised the pageants, plays and pastorals so prettily presented.'

Every language probably has its tongue-twisters and they are a very useful aid to pronunciation and intonation, but such an excessive use of alliteration would be disastrous if used for anything but comedy. In fact alliteration should always be used judiciously and only when it is essential to the style of the writing; when the use of words becomes an aim in itself then writing ceases to be literature.

Although conveying meaning accurately and imaginatively is the primary aim of literature, like alliteration, onomatopoeia is a means of enhancing the writing by sound effects.

G Onomatopoeia

The sound echoes the sense of a word: crisp, crack, chatter, pop, cool, drone, smooth, etc. Sometimes the effect is produced by the vowel sounds, sometimes by the consonants and sometimes by a combination of both. Consider this extract from a poem by Tennyson where the vowel and consonant sounds are equally important in achieving a sound picture:

'The moan of doves in immemorial elms,
And murmur of innumerable bees'

Oscar Wilde uses some of the same vowel and consonant sounds in his onomatopoeic treatment of bees in summer:

'The sullen murmur of the bees shouldering their way through the long unmown grass, or circling with monotonous insistence round the dusty gilt horns of the straggling woodbine, seemed to make the stillness more oppressive.'

But here the image is expressed very differently; Tennyson's warm, drowsy, richly evocative country scene has become sultry and overblown. You might like to consider how Wilde produced this change – which words and sounds built up the picture?

Like alliteration, onomatopoeia has been used throughout all the periods of English literature and often the two are used together to produce vivid sound pictures:

'Full fathom five thy father lies;
Of his bones are coral made;
Those are pearls that were his eyes:
Nothing of him that doth fade,
But doth suffer a sea-change,
Into something rich and strange.'

Shakespeare's haunting sea-picture in 'The Tempest' can be contrasted with Gerald Manley Hopkins' image of the sea in 'The Wreck of the Deutschland' (try saying this aloud):

'And the sea flint-flake, black-backed in the regular blow,
Sitting Eastnortheast, in cursed quarter, the wind;
Wiry and white-fiery and whirlwind-swivelled snow
Spins to the widow-making unchilding unfathering deeps.'

In prose, writers have also used onomatopoeia and alliteration together for sound and visual scenes. Here is one of Virginia Woolf's impressions of the sea, from her novel 'The Waves':

'The waves massed themselves, curved their backs and crashed. Up sported stones and shingle. They swept round the rocks, and the spray, leaping high, spattered the walls of a cave that had been dry before, and left pools inland, where some fish stranded lashed its tail as the wave drew back.'

How effective do you think Virginia Woolf was in her use of onomatopoeia and alliteration? Could the same impression of the sea have been achieved in any other way?

Exercise 4

Comment on the use of alliteration and onomatopoeia in the following extracts and say how effective you think the writers have been in imaginatively communicating their feelings and thoughts.

1   1872 August 10th. I was looking at high waves. The breakers always are parallel to the coast and shape themselves to it except where the curve is sharp however the wind blows. They are rolled out by the shallowing shore just as a piece of putty between the palms whatever its shape runs into a long roll. The slant ruck or crease one sees in them shows the way of the wind. The regularity of the barrels surprised and charmed the eye; the edge behind the comb or crest was as smooth and bright as glass. It may be noticed to be green behind and silver white in front; the silver marks where the air begins, the pure white is foam, the green, solid water. Then looked at to the right or left they are scrolled over like mouldboards or feathers or jibsails seen by the edge. It is pretty to see the hollow of the barrel disappearing as the white comb on each side runs along the wave gaining ground till the two meet at a pitch and crush and overlap each other.

(*Journal* Gerald Manley Hopkins)

2   She should have died hereafter;
      There would have been a time for such a word.
      Tomorrow, and tomorrow, and tomorrow,
      Creeps in this petty pace from day to day,
      To the last syllable of recorded time;
      And all our yesterdays have lighted fools
      The way to dusty death. Out, out, brief candle!
      Life's but a walking shadow, a poor player,
      That struts and frets his hour upon the stage,
      And then is heard no more; it is a tale
      Told by an idiot, full of sound and fury,
      Signifying nothing.

(*Macbeth* Shakespeare)

3   And what sort of stream was it? Was it like an Irish stream, winding through the brown bogs, where the wild ducks squatter up from among the white water-lilies, and the curlews flit to and fro, crying 'Tullie-wheep, mind your sheep'; and Dennis tells you strange stories of the Peishtamore, the great bogy-snake which lies in the black peat pools, among the old pine-stems, and puts his head out at night to snap at the cattle as they come down to drink?

    No .... It was such a stream as you see in dear old Bewick; .... A full hundred yards broad it was, sliding on from broad pool to broad shallow, and broad shallow to broad pool, over great fields of shingle, under oak and ash coverts, past low cliffs of sandstone, past green meadows, and fair parks, and a great house of grey stone, and brown moors above, and here and there against the sky the smoking chimney of a colliery. You must look at Bewick to see just what it was like, for he has drawn it a hundred times with the care and love of a true north country-man.

(*The Water Babies* Charles Kingsley)

169

4 Then quickly rose Sir Bedivere, and ran,
  And leaping down the ridges lightly, plunged
  Among the bulrush-beds, and clutch'd the sword,
  And strongly wheel'd and threw it. The great brand
  Made lightnings in the splendour of the moon,
  And flashing round and round, whirl'd in an arch,
  Shot like a streamer of the northern morn,
  Seen where the moving isles of winter shock
  By night, with noises of the northern sea.
  So flashed and fell the brand Excalibur.

        (*The Idylls of the King* Alfred Lord Tennyson)

5 It is known only to the inhabitants of the quarter. To find it you must penetrate a
winding passage, wedged between high walls of dismal brick. Turn to the right
by the blue-lettered advertisement of Kop's Ale, and again to the left through
the two posts, and you come to Pleasant-court.

 There are thirteen houses in Pleasant-court – seven on the one side, and six on
the other. They are alike, every one; low-walled as country cottages; built of
blackish brick, with a six-foot plot before each, and slate roofs that glimmer wanly
on the wet, winter mornings.

 But winter is not the season to see Pleasant-court at its best. The drain-sluice
is always getting choked, so that pools of mud and brown water loiter near the
rickety fence that flanks each six-foot enclosure ...

 In the summer, however, everyone smartens up, and by the time that sultry June
days have come, Pleasant-court attempts a rural air. On the left-hand side a jaded
creeper pushes its grimy greenery under the windows; some of the grass plots grow
quite bushy with tough wizened stalks; and the geranium pots at No 7 strike
flaming specks of vermilion.

        (*Pleasant Court* Hubert Crackanthorpe)

6 Next comes the dull disciple of the school,
  That mild apostate from poetic rule,
  That simple WORDSWORTH, framer of a lay
  As soft as evening in his favourite May,
  Who warns his friend 'to shake off toil and trouble
  And quit his books, for fear of growing double';
  Who, both by precept and example, shows
  That prose is verse, and verse is merely prose;
  Convincing all, by demonstration plain,
  Poetic souls delight in prose insane.

        (*On Wordsworth* Lord Byron)

WRITTEN SKILLS **B**

Literary Appreciation

Remember when you are studying a piece of writing you should be considering it in
its entirety; you should be asking yourself the following questions: What is it about?
How is it said? Is it successful? The figurative language can only be considered within
the framework of the author's intention; if it clarifies a thought, enhances a scene or
generally adds a vivid impression or sound to the writing then its use has been effective.

Unit six

This is what the American writer Henry James had to say about literary criticism: 'To criticise is to appreciate, to take intellectual possession, to establish a fine relation with the criticised thing and make it one's own.'

Often in the Cambridge Proficiency examination, in Section B of Paper 3, you will be required to study a piece of prose and comment on it. There are generally questions on the content of the passage, the language used, the effectiveness of any figurative language and the overall tone or style of writing. So the best way to tackle the question is to read the passage through once just for general understanding of the subject matter. Then go back and read it again for language, noticing any particular vocabulary or figurative devices the writer might have used. Next, read through the questions that have been set on the passage and finally, read each paragraph of the passage separately – linking it to any questions it refers to. Here is a representative passage with the questions worked for you.

> Literary criticism can be no more than a reasoned account of the feeling produced upon the critic by the book he is criticising. Criticism can never be a science: it is, in the first place, much too personal and, in the second, it is concerned with values that science ignores. The touchstone is emotion, not reason. We judge a
> 5 work of art by its effect on our sincere and vital emotion, and nothing else. All the critical twiddle-twaddle about style and form, all this pseudo-scientific classifying and analysing of books in an imitation-botanical fashion, is mere impertinence and mostly dull jargon.
>
> A critic must be able to *feel* the impact of a work of art in all its complexity
> 10 and its force. To do so, he must be a man of force and complexity himself, which few critics are. A man with a paltry, impudent nature will never write anything but paltry, impudent criticism. And a man who is emotionally educated is rare as a phoenix. The more scholastically educated a man is generally, the more he is an emotional boor.
> 15 More than this, even an artistically and emotionally educated man must be a man of good faith. He must have the courage to admit what he feels, as well as the flexibility to know what he feels.... A critic must be emotionally alive in every fibre, intellectually capable and skilful in essential logic, and then morally honest.
>
> Then it seems to me a good critic should give his readers a few standards to go
> 20 by. He can change the standards for every new critical attempt, so long as he keeps good faith. But it is just as well to say: This and this is the standard we judge by.
>
> (D. H. Lawrence)

1 What are the qualities, according to this passage, of a 'good critic'?

A 'good critic' should be a man of force and complexity and be artistically and emotionally educated. He should feel the impact of the work he is reviewing and not judge it intellectually. He must be morally honest and have the courage of his convictions to say what he feels about the work. To sum up, he should be sensitive and emotionally aware, intellectually able, rigorous in applying logic and morally honest.

2 What does the author mean by 'The touchstone is emotion not reason' (line 4)?

The author means the criterion for judging the work should be an emotional reaction, something felt, not a rational or logical thought process. The use of 'touchstone' instead of a word like 'criterion' in connection with emotion is more appropriate to the writer's feelings about criticism. 'Criterion' is a neutral unemotive word, more suitable to be connected with 'reason', while 'touchstone' suggests an intuitive basis for judgment – the word has rather magical, unreasoned connotations – touching stones for luck, the feeling of instinctive power contained in ancient stones; the touchstone used to be the standard for assessing the purity of gold and silver – the unknown power of this stone deciding the fate of exotic metals. Therefore it expresses very vividly the author's conviction that emotion is the only sure guide to criticism as it is a powerful, instinctive force like the touchstone.

3   How far do you think this passage expresses the personal opinion of the author and how far it is an objective statement?

It appears far more a personal opinion as the author makes no attempt to back up his strongly expressed opinions with quotations or examples. In line 6 he dismisses the whole of the literary tradition of critical appreciation as 'twiddle-twaddle' or rubbish, without considering whether it could add any dimension to the understanding of a work when combined with personal, emotional opinion. In line 9 he uses 'must' when giving his opinion where an author expressing his point of view more objectively would probably use 'should'.

4   In the sentence, 'A critic must be able to *feel* the impact of a work of art in all its complexity and its force' (line 9), why is the word *feel* emphasised?

Because the author feels very strongly the importance of 'feeling' as opposed to 'reasoning' in literary criticism, he wants to emphasise the personal, subjective approach – the feel for something.

5   What effect does the author achieve in the phrase 'emotionally alive in every fibre' (line 17)?

By the use of the word 'fibre' in conjunction with 'emotionally alive' the author produces an urgent, vivid picture of the necessity for the critic to use all of his emotional depth, down to the 'fibre', where the deepest levels of emotion are experienced – the skin and flesh stripped away exposing the 'fibre', the living emotional depths.

6   What is the author's purpose in using the phrases 'pseudo-scientific classifying' and 'in an imitation-botanical fashion' (lines 6–7)?

The deliberately used 'scientific classifying' and 'botanical' (scientific words) in connection with 'pseudo' and 'imitation', words which mean 'false', show the author's opinion about the wrongness of this approach to criticism. It is not the 'true' way, which is the emotional approach, but a 'false' (pseudo/imitation) method.

7   Summarise in 50–100 words Lawrence's attitude to literary criticism and critics.

Literary criticism is not a scientific exercise. It is a personal and emotional evaluation of the effect of a work of art on the critic. Literature cannot be scientifically analysed and classified.

Few men have the ability to open themselves up emotionally to a work of art; criticism is not an intellectual judgement. The 'good critic' has the courage and flexibility to admit and to know what he feels. He should provide his reader with standards to judge by.

From the above example of literary criticism you will see that the main response to the passage comes from an understanding of what the author is saying and an imaginative comprehension of his feelings as expressed through the language he uses. Do you agree with Lawrence's attitude to literary analysis?

Unit six

Read the following passages and then answer the questions. The first is by Oscar Wilde; the second by John Ruskin.

Passage A

The play was good enough for us, Harry. It was *Romeo and Juliet*. I must admit that I was rather annoyed at the idea of seeing Shakespeare done in such a wretched hole of a place. Still, I felt interested in a sort of way. At any rate, I determined to wait for the first act. There was a dreadful orchestra, presided over
5 by a young man who sat at a cracked piano, that nearly drove me away, but at last the drop-scene was drawn up, and the play began. Romeo was a stout elderly gentleman, with corked eyebrows, a husky tragedy voice, and a figure like a beer-barrel. Mercutio was almost as bad. He was played by a low-comedian, who had introduced gags of his own and was on most friendly terms with the pit. They
10 were both as grotesque as the scenery, and that looked as if it had come out of a country booth. But Juliet! Harry, imagine a girl, hardly seventeen years of age, with a little flower-like face, a small Greek head with plaited coils of dark-brown hair, eyes that were violet wells of passion, lips that were like the petals of a rose. She was the loveliest thing I had ever seen in my life. You said to me once that
15 pathos left you unmoved, but that beauty, mere beauty, could fill your eyes with tears. I tell you, Harry, I could hardly see this girl for the mist of tears that came across me. And her voice – I never heard such a voice. It was very low at first, with deep, mellow tones, that seemed to fall singly upon one's ear. Then it became a little louder, and sounded like a flute or a distant oboe. In the garden scene it had
20 all the tremulous ecstasy that you hear just before dawn when nightingales are singing. There were moments, later on, when it had the wild passion of violets. You know how a voice can stir you … Harry, I do love her. She is everything to me in life. Night after night I go to see her play. One evening she is Imogen, and the next evening she is Rosalind. I have seen her die in the gloom of an Italian
25 tomb, sucking the poison from her lover's lips. I have watched her wandering through the forest of Arden, disguised as a pretty boy. She has been mad, and has come in the presence of a guilty king, and given him bitter herbs. She has been innocent, and the black hands of jealousy have crushed her reed-like throat. I have seen her in every age and every costume. How different an actress is! Harry! why
30 didn't you tell me the only thing worth loving is an actress?

1 Compare the writer's use of language before the entrance of Juliet (line 11) with his description of her (lines 11–21)
2 What does the writer mean by the phrase 'a wretched hole of a place' (line 3) and why is the phrase appropriate?
3 Which phrases indicate that the actor playing Mercutio was wrong for the part?
4 Explain the following.
a the drop-scene was drawn up (line 6)
b plaited coils (line 12)
c tremulous ecstasy (line 20)
d a voice can stir you (line 22)
5 Why do you think the writer uses similar phrases: 'violet wells of passion' (line 13) and 'the wild passion of violets' (line 21) to describe both the girl's eyes and voice?
6 What is the significance of the word 'singly' in line 18?
7 Summarise in 50–100 words Wilde's impression of the actors and their effect on him.

Passage B

You sent for me to talk to you of art; and I have obeyed you in coming. But the main thing I have to tell you is this, – that art must not be talked about. The fact that there is talk about it at all, signifies that it is ill done, or cannot be done. No true painter ever speaks, or ever has spoken, much of his art. The greatest
5   speak nothing. Even Reynolds is no exception, for he wrote of all that he could not himself do, and was utterly silent respecting all that he himself did.

The moment a man can really do his work he becomes speechless about it. All words become idle to him – all theories.

Does a bird need to theorise about building its nest, or boast when it is built?
10 All good work is essentially done that way – without hesitation, without difficulty, without boasting; and in the doers of the best, there is an involuntary power which approximates literally to the instinct of the animal – I am certain that in the most perfect human artists, reason does not supersede instinct but is added to an instinct.... But be that as it may – be the instinct less or more than that
15 of inferior animals, still the human art is dependent on it first, and then upon an amount of practice, of science – and of imagination disciplined by thought, which the true possessor of it knows to be incommunicable, and the true critic of it, inexplicable, except through long process of laborious years.

But in a slow way art can be taught – if you have faith in your guide. But in
20 what teacher of art have you such faith? Certainly not in me; for, as I told you at first, I know well enough it is only because you think I can talk, not because you think I know my business, that you let me speak to you at all. If I were to tell you anything that seemed to you strange you would not believe it, and yet it would only be in telling you strange things that I could be of use to you.
25 But you would not believe it, just because the thing that would be of real use would displease you. Suppose I were to tell you, in the strongest terms I could use, that Gustave Doré's art was bad – bad not in weakness – not in failure – but bad with dreadful power; that so long as you looked at it, no perception of pure or beautiful art was possible for you. Would you believe me? Would you look
30 at Gustave Doré less? Rather more, I fancy. On the other hand, I could soon put you in a good humour with me, if I chose. I know well enough what you like and how to praise it to your liking. I could talk to you about moonlight, and twilight, and spring flowers, and autumn leaves – how delicious! Old as I am, I could play you a tune on the harp yet, that you would dance to. But neither you nor I should
35 be a bit wiser; or, if we were, our increased wisdom could be of no practical effort. Art is neither to be achieved by effort of thinking nor explained by accuracy of speaking. It is the instinctive and necessary result of powers which can only be developed through the mind of successive generations, and which finally burst into life under social conditions as slow of growth as the faculties they regulate.

1   Compare the writer's treatment of his theme in paragraph 1 (lines 1–6) with that in paragraph 4 (lines 19–40).
2   Explain the phrase 'all words become idle to him' (lines 7–8).
3   What does the writer consider most important to human art?
4   To what do these expressions refer?
a   the doers of the best (line 11)
b   long process of laborious years (line 18)

5   Why does the writer refer to art as 'incommunicable' by the artist and 'inexplicable' by the critic (lines 17–18)?
6   What is the significance of the phrase 'dreadful power' (line 8)?
7   To what does 'it' refer (line 32)?
8   Comment on 'I could play you a tune on the harp yet, that you would dance to' (lines 33–34).

9 What is meant by 'practical effort' (lines 35–36)?

10 Summarise in 50–100 words Ruskin's views on the teaching of art.

Passage C

> If music be the food of love, play on,
> Give me excess of it, that, surfeiting,
> The appetite may sicken and so die.
> That strain again! It had a dying fall;
> 5 O, it came o'er my ear like the sweet sound
> That breathes upon a bank of violets,
> Stealing and giving odour! Enough, no more;
> 'Tis not so sweet now as it was before.

(Twelfth Night Shakespeare)

1 What do you think Shakespeare meant by, 'If music be the food of love' (line 1)?
2 Why should the appetite 'sicken and so die' (line 3)? Which 'appetite' is Shakespeare referring to?
3 Explain the following.
   a surfeiting (line 2)   **b** strain (line 4)   **c** a dying fall (line 4)
   d giving odour (line 7)
4 Pick out the words and phrases that are connected with
   a sound   **b** smell
5 What difference in meaning is there in 'sweet' (line 5) and 'sweet' (line 8)?
6 The speaker says 'play on' (line 1) and 'Enough, no more' (line 7). What could be the reason for this change of mood?
7 Summarise in about 50 words the feelings about love expressed in this passage.

REMINDER **6**

Participle Phrases

With ——**ed** or ——**ing** in every case
Put the phrase in its proper place

1 Participle phrases are formed with the **Present Participle '——ing'** or the **Past Participle '——ed'/or irregular form.** They are not complete sentences as they do not have a Subject + Verb of their own.

Phrases with the **Present Participle** are sometimes confused with the Gerund. The most important point to remember about this is that the Participle phrase cannot have a Possessive case, as the Gerund can:

I have always admired *his painting*. (Gerund)
I watched *him painting* her portrait. (Participle: while he was painting)

Examples of Participle phrases
Present: We saw the old monk *walking* in the cloisters, *counting* his beads.
Perfect: *Having seen* the cathedral, we decided to visit the museum.
Past: We entered a great hall, *hung* with priceless tapestries.
(This is really a concealed Passive, i.e. 'a great hall which was hung with priceless tapestries.')

2   When using Participle phrases, it is necessary to place them as closely as possible to the Subject or Object to which they refer, otherwise confusion or absurdity may result.

Example

He presented the miniature to the Queen wrapped in velvet.
That means that the Queen was wrapped in velvet!
Correct to   He presented the miniature, *wrapped in velvet*, to the Queen.

Exercise 1

Put the Participle phrases in the following sentences into their correct place, making any necessary changes including punctuation.

1   We were late for the first act of the opera having been delayed by the traffic.

   ....

2   Carved by Grinling Gibbons, the house contains a fine example of a mahogany overmantel.

   ....

3   We noticed Impressionist paintings filled most of the walls visiting the State Gallery.

   ....

4   After having composed the Water Music, George IV commissioned Handel to write the Music for the Royal Fireworks.

   ....

5   Covered in dust, the old lady took the medallion from the back of the cupboard where it had lain for more than fifty years.

   ....

6   I decided not to see the film having a horror of violence.

   ....

7   Still weaving on an eighteenth-century loom, we went to see an old woman in the Highlands.

   ....

8   Lying on a stall in Portobello Market my brother found this anthology of poetry.

   ....

9   The museum was destroyed by fire exhibiting prehistoric remains.

   ....

10 Living in Pompeii, this ornamental comb once belonged to a young woman.

   ....

Exercise 2

Complete the following sentences, taking care to attach the participle to a suitable noun.

1   Having become interested in Rembrandt's paintings ....
2   Being too tired for any more sightseeing ....
3   Wrapped in layers of yellowing newspaper ....
4   Carrying an easel under his arm   ....
5   Having lost our way to the ruins ....
6   Designed in the thirteenth century ....
7   Lying on the pavement ....
8   Having an irrational dislike of classical music ....
9   Undiscovered for centuries ....
10 Staring into the shop window ....

Unit seven Government and Law

ORAL SKILLS A

Intensive Listening

	Presenter	Now we're taking you over to the House of Commons for **'That's the Question'**, the programme in which you will hear the Prime Minister answering questions of national importance from Members of all parties. Today we are likely to hear
5		questions on the Sunday closure of museums, the American air base at Puddledown, and the strike of women workers at a factory in North Wales. **That's the Question:**
		[Sound of voices raised in discussion]
	Speaker	Mrs Alice Betters, Member for Whitechapel East.
10	**(House of Commons)**	
	Presenter	Conservative.
	Mrs Betters	Is the Prime Minister aware that the closing of the Whitechapel Museum and the East London Art Gallery on Sundays will
15		result in serious social deprivation in the area, particularly for old-age pensioners for whom these museums have offered a

		meeting place for the last fifty years, to say nothing of the large number of part-time students who, owing to their working commitments, are frequently only able to visit the
20		museums on Sundays?
	Prime Minister	I would remind the Right Honourable Member for Whitechapel East that, much as we all sympathise with the problems of pensioners in our society, the purpose of a museum is not to provide a free meeting place....
25		[Cries of 'Shame']
	Speaker	Order, Order!
	Prime Minister	As far as part-time students are concerned, there are a number of other museums open on Sundays which would no doubt serve their purpose equally well. However, as I understand it
30		the problem with the Whitechapel Museum and the East London Art Gallery is largely a question of staffing and this is a matter for the appropriate local authority.
	Speaker	Mr Gordon Box, Member for Puddledown.
	Presenter	Labour.
35	**Gordon Box**	The Prime Minister will doubtless have received the petition signed by five thousand of my constituents in protest against the Government's decision to allow an American Air Training Station to be based on the old war-time airfield at Puddledown. This is a quiet, rural area, justly famed for its beauty and
40		visited by thousands of tourists during the season from whom the local people derive a considerable part of their income. I am astonished, not to say alarmed, at the Government's bland disregard of the wishes of the people in this matter. It would seem that in the appalling economic situation into which the
45		present Government has so shamelessly plunged us ......
		[Angry uproar among Members]
	Speaker	... so shamelessly plunged us, the total disruption of people's lives is a secondary consideration when it comes to making a quick dollar.
50		[Cheers from Opposition]
	Prime Minister	My honourable friend would probably do well to get his facts right before levelling accusations at the present Government. The question of the American Air Training Station at Puddledown first arose in the lifetime – admittedly short –
55		of the last Government ...
		[Laughter]
		and was agreed in principle then. Opinion was canvassed in the area and it was generally considered that the local residents stood to gain rather more from having the Americans
60		permanently based in their area than from the seasonal visits of coach parties of transatlantic visitors. It is regrettable that the constituents Mr Box refers to did not take the matter up with the Government then in office.
	Speaker	Mr Harold Adams.
65	**Presenter**	Leader of the Opposition.

Harold Adams	In the midst of her other urgent labour problems, has it entirely escaped the Prime Minister's notice that there are at this moment five hundred women packers on strike at the Pontriff Cereal Company in North Wales? This in effect means

70   that the distribution of breakfast cereals over half the country, if not nationwide, has virtually halted. Since at the current rate of inflation breakfast cereals are probably going to be all the majority of us will be able to afford for dinner, let alone breakfast, I should be glad to know what the Prime Minister

75   intends to do about it.

[Laughter]

Prime Minister   I should find it a matter of extreme regret if the Leader of the Opposition were reduced to living entirely on breakfast cereals. And, if such were the case, I should consider it a privilege to

80   invite him to dine at No. 10 – to bury our differences, so to speak, under a mound of sausages and mash –

[Laughter. Cries of 'Shame']

Harold Adams   The Prime Minister with her customary elusiveness has succeeded in evading the question.

85 **Prime Minister**   The Right Honourable gentleman must realise as well as I do that the strike of packers at the Pontriff Cereal Company is at the moment entirely a union matter. It would not be appropriate for the Government to take any action at this stage....

Exercise 1

Listen to the extract again then answer or complete the following.

1   Mrs Betters said that the closing of the museum and art gallery ....
2   Why did Mrs Betters think that part-time students would be particularly affected?
....
3   What did the Prime Minister say about the purpose of a museum and what suggestions did she make for part-time students?
....
4   Gordon Box reminded the Prime Minister that five thousand of his constituents ...
....
5   Gordon Box expressed alarm because ....
6   How in Gordon Box's opinion did the Government rate the disruption of people's lives?
....
7   With regard to the American Air Training Station at Puddledown, the Prime Minister pointed out that ....
....
8   What, at the time of the last Government, was the feeling of the local residents about the American Air Training Station?
....
....
9   The Prime Minister regretted that Mr Box...
10   What did Harold Adams say had been the immediate effect of the strike of women packers at the Pontriff Cereal Company?
....

11 Harold Adams felt that at the current rate of inflation ....

....

12 What invitation did the Prime Minister issue to Harold Adams?

....

13 What criticism of the Prime Minister did Harold Adams make in response to this invitation?

....

14 The Prime Minister did not think it right for the Government to take any immediate action about the strike because ....

....

Note the following expressions used in the text.

1 to say nothing of (line 17)   if not (line 71)
   not to say (line 42)   let alone (line 73)

These expressions are rather similar in meaning and refer to a fact already known or extremely probable, which adds force to the main statement. Here are some additional examples.

The Government are unlikely to increase pensions this year, *let alone* child benefits.
His salary is hardly enough to meet his rent, *to say nothing of* his rates.
His speech will probably be very lengthy, *if not* boring.
I find the licensing laws very complicated, *not to say* almost impossible to understand.

2 **a**   as far as ... are concerned (line 27)   *with regard to*
    b   no doubt/doubtless (lines 28–35)   *assumed to be a fact*
    c   when it comes to ... (line 48)   *in the event of*
    d   do well to ... (line 51)   *would be advised to*
    e   stood to gain ... (line 59)   *could only profit by*
    f   if such were the case ... (line 79)   *in this unlikely situation*
    g   so to speak ... (line 80)   *for want of a better expression*

Exercise 2

Choosing the most suitable phrases from the ones given, make sentences to express the following. Try to use a different expression for each sentence.

1 People living in the village of Puddledown will be inconvenienced and very probably lose a great deal of trade if the Air Training Station is established there.

2 The Government's agricultural policy will certainly cause food prices to rise as well as reducing exports.

3 The increase in National Insurance contributions will cause dissatisfaction among employers without taking into account the effect it will have on the workers' pay packets.

4 I suppose we have to accept the Government's pay guidelines, but with regard to the miners, I think some special provision should be made.

5 The Minister of Agriculture stated that the farmers must inevitably profit by the new import restrictions.

6 It doesn't seem very likely that mortgage rates will go down, but if this did happen, it would be advisable for present tenants to make every effort to buy the houses they occupy.

7 The local residents are not unsympathetic to the immigrants' housing problem but if they were asked to provide accommodation for them in their own homes, they would probably object.

8 I don't quite know how to describe my boss, but he is, for want of a better expression, very old-fashioned.

9 Although there has so far been no official statement, it must be assumed that the local authority have already come to a decision about the Sunday closing of the museum.

10 If something is not done quickly, the strike of ambulance men in Banchester will soon spread all over the county and very likely over the whole country as well.

ORAL SKILLS **B**
Dialogue

 Listen to the following dialogue between a magistrate and a young man who has been charged with driving while under the influence of drink.

Exercise 1

For each of the questions 1–4 put a tick in the appropriate boxes.

1 What is the attitude of the magistrate towards the accused?

    A Puritanical

    B Intolerant

    C Sceptical

    D Compassionate

A	
B	
C	
D	

2 Which of these reasons does the accused offer as plausible excuses?

    A The position of the school

    B The breathalyser test

    C An inaccurate speedometer

    D Police officiousness

    E Small amount of liquor consumed

    F A faulty steering wheel

A	
B	
C	
D	
E	
F	

3 How does the accused behave in court?

    A He tries to ingratiate himself

    B He makes fun of the magistrate

    C He borders on insolence

    D He appears ill at ease

A	
B	
C	
D	

4 To which of the accused's remarks does the magistrate take particular exception?

    A It sort of backs me up

    B A machine can't lie, can it?

    C You must be joking

    D They're just trying to put it over on me

A	
B	
C	
D	

Exercise 2

A Now match the following expressions used to their meanings.

1	*keep to*	*A*	postpone it
2	*run the risk*	*B*	supports what I say
3	*backs me up*	*C*	observe the rule
4	*go by*	*D*	finding fault with
5	*go wrong*	*E*	have it checked/repaired
6	*playing up*	*F*	incur the danger of
7	*have it seen to*	*G*	become defective
8	*put it off*	*H*	causing trouble
9	*put it over on me*	*I*	make me believe
10	*picking on*	*J*	judge from

B   Now re-phrase the following sentences using one of these verbal expressions as appropriate.

1   I don't understand politics, I can only judge from what I read in the papers.
2   My husband is always finding fault with his secretary, although I'm sure she does her best.
3   I'd rather you drove because I'm a bit out of practice and I wouldn't want to be the cause of an accident.
4   I'm afraid there's something the matter with this tape recorder.
5   Whatever he introduces, the Chancellor can count on the support of the Cabinet.
6   Whenever I am driving in a foreign country, I take care not to infringe the parking regulations.
7   I really must get someone to repair the garage door.
8   I don't believe everything Councillor Morgan says about the plans for the new hospital, but he's very clever in the way he manages to convince people.
9   I heard on the radio that the Summit Meeting had been postponed till next week.
10   Our telephone system has been giving so much trouble lately, I think I shall have to call the Engineers.

Exercise 3

Listen to the two statements and answer these questions:

Statement 1: (Magistrate)

What reason did the magistrate give for putting the young man on probation?
What warning did he give the young man?
What reproof did he give him?

Statement 2: (Minister of Education)

What did the Minister say about the pass grades in CSE and GCE examinations?
What did he say would be substituted for them?
How did he say this decision had been arrived at?

ORAL SKILLS **C**
Photograph for Discussion

Look at this photograph of the Old Bailey (the Central Criminal Court) and be prepared to talk about it.

Questions

1 Describe the building in the picture.
2 Why do you think the figure at the top is holding a pair of scales?
3 Is this a modern style of architecture?

Topics

Justice.
Increased crime in modern society.
Punishment of wrong-doers.

ORAL SKILLS **D**
Reading Aloud

Study this text. Answer the questions that follow and then read it aloud.

I should like the Jury to take into consideration the extreme stress under which the accused was suffering at the time he committed the robbery, a burden of debts which were incurred not for himself but for the greater relief of a dying wife. In such circumstances, Members of the Jury, would not you or I, weighed down by anxiety and intolerable pressures at home, have been ready to risk prison – I would even go so far as to say, our lives – in order to bring some comfort to the woman we loved?

Who is speaking and where?
Who is he speaking about?
What extenuating circumstances does he put forward?

ORAL SKILLS **E**
Group Discussion

Prisons

need for reform   punishment v. rehabilitation   aftercare of prisoners

USE OF ENGLISH **A**
Revision of Direct/Indirect Speech

A Direct

1   The **Direct** words of a speaker are placed between inverted commas '……' preceded by a comma, question/exclamation mark as required before *he said, she asked, they exclaimed,* etc.

If the speaker continues, then the inverted commas are opened and closed again in the same way:

'I understand that there has been an encouraging fall in the unemployment figures during the last six months,' the Prime Minister said, 'but I shan't have the exact figures available until early next week.'

In Direct statements with *said,* it is possible to invert the order of the verb and subject: '……,' *said the Prime Minister.* But this cannot be done with questions and the form should be avoided with other verbs.

2   In **Direct Dialogue** only the names of the speakers are given, followed by a colon. Inverted commas are not used.

Prime Minister: There has been an encouraging fall in the unemployment figures during the last six months.

Member of Parliament: When will the exact figures be available?

N.B. This form is commonly required in examinations when the candidate is asked to write a Dialogue.

3 Except for some very formal or emphatic pronouncements, short forms, i.e. *don't, can't, I've,* etc. should be used for Direct Speech as this is the way people really talk.

Exercise 1

1 Write a short dialogue between yourself and a Traffic Warden who has just told you that you are in a Non-parking zone.

2 Write a short statement made by a Government official on the necessity to increase the tax on petrol by 2p a gallon.

B Indirect

1 The two general rules for changing **Direct** to **Indirect Speech,** that is, reporting something that *was or is being said* are:

    a If the reporting verb is in a Present Tense – *he says/he is saying* then the tenses remain unchanged.

    Example

    '*I hope* to stand as a Labour candidate in the next General Election.'

    'What's he saying?'

    'He says/is saying *he hopes* to stand as a Labour candidate in the next General Election.'

    N.B. Careful attention must, however, be paid to the change of *pronouns* where necessary. In the example given above '*I*' changes to '*he*'.

    b If the reporting verb *say, ask,* etc. is in the Past Tense then the tenses in the **Direct Speech** change to their equivalent Past Tenses.

    Example

    'The Queen *will* open Parliament on the 5th October,' Mr Brown said.

    Mr Brown said that the Queen *would* open Parliament on the 5th October.

2 **Orders, instructions, requests** are commonly used with an Infinitive structure (see also page 155).

If introduced with *tell, order, ask,* etc. they must have a Person Object:

'Be quiet!'

He told us *to be quiet.*

'Would you mind not making so much noise?'

He asked us *not to make* so much noise.

BUT

If the speaker is making a personal request then the **Indirect Speech** form becomes:

Subject + Reporting Verb + 'IF' + Subject + Request

'Can I borrow your radio?'

She asked *if she could* borrow my radio.

3 **Indirect Questions**

Remember that when Indirect Questions are reported, they form two sentences connected by a Question Word, i.e. *how, where, when, if* etc.

Examples

'When is the next General Election?'

He *asked* me *when* the next General Election *was.*

'Did you vote for the Conservative candidate?'

He *wanted to know if* I *had voted* for the Conservative candidate.

'How long will it be before they publish the results of the referendum, Father?'
John asked.

John *asked* his father *how long* it *would be* before they *published* the results of
the referendum.

4 Time/Date Changes

Care must be exercised in changing *today* to *that day, last week* to *the week before,*
etc. Such changes are a simple matter of common sense. If someone says that he
visited the House of Commons *last week*, and it was in fact *last week* that he did this,
then it makes nonsense to report his visit as '*the week before*'.

Examples

a 'The Chancellor of the Exchequer is making his Budget Speech *today*.'
  'What did you say?'
  'I said the Chancellor of the Exchequer was making his Budget Speech *today*.'

b Extract from Budget Speech made six months ago:
  'I am proposing to increase the tax on cigarettes by 2p for 20 *as from today*.'
  – 'Do you remember if the tax on cigarettes was increased in the last Budget?'
  – 'Yes, the Chancellor said he was going to increase it by 2p for 20 *as from that
  day*.'

5 Should/Would/Could/Might/Ought

do not change to the Perfect when reported, as to do so would completely alter
the sense:

'I could take the matter up with my MP.'   (possible future)
He said he *could take* the matter up with his MP.

Note difference in sense:
He said he *could have taken* the matter up with his MP.   (was possible but not done)

'I might be able to check that reference if I went to the library.'
She said she *might be able* to check that reference if she *went* to the library.
(possible future)

Note the difference:
She said she *might have been able* to check that reference if she *had gone* to the
library.   (was possible but not done)

Exercise 2

Put the following sentences into Indirect Speech.

1 'Don't interrupt while the Mayor is speaking, children,' said the teacher.
  'There will be plenty of time for questions later.'
2 'You would have to work very long hours as a Probation Officer, Harry,' the
  Careers master explained, 'but there is a great deal of satisfaction to be got out of
  the work.'
3 'It says in the paper,' said Philip, 'that an undertaker was given a parking ticket
  for leaving his hearse on a yellow line while he went into a house to collect the
  body for the funeral service.'
4 'I'm sorry but you can't watch that jazz programme on TV tonight, Johnny,' said
  his mother. 'Your father wants to listen to the Party Political Broadcast.'
5 'I must get up early tomorrow,' said Mary. 'I'm going to watch the Changing of
  the Guard at Buckingham Palace.'

6 'When is my case likely to be heard?' Mr Simpkins asked his solicitor.

7 'If you want to know what I think,' said Mr Barnes, looking at his rates demand, 'the Council ought to have something better to do with its time than trying to bleed the residents out of every penny they've got.'

8 'How long do you think it will be before there's another General Election?' Peter asked me. 'I should like to be able to vote but I'm not eighteen till after Christmas.'

9 'Take this letter,' Mr Hill told his secretary, 'and see that it is delivered personally to the Minister of Education.'

10 'Do stop arguing about politics,' said Mother, 'and come and have your supper. I put it on the table ten minutes ago. It must be cold by now.'

USE OF ENGLISH **B**
Variations and Special Uses

The common reporting verbs: *say, tell, ask* are frequently varied to prevent too much repetition and there is often difficulty in converting Greetings and Responses, Exclamations, Expressions of Emotion and Colloquial Idiom into Indirect Speech. The following notes may serve as a guide.

Simple Statements	*Introducing verbs :* say, state, tell, announce, declare, inform, assert, etc.
Questions	*Introducing verbs :* say, enquire, want to know
Orders/Requests/ Instructions	*Introducing verbs :* tell, order, command, direct
Suggestions	*'How about ...?' 'Why don't we ...?' 'Let's ...'*, etc. suggest, propose, recommend, advise, etc.
Encouragement	*'Come on !' 'Keep going'*, etc.; encourage, urge
Greetings and Polite. Phrases and Responses	*'Good morning', 'Good night', 'How are you?'* *'Please', 'Thank you', 'That's very kind of you'*, etc. These expressions can usually be omitted from the Indirect Speech, but if necessary the following verbs can be used to convey the sense. 'Good morning' – he *greeted* me 'How are you?' – he *asked after* me 'Please' – he *asked politely* 'Thank you' – he *thanked* me 'That's very kind of you' – he *thanked me for my kindness/help*
Refusals/Denials	*'I didn't', 'I won't', 'I flatly refuse to'*, etc. refuse, deny, repudiate, etc. 'I didn't exceed the speed limit.' He *denied exceeding* the speed limit. 'I won't take the breathalyser test!' He *refused to take* the breathalyser test.

Unit seven

| Exclamations/Expressions of emotion: Anger, Regret, Surprise, etc. | exclaim, sigh, regret, scream, laugh, cry, etc. as appropriate to the sentence. The reported sentence may then need some other slight changes to keep its sense and balance: |

'Oh dear,' said Mr Bates, 'I've still got five more letters to write.'

Mr Bates *sighed because* he still had five more letters to write.

'I'm terribly sorry I couldn't get to the meeting.'

He *apologised for being unable to attend* the meeting.

'If you report this to the Police, I'll kill you!'

He *threatened to kill me if I reported it* to the Police.

Students will be able to think of a variety of verbs that will express these and expressions of a similar kind.

Exercise 1

Put the following situations into Direct Speech.

Example

John wished he were old enough to vote in the next General Election.

'*I wish I were old enough to vote in the next General Election,*' said John.

1   His father suggested that Peter should take a Law degree if he wanted to go into politics.

2   The new MP was very worried when he found he had left the notes of his maiden speech at home.

3   He was surprised to hear that the vandals were only put on probation.

4   The magistrate warned the boy not to get into trouble again.

5   Mrs Brown was delighted to hear that her husband had been elected to serve on the local council.

6   The policeman reassured the lost child and told her that he would soon find her mother for her.

7   The speaker apologised for not having checked the latest unemployment figures.

8   The shopkeeper thought there was something rather suspicious about the two men waiting outside his shop.

9   It's a matter of complete indifference to Mr Jones whether the Government increases the tax on tobacco or not. He doesn't smoke.

10   Mary regretted not having taken her driving test years ago. She knew she would never pass it now.

11   Old Mrs Jones was delighted when she learnt that the retirement pensions were to be increased.

12   Mr Stevens found it hard to believe that his son was going to vote Conservative.

13   In view of the size of Mrs Harrison's estate, the solicitor considered it unfortunate that she had not made a will before she died.

14   The woman uttered a scream of pain. She had cut her finger on the carving knife.

15   Alan protested that it was not due to his negligence that the thieves broke into the house. He had locked and bolted all the doors and windows before he went out.

Exercise 2

Following is an extract from a speech made by Joseph Hart MP to his constituents in an area where juvenile crime has significantly increased. Read the extract carefully and then answer the questions. Use Indirect Speech forms for your answers.

I'm afraid we have to accept the fact that criminals are getting younger all the time, but unfortunately the offences they commit are becoming proportionately more serious. I only wish we didn't have to admit this but, in doing so, we must first ask ourselves what's wrong with our society that our children apparently
5 couldn't care less about law and order. The day of the sneak thief who stole a couple of apples off a barrel or nicked a packet of sweets from a chain store are virtually over. I had occasion to say this to a young offender the other day. 'Sweets from a chain store?' he said, 'you must be joking. That's kid's stuff.' I may add that he was aged eleven. In other words, today's young criminals would find it
10 laughable to risk being caught for petty theft of this description. They've got enough money in their pockets to buy the sweets they want, anyway. I think we have come to the point where it's all too easy to put the blame on anyone but ourselves. Faced as they are with a society that frequently rejects them on the grounds of colour, race or low academic ability, these children turn to crime as
15 a means of boosting their self-esteem. Nurtured on films and TV glamorising the role of the criminal, they are quick to identify with these anti-heroes. It is a matter of increasing concern to the Police and magistrates that the Children and Young Persons Act, 1969 is becoming inadequate to deal with the rise in juvenile crime. Because the emphasis has been placed on the cause and treatment
20 of their delinquency, rather than on old-fashioned methods of punishment, the children themselves are well aware that there is very little that can be done to prevent them continuing to mug, vandalise and in some case even cause the death of those they choose to terrorise. I don't like the look of this situation any more than you do. In our own interests and in those of our children and grandchildren,
25 we cannot continue to take the 'it's nothing to do with me' attitude we have adopted for so long. We must unite in a common demand for harsher and more disciplined methods against these young offenders....

1 What did the speaker have to say about the age of the criminals in relation to their offences?

2 How did one young offender react to the idea of stealing sweets from a chain store?

3 What reasons did the speaker give for children turning to crime?

4 Why did the speaker feel the Police and magistrates were becoming increasingly concerned?

5 In what way did the speaker believe that the emphasis in dealing with delinquents was misplaced?

6 What did he feel added to the children's contempt for the law?

7 How did the speaker describe the public's attitude to child crime?

8 What particular kinds of child crime did he refer to?

9 State any points made by the speaker with which you disagree.

10 Summarise in 50–100 words the main points of Joseph Hart's speech. Begin your summary:

In a speech to his constituents Joseph Hart stated …

USE OF ENGLISH **C**

Gap-filling

Fill each of the numbered blanks in the following passage with one suitable word.

People often ………(1) to give information about serious………(2) to the Police because they fear ………(3). This is particularly ………(4) if the suspect is someone they know or a popular figure in the community. In the case of a friend they may even try to cover ………(5) for them in the ………(6) belief that they are acting ………(7) of loyalty. It takes long and patient work on the ………(8) of the Police to educate the public to come ………(9) with information, ………(10) trivial it may seem, and to ………(11) them that anything they report will be kept entirely ………(12). 'I don't want to get ………(13) up in it' is a common ………(14) for not reporting ………(15) circumstances. Unfortunately what these people do not always ………(16) is that by ………(17) information they may be ………(18) the lives and property not only of ………(19) but of many of those most vulnerable ………(20) of our society.

'Government can exist without law, but law cannot exist without government.'
('Unpopular Essays' – Bertrand Russell)

The interior of the House of Commons

WRITTEN SKILLS **A**
Debates and Discussions

For and Against

When you take part in a debate or discussion you should be able to present your side of the case convincingly, whereas if you speak or write on a particular topic you need to be able to present both sides clearly.

In a debate, therefore, you need have only the facts and information relating to the point of view that you wish to present. Of course it helps if you have considered in advance any possible arguments the opposing side may put forward; you are then in the position to demolish them as soon as they appear. A good analogy is a game of chess; you must plan your own attack carefully, but at the same time anticipate and counter your opponent's moves. However, speaking or writing on a given topic is equivalent to playing both sides of the game of chess yourself; your arguments attack and counter-attack each other until at the end a truce is declared and the winner is named. In other words, you present both sides of an argument, sum up and then state your own position.

So, let's see how this works out in practice. First, debates.

Debates

Debates are generally rather formal and have a standard method of procedure:

1　**The Chairman** – Opens the debate, announces the subject under discussion, introduces the first speaker (the proposer of the motion) and calls upon him or her to speak. Other duties of the Chairman are to keep order during the debate; to discourage irrelevance and keep the speakers to the point; and to take the vote at the end – he has the casting vote in the event of a tie.

2　**The Proposer** – The first speaker, presents the motion (subject under discussion) and makes a strong case in support of it. Generally has strong feelings or/and views on the motion. Other duties: sums up the arguments in favour of the motion at the end of the debate; answers chief points made against the motion.

3　**The Opposer** – In some debates the proposer is immediately followed by his seconder (chief supporter), but often the opposer speaks next. The opposer, often the second speaker, presents the opposing point of view. Attacks the proposition (motion), without being led into side issues. Other duties: should throw out hints for the audience to develop; sums up the opposing case at the end of the debate.

4　**Seconder of the proposition** – Supports the proposer, adding any new points in support of the motion; defends the motion from attack of the opposition and answers any questions.

5　**Seconder of the opposition** – Supports the opposer, adding any new points against the motion; attacks the proposition and replies to questions about the opposition.

6　After the seconders have spoken, the meeting is generally thrown open to the House (audience). People wishing to say something raise their hands and the Chairman then invites them to speak in turn. A time limit is usually put on each speaker so that as many people as possible get the chance to say something. Long speeches are discouraged so that more time can be given to 'open' debate.

7   At the end of the debate, after the summing up, a vote is taken – all members of the audience and the speakers voting 'for' or 'against' the motion – only the Chairman abstains.

8   **Tellers** – Two tellers count the votes, those in favour of the motion first and then those against. If there is a tie (draw) the Chairman uses his casting vote.

9   The Chairman declares the motion 'carried' or 'lost' accordingly, thanks the speakers, etc. and closes the debate.

10 **Secretary** – Records vote in minutes. A secretary is present at debates when they are a regular occurrence of a society or association. He keeps the minutes (record) of the debate and also reads out the minutes of the last debate at the beginning.

Here is an example of a debate held by a society which helps ex-prisoners. The motion is 'Prisons are useless as a means of reforming criminals', and the proposer is Ms Ann Foster, a social worker and prison visitor. Mr Richard Black, a prison governor, is the opposer of the motion. The Chairman has opened the meeting, the Secretary has read the minutes of the last meeting, then the Chairman introduced Ms Foster who rose to propose the motion. This is what she said. Notice how she starts her speech.

Mr Chairman, Ladies and Gentlemen, I have always held the opinion that prisons should be instrumental in helping a criminal reform and change his way of life. Unfortunately, our present prison system only makes the prisoner worse, hence the large number of prisoners who return 'inside' again and again. I should
5   like to draw your attention to several serious defects in the prison system. Consider the rigid discipline that is enforced; surely it must destroy all independence in the prisoners so that they become completely dependent on society when they are released – their self-reliance utterly destroyed. In the same way the dull, monotonous work they do in prison does nothing to build up
10 their self-confidence or give them a pride in themselves. Instead of being taught a skill or a trade which would help them to get a job when they leave, they are given unskilled, low-grade work of no value to them or to the world outside. Similarly, there is little opportunity for the prisoners to study or take part in creative activities, therefore they rarely develop their mental or creative abilities.
15 In fact, they spend long hours locked up in their cells with little to occupy themselves. The resultant feelings of frustration and rebellion are further aggravated by the almost complete lack of physical exercise; I understand that only half an hour a day is not uncommon in some prisons. Not surprisingly, the physical health of many prisoners deteriorates, a condition not helped by the
20 general poor quality of prison food.
    A few isolated examples of prison reform can be quoted: more exercise, better recreational facilities, less mindless discipline; but, in general, prisons are still places of punishment solely and few efforts are made to help reform the prisoners or equip them for life 'outside'. It is hardly surprising that 60% of all criminals
25 return to prison in less than five years from release. After all, the prison system as it stands today only serves to reinforce the prisoners' feelings of hostility to society for punishing them and strengthens their belief that 'the world owes them a living.'

Exercise 1

1   Make a list of Ms Foster's points in support of the motion. By the side of each point write 'agree' or 'disagree', according to your own personal opinion.
2   Choose the point you agree with most and say or write why you agree.

3 Choose the point you disagree with most and write down a question to be addressed to Ms Foster during the debate. Begin: 'I should like to ask the proposer of the motion ...'

Now here is how Mr Black presented the opposition to the motion.

'Now, there's another side to this question ...' he began.
At this point he was interrupted by the Chairman. Do you know why?
He continued:

I'm sorry. Mr Chairman, Ladies and Gentlemen, I should like to show you the other side of the rather grim picture presented so vividly by the Honourable Proposer of the motion. As you may be aware I have been a governor in Her Majesty's Prison Service for over twenty years and during that time I have seen
5   little evidence of the depressing conditions in prison as described. It is true that some of the older prisons, which I hasten to add are mainly being rebuilt, are unable to offer all the facilities to prisoners that they would wish, but on the whole, governors and prison officers alike are united in their efforts to help the prisoners adjust to life both 'inside' and 'outside'.
10   It is of course regrettable that old-fashioned buildings and overcrowding sometimes lead to prisoners being kept in their cells longer than would normally be desirable, but in those cases where it is unavoidable the number of hours worked every day is reduced slightly and a longer period of physical recreation is allowed. Until more money is earmarked by the Government for the building and
15   rebuilding of prisons, I'm afraid these conditions will prevail in a very small number of prisons.
   I think that we should not forget that a man is only sent to prison because he has offended against society; and society, in which you live, demands to be protected. Don't forget, also, that most first or second offenders never get as
20   far as prison; it is only the more dangerous criminals or persistent offenders who are sent down. Therefore the people most likely to end up in prison are either the hardened criminals who have made a life of crime, or the violent, or the corrupters of youth (be it through sex or drugs). As you can imagine, these prisoners are not the most rewarding material to work on. Most prisons are
25   badly understaffed, which means each prison officer is overworked and underpaid as they are always telling me, so their task of reforming prisoners is not an easy one. The prisoners, often against their will, are encouraged to take up an interest in prison – it doesn't matter whether it's studying for their own satisfaction (and all prisons nowadays have libraries and offer educational courses), entertaining
30   (and most prisons put on their own shows, devised, produced, scripted and performed by the prisoners) or playing some kind of game or sport (generally there is a football team they can join or a darts team or chess or draughts are available). Everything is done to encourage the prisoners to keep in contact with the life 'outside'. In the more modern prisons, trusted prisoners are allowed home
35   for weekends so they are not cut off from their families and friends and rehabilitation into society is easier when they are released. These open prisons have proved very successful and are a move in the right direction for the future.
   The Honourable Proposer mentioned 'rigid discipline', but I think if she studied the problem of violence a little more closely she would realise that
40   some criminals only recognise a force greater than their own. If they are not made to conform to society inside prison by a fairly strong, I would not say 'rigid' discipline, then they would take over the running of the prison themselves; one can imagine with what consequences! Like all organisations there must be some

45 rules and regulations in prison and when they apply to a one-sex society, whose
members are often violent or anti-social, then I think strong discipline is justifiable.

Over the question of food I will draw a veil, for although it is eatable (I eat it
myself) and based on a balanced diet, like British Rail, it leaves a lot to be desired.
It is certainly better than school meals, most staff canteens and a large number of
hotels – so, in fact we get very few complaints – and it doesn't lead to physical
50 deterioration!

To the more serious accusation that the present-day prison system alienates
prisoners from society I can only reply from my own experience. I can truthfully
say that I have never heard a prisoner express the opinion that he was more
hostile to the world after being in prison than he was before going in. In fact, many
55 of them leave with a better understanding of themselves, better educated, less
inhibited and more confident. And they certainly don't seem to resent the
discipline – after all, they wouldn't come back in again if they did, would they?

Therefore, Mr Chairman, Ladies and Gentlemen, I oppose the motion and
I do believe that prisons can be useful in reforming prisoners.

Exercise 2

1   Give in your own words the most important statements made by Mr Black, the
opposer.
2   Which statement, in your opinion, was the most effectively expressed? Why?
3   Mr Black completely ignored one of the points of the previous speaker. What point
was it and what motive could he have had for ignoring it?
4   What kind of man do you think Mr Black is, judging by this speech?

Exercise 3

Make notes for the speeches of the seconders – try and think what new points could be
added to the argument on both sides. Decide which side you would like to speak for,
then deliver the speech to the class or write it out in full.

Exercise 4

Imagine you are in the audience of this debate. Think of questions you would like to
ask and who you would address them to. Ask them in the class or write them down for
discussion.

Role Playing

Form a Debating Society in your class. Elect a Chairman, then get your teacher to
write down some motions on pieces of paper and write either 'proposer' or 'opposer'
on each piece. Each motion should have both a proposer and an opposer. Each student,
except the Chairman, selects one of the papers and prepares a speech 'for' or 'against'
the motion. A different motion could be debated every week – the class must be
prepared to propose, second and discuss the motion in open debate. A time limit of two
minutes should be set on each speaker. Don't forget how to open and close the debate
and always to address the Chair when you speak. Take a class vote at the end of every
debate and get tellers to count the votes. Don't forget, Chairman, you have a casting
vote! All motions should be declared 'carried' or 'lost' and the result minuted by the
Secretary.

Here are some suggested motions.

1   The law on drinking and driving should be enforced more strongly.
2   It's a poor criminal who cannot make a good living from crime.
3   The increase in violence is threatening the stability of modern society.

All debates are conducted in roughly the same way (see the Parliamentary debate at the beginning of this Unit) and the structure of a debating society can be paralleled in Parliament and to a certain extent in the High Court.

Debating Society	Parliament	High Court
The Chairman	The Speaker	The Judge
Proposer of motion	Front-benchers: Government Minister	Barristers: Counsel for Prosecution
Opposer of motion	Opposition Minister	Counsel for Defence
Seconders	MPs (Back-benchers)	Witnesses
Speakers (from the floor)	MPs (from the floor of the House)	Jury (don't speak)
Vote taken	Division (vote taken) (Party Whips' direction)	Verdict given (Judge's direction)
Tellers count votes/hands	Tellers count votes	Jury Foreman gives verdict
Chairman announces result	Speaker declares result	Judge passes sentence
Motion 'Carried' or 'Lost'	'Ayes' or 'Noes' have it	'Guilty' or 'Not Guilty'
Chairman addressed as: *Mr Chairman*	Speaker addressed as: *Mr Speaker*	Judge addressed as: *M'Lud* (*My Lord*)
Proposer addressed as: *The Honourable Proposer/ Lady/Gentleman*	Ministers addressed as: *Prime Minister/Minister for ...*	Counsel addressed as: *My Learned Friend*
Opposer addressed as: *The Honourable Opposer/ Lady/Gentleman*	MPs addressed as: *The Honourable (Hon) Member*	Witnesses addressed: by name

A debate in Parliament generally follows the second reading of a Public Bill in the process of making the Bill into an Act. The Bill has to go through five stages in the House of Commons and five stages in the House of Lords before it receives the Royal Assent and becomes an Act of Parliament and finally law. The Second Reading, when the Bill is debated in the House of Commons, is the most crucial stage as if it is thrown out then it may never be presented again, or at least not in the same form.

WRITTEN SKILLS **B**

Trials

Although trials, particularly in the High Court, are far more serious affairs than debates, they possess something of the same character. The barristers (Counsel) take the opposing sides – Prosecution (representing the Crown (Regina/Rex)) and Defence (representing the accused). It is the job of the Prosecution to produce enough evidence to prove that the Law has been broken and that the accused is guilty, while the Defence Counsel has to prove that his client has not broken the law and is innocent. The Judge acts rather like a chairman but has more power as he is able to direct the Jury and pass sentence on the accused if found guilty. Witnesses for both the Crown and Defence can be called to present evidence, providing support similar to seconders in a debate. Voting is represented by the verdict which is passed on the accused by the twelve members of the jury who decide if he is innocent or guilty; if the defendant is found guilty then the judge passes sentence (decides the punishment). A shorthand writer in the court takes down every word that is spoken, a function that roughly corresponds to the secretary taking minutes at a debate. In the trial therefore you have the same idea of two opposing sides, as in a debate, presenting the 'pros' and 'cons' or 'for' and 'against' a case.

In the following case notice which evidence (points) is for the accused and which against:

The accused (Mr X) drove his van at high speed across the road junction ignoring an illuminated Halt sign and collided with another vehicle (a car) which overturned. The driver of the car was killed and Mr X badly injured when his van went on to hit a lamp-post.

For the defence Mr X's Counsel contended that he had been unconscious at the time of the accident as the result of being overcome by a sudden illness. In hospital after the accident Mr X said that he could not remember what had happened. Medical evidence was produced to show that Mr X had been suffering from ill-health prior to the accident and had had one previous black-out.

The case presented by the Prosecution stated that Mr X had been driving dangerously and had failed to conform to a road traffic sign, thereby breaking two sections of the Road Traffic Act. He had also caused the death of a person by his dangerous driving and was therefore charged with manslaughter.

Let's see how the evidence divided into 'for' and 'against' Mr X.

R.v.X. (*Regina versus Mr X*)

Defence (for)	**Prosecution (against)**
Unconscious at time	Driving dangerously
Didn't remember what happened	Ignored Halt road sign
Ill health before accident	Caused death of person by dangerous
Previous black-out	driving (manslaughter)

What verdict do you think was given?

In fact the case continued as follows:

The jury found that the defendant must have exercised skill in order to reach the road junction but were of the opinion that he was not conscious of what he was doing for some little time before reaching the junction and was not capable of forming any intention as to his manner of driving. But since there was an absolute prohibition against dangerous driving, the defendant's intention in relation to the driving was immaterial, therefore he was found guilty. If it could have been proved that he had had a stroke or an epileptic fit then he would have been considered as not driving at all. For even if a man is seated in the driver's seat with his hands on the wheel he may be in such a state of unconsciousness that he cannot be said to be driving. But in Mr X's case this state of unconsciousness could not be proved.

Exercise 1

Consider the following cases and divide the evidence into 'for' or 'against' the accused, then choose Defence and Prosecution teams and present the cases, either spoken or written. You might like to choose a jury and judge and give a verdict at the end.

(All these cases are fictitious)

1   R. v. Potter

Miss Potter took an examination (BA) in place of her friend and passed (having signed all the examination papers in her friend's name); she then received the degree certificate in her friend's name. Her friend, on the strength of this certificate, obtained a very well paid, prestigious job. Miss Potter was charged with forgery and uttering forged documents (the examination papers); her friend was also charged as an accessory to the act. In their defence they admitted the facts but submitted that it was not forgery as none of the documents were false (i.e. the examination papers were genuine). Miss Potter alleged that she had no intention of deceiving anyone; she was just helping her friend who was unable to take the examination due to illness. She only signed her friend's name because the examination papers were assigned to that name. There was no guarantee that she would pass the examination any more easily than her friend who, indeed, had had every expectation of passing herself.

The Prosecution submitted that as Miss Potter had submitted documents with intent to defraud, it was forgery. Even though the documents were not false in so far as they were genuine examination papers, they were plainly false in that they were not signed by the person who purported to sign them. Evidence of illness did not excuse a deliberate intention to deceive.

2   R. v. Pemberton

Mr Pemberton had been drinking in a public house and when he left he got involved in a fight outside. He picked up a large stone and threw it at the person he had been fighting. He missed the person aimed at and the stone broke a window in the public house. The landlord thereupon accused him of malicously damaging his property. The defendant stated that he had intended to hit the person at whom he had aimed the stone and that he did not intend to break the window. He could only assume that his aim had been wide as he had been rather drunk at the time. The Prosecution inferred that Mr Pemberton had been reckless at the time and that he knew that the natural consequence of his act might have been to break the glass of the window, especially if he suspected that his aim was impaired by drink.

3   R. v. Williams

The accused was charged with murder of his two-year-old son, whose throat he had cut. The child was very seriously ill, in great pain, and likely to die at any time. The accused had come home from business abroad and had found his wife was absent and had left the child unattended and uncared for and he had become uncontrollably angry, in course of which he had killed the child who was screaming with pain. His defence was provocation, in that his wife's conduct had caused him to lose all self-control, also he had wanted to put his son out of his misery; he therefore pleaded manslaughter. The Prosecution argued that provocation by one person, leading the accused to form the intent to kill another, was not sufficient to reduce the crime of murder to manslaughter.

4   R. v. Smith

The accused took a handbag, searched through it, appeared to find nothing of interest to him so replaced it intact. He was charged with theft of the bag and its contents. In defence, Smith said that he had not stolen the bag as he had replaced it intact – he had only been looking for some matches. The Prosecution submitted that taking any property without permission constitutes theft; the fact that the accused found nothing of interest in the bag and returned it was immaterial.

5   R. v. Holliday

The defendant was charged with the infliction of grievous bodily harm upon his wife. It appeared that in order to escape her husband Mrs Holliday had climbed out of a window, fallen and broken her leg. The accused was known to be a brutal man who frequently beat his wife, and the Prosecution argued that his wife was so scared of him that she had climbed out of a first-floor window and so fallen and injured herself. Holliday alleged that he and his wife had been 'messing about' near the window and she had slipped and fallen out.

WRITTEN SKILLS C

Composition – Discussion

A discussion-type composition needs careful preparation. Write down your list of points for or against the argument, arrange them in good order and then write three or four paragraphs setting out your arguments clearly and finish with a conclusion that gives your opinion on the subject. Suppose we consider the following composition: '*The only way to control crime is to bring back capital punishment*'. Consider the 'pros' and 'cons' of the case.

Pros

Crime increasing every year
More violent crime
Criminals respect strong laws
Moral basis (eye for an eye)

Reflects strong government
Acts as deterrent to murder

Cons

Crime increases with population rise
No more violent crime per population
Criminals make own laws
Inhumane – men must help each other and forgive
Reflects authoritarian government
Does not act as a deterrent

The resultant composition might look something like this:

Recently there has been a re-emergence of the question of capital punishment. Opinion polls in Britain inform us that half the population are in favour of the return of the death penalty, but just how effective would it be?

The woe-mongers cry that crime is becoming more violent and increasing on an alarming scale. Is this really true though? Surely, as the population increases so proportionally will crime. The same is also true for violence; more violence is to be expected as the world becomes more densely populated.

If we consider whether the ancient religious law of inflicting the same punishment on the wrong-doer as he committed is applicable in modern society, then we also have to take into account the equally strong religious law which urges us to show compassion and forgiveness. In fact it is a fallacy that people can be changed by having strict rules imposed on them; their anti-social instincts can be suppressed for a while but will break out again more strongly later. Therefore any sort of authoritarian government does not generally denote strength but fear and the criminal will find means of breaking any law, the stronger the better in his eyes; for he will firmly array himself against law and order in an inflexible society.

As to the final question of whether capital punishment acts as a deterrent – well, rather to everyone's surprise it was discovered that there was no increase in murder or other violent crimes when the death penalty was abolished. So, the increase in violent crime must have another cause and sociologists suspect it is contained in our modern overcrowded technological society.

Therefore, to sum up, it seems that to bring back capital punishment would not help to control crime as there are deeper underlying causes. Abolishing the death penalty had little effect on the rate of crime in the past, so there is no reason to assume that reinstating it would diminish the crime rate now.

Unit seven

Exercise 1

Here are some strongly opposing points of view; consider them and then jot down any points you can think of under each viewpoint.

1 a Taking another person's life is never justifiable.
   b There are extenuating circumstances for all actions.
2 a The Law is an ass.
   b The Law embodies the wisest, most just principles of society.
3 a The penalties against drug-taking should be increased as the practice is undermining society.
   b Drugs should be legalised as they do less harm than smoking tobacco or drinking alcohol.
4 a Censorship protects people against moral corruption.
   b Censorship should be abolished and people be allowed to decide for themselves.
5 a No crime should go unpunished.
   b Criminals should be helped, not condemned.

Exercise 2

Here is an extract from 'An Enquiry into the Causes of the late Increase of Robbers, 1750' by Henry Fielding.

Though most of the rogues who infest the public roads and streets, indeed almost all thieves in general, are vagabonds in the true sense of the word, being wanderers from their lawful place of abode, very few of them will be proved vagabonds within the words of the act of parliament. These vagabonds do, indeed, get their
5   livelihood by thieving ... and have their lodgings not in alehouses, etc. but in private houses, where many of them resort together, and unite in gangs, paying each 2d per night for their beds.

Mr Welch, the high-constable of Holborn, in the execution of search-warrants, rarely finds less than twenty of these houses open for reception of all comers at
10 the latest hours; in one of these houses and that not a large one, he has numbered fifty-eight persons of both sexes, the stench of which was so intolerable that it compelled him in a short time to quit the place.

If one considers the destruction of all morality, decency, and modesty; the swearing and the drunkenness which is eternally carried on in these houses, on the
15 one hand, and the excessive misery and poverty of most of the inhabitants on the other, it seems doubtful whether they are more the objects of detestation or compassion, for such is the poverty of these wretches, that upon searching all the above number, the money found upon all of them did not amount to one shilling (5p); and I have been credibly informed that a single loaf has supplied a whole
20 family with provisions for a week. Lastly, if any of these miserable creatures fall sick ... they are turned out in the streets where, unless some parish officer of extraordinary charity relieves them, they are sure miserably to perish, with the addition of cold and hunger to their disease....

The wonder in fact is that we have not a thousand more robbers than we have;
25 indeed, that all these wretches are not thieves must give us either a very high idea of their honesty, or a very mean one of their capacity and courage.

1 List the points that would make you expect the poor to also be thieves.
2 Make your own points and then write a paragraph on why you think some of the poor remained honest.
3 Do you think things have changed much in the last two hundred and thirty years?

Exercise 3

Write a composition of about 300 words on one of the following.

1 Should the individual citizen have a say in his government?
2 Which would you rather be, a politician or a lawyer?
3 'Stone walls do not a prison make, Nor iron bars a cage.'
4 Is it possible to solve the problem of crime without eroding individual freedom?
5 Some corruption is to be found in all legal systems.
6 'It is the purpose of a government to see not only that the interests of the few are protected, but also that the welfare and rights of the many are conserved.'
7 All prisons should be abolished and criminals trained to do social work.
8 To rob the rich to give to the poor is perfectly justifiable.

WRITTEN SKILLS **D**
Reading Comprehension

Exercise 1

Choose the most suitable word or phrase for each of the following sentences, using the letter A, B, C or D to indicate your choice.

1 In Scotland, minor cases are .... without a jury in the Sheriff courts.
   A tested   *B* examined   *C* tried   *D* considered

2 If you can't afford to employ a solicitor, then you should apply for legal ....
   A assistance   *B* aid   *C* help   *D* attendance

3 George Black is .... as a Labour candidate in the next election.
   A standing   *B* sitting   *C* contending   *D* entering

4 In the case of personal injury, the offender may be ordered to pay ....
   A recompense   *B* retribution   *C* restitution   *D* compensation

5 Parliament will .... the Chancellor's Budget proposals next week.
   A discuss   *B* argue   *C* criticise   *D* debate

6 Eighteen is the .... voting age in Great Britain.
   A minimum   *B* minimal   *C* competent   *D* maximum

7 Cases involving young people under 17 are heard in specially constituted .... courts.
   A junior   *B* youth   *C* infantile   *D* juvenile

8 If you want to vote, you must make sure that your name is on the electoral ....
   A list   *B* roll   *C* rota   *D* table

9 The election of the new chairman for our union branch will be conducted by secret ....
   A process   *B* poll   *C* vote   *D* ballot

10 Paul was convicted of dangerous driving and his licence was ....
   A endorsed   *B* stamped   *C* undersigned   *D* invalidated

Unit seven

11 It is Government .... to give special aid to industrial development.
A proposal *B* programme *C* prospectus *D* policy

12 If a man is legally separated from his wife, is he still .... for her debts?
A answerable *B* liable *C* bound *D* chargeable

13 Under the existing laws, all persons selling alcoholic liquor must be ....
A authorised *B* sanctioned *C* licensed *D* legalised

14 Although there is no official censorship, the Press in Britain is still .... the laws of the land.
A controlled by *B* subject to *C* accountable to *D* restrained by

15 A .... for the devolution of Cornwall was defeated in the House of Commons last night by a majority of 33.
A statute *B* law *C* bill *D* motion

16 According to the latest .... poll, the Opposition is likely to have a landslide in the next General Election.
A enquiry *B* opinion *C* question *D* impression

17 After two hours the jury were still unable to reach a unanimous ....
A verdict *B* decision *C* judgment *D* conclusion

18 .... of the children was awarded to Mrs Black following her divorce.
A care *B* guardianship *C* control *D* custody

19 A .... was held to determine the wish of the people regarding entry into the Common Market.
A questionnaire *B* representation *C* referendum *D* suffrage

20 The new Member for Burlington will make his .... speech in the House of Commons on Friday.
A introductory *B* virgin *C* initial *D* maiden

21 Wearing seat-belts when driving is now .... by law.
A compulsive *B* forcible *C* compulsory *D* involuntary

22 He was accused of being drunk in .... of a car.
A charge *B* possession *C* use *D* usage

23 The accused had two previous .... for theft.
A sentences *B* penalties *C* condemnations *D* convictions

24 The motion for the increase in pension contributions was .... by 45 votes.
A denounced *B* defeated *C* denied *D* demoted

25 The Jury listened attentively to the case for the ....
A indictment *B* accusation *C* prosecution *D* arrest

REMINDER **7**
Participle Adjectives

When you use them
Don't confuse them

Students sometimes find it difficult to distinguish the use of **'To be'** + **Past Participle** and **'To be'** + **Present Participle** when these are used as Adjective forms. The following notes may be useful.

1 **'To be'** + **Past Participle** describes how a *person* is affected by the *Object* of the sentence. It is really a form of Passive:

I *am interested in* politics.
He *was bored by* the Minister's speech.

2 **'To be'** + **Present Participle** describes the quality of the *Subject* or *Object* itself. In fact the Participle Adjective placed in front of the Noun in the normal way gives the same meaning:

His speech *was very interesting*   That book *is very boring*.
(He made *an interesting speech*.)   (That is *a very boring book*.)

2 **Past Participles** used as Adjectives are normally followed by a Preposition: *interested in* , *bored by*, etc.

Following are 20 of these *Participle Adjective* forms most commonly confused.

absorbed in	absorbing	distressed by/at/about	distressing
alarmed at/by	alarming	embarrassed by/at	embarrassing
amazed at/by	amazing	excited about/by	exciting
amused at/by	amusing	exhausted by	exhausting
annoyed at/by	annoying	interested in	interesting
astonished at/by	astonishing	irritated by	irritating
bored by	boring	pleased at/by	pleasing
confused by	confusing	puzzled by	puzzling
disappointed by/at	disappointing	shocked at/by	shocking
disgusted at/by	disgusting	surprised at/by	surprising

Exercise 1

In the following sentences insert the correct Participle Adjective form of the word given and a preposition where necessary.

Example

I was .... the way he spoke to you.
ANNOY
I was *annoyed at* the way he spoke to you.

1   It was .... for John to have to admit he had had his driving licence endorsed.
    EMBARRASS
2   I was .... the way those hooligans behaved at the football match.
    SHOCK
3   I never listen to Party Political Broadcasts because they're so ....
    BORE

4 The local residents are extremely .... the indifference with which their protest about the new motorway has been received.
IRRITATE

5 I am very .... the new licensing laws because they seem so complicated.
CONFUSE

6 The Stephensons are very .... not being able to obtain planning permission to build an extension to their house.
DISAPPOINT

7 The recent increase in unemployment figures is very ....
ALARM

8 Is he really so .... his work that he can't even answer the telephone?
ABSORB

9 Those all-night sittings at the House of Commons are very .... for the MPs.
EXHAUST

10 I am very .... the result of the next General Election.
EXCITE

Exercise 2

Using Participle Adjective forms, rewrite the following sentences, keeping as closely as possible to the original meaning. The beginning of each answer is given.

Example

It is very exciting to know that I shall be old enough to vote in October.
I am ....
I am very excited about being old enough to vote in October.

1 The telephone operator was so irritating that Mr Barnes put down the receiver.
Mr Barnes was ....

2 The Minister said he was very disappointed at the attitude of the union leaders to the new pay guide-lines.
'The attitude ....

3 'The new immigration laws are disgusting,' said John.
John said he..

4 The news of the President's assassination was so shocking that many people refused to believe it at first.
Many people were ....

5 Professor Barnes is so absorbed in his research into the psychology of politics that he spends nearly all his time in the university library.
His research into the psychology of politics is ....

6 The Magistrate declared that he was astonished at the young offender's apparent indifference to the consequences of his crime.
'Your apparent indifference ....

7 John said it was very annoying being stopped by the Police when he was driving his girl friend home.
'I was ....

8 'Don't you think the prospect of a General Election is exciting?'
'Aren't you..?

9 Listening to parliamentary debates is not usually very amusing.
I am not ....

10 John said the election procedure was very interesting.
'I was ....

Unit eight Relationships

ORAL SKILLS **A**

Intensive Listening

Read or listen to the following story and then answer the questions that follow it.

Reader The hills rose steeply on either side, forming a kind of gully through
which the road snaked its way to emerge at last into more open country
and the broader, flatter highway leading to the capital. It was not
forest land, but there were clumps of trees and bushes and rough
5 boulders where a man might conceal himself with little danger of being
seen from the road. Two men lay hidden there now, one on either side
of the gulley, waiting for the same thing but each with a different
purpose. The older of the two, Tomas, was a hired assassin, a man,
trained in the art of killing, who had no interest in his victims beyond
10 the price of their lives. A cool, methodical man, a brilliant marksman,
who prided himself on his efficiency and charged accordingly. The
other, Toni, not yet twenty, was an idealist. His idealism accepted
blindly the concepts of terrorism and violence as a means of achieving

the brave new world in which he believed. Death for him held no reality, as it did for Tomas. To kill was to rid the world of evil, to be killed a magnificent gesture, a martyrdom to his cause. From this it will be seen that, to those to whom he had sworn his allegiance, he was not only useful but expendable.

The two men had been waiting for two days. Each, as has been said, with a different objective. About an hour before dusk that day or the next day, Carlos Perez, thief, convicted murderer and self-appointed leader of the People's Freedom Party, would come riding along this road with his chief of staff, Augusto Mendoza. They would be dressed as peasants and riding on donkeys – indeed, it is doubtful if they would have been capable of riding anything else. The plan, which had been carefully thought out, was for them to enter the capital inconspicuously, rally their supporters, which included most of the working population of the city, and seize control by blowing up the presidential palace with, it was to be hoped, the President and his staff, and shooting indiscriminately anyone who seemed likely to cause trouble about it. Tomas, in the pay of Augusto Mendoza, had been hired to assassinate Perez, who was suspected of corrupt negotiations with foreign powers. Toni, dedicated servant of the People's Freedom Party, was to kill Mendoza, already known to be plotting against their glorious leader, Carlos Perez. Neither Tomas nor Toni, however, had allowed for the dangerous streak of pride in Mendoza.

Tomas had not been on the hill more than an hour or so before he realised there was a man on the other side. It did not take him long to guess why he was there. Using binoculars, he watched him at intervals, deducing that he was young, nervous and, from the way he handled his gun, probably an inexpert shot. Once or twice he trained his own rifle on him, calculating the split second it would take to kill him and working out the exact moment when this should be done to prevent the killing of Mendoza. The distraction would be useful in timing the moment to kill Perez.

Two more days passed and Tomas, bored and irritated by the delay, took to watching Toni more frequently. One morning, when Toni crept from his hiding place to fetch water from a stream, Tomas, caressing his rifle, stepped forward boldly and shouted a greeting across the ravine. Toni fell flat on his face, scratching his cheek on a tangle of brambles. After a while he lifted his head and saw Tomas still standing there. Tomas raised his rifle in mock salute. Toni, conditioned only to distrust those he had been taught to distrust, scrambled to his feet and returned the salute. His heart was filled with relief and gratitude to his masters for sending this support. Nothing could possibly go wrong now. He, too, picked up his rifle and made little jabbing motions with it towards the ravine and threw back his head and laughed.

It was another two days before Perez and Mendoza came. During this time Tomas and Toni exchanged daily greetings, shouting things to each other across the ravine that neither could hear, making signs and gestures. Tomas, who was something of a mimic, imitated the waddling duck-like walk of Mendoza and Toni clapped and laughed. Not to be outdone he, too, mimicked Mendoza and clutching his chest, fell to the ground, writhing in agony, just as he had seen men do in the films.

65   It was almost dusk when Perez and Mendoza appeared, clip-clopping
on their donkeys along the road through the gulley. The factor the two
watchers had not allowed for was Mendoza's son, Mario. Mendoza had
persuaded Perez to allow Mario to accompany them as bodyguard, but
the fact was that the boy was young and strikingly handsome and with
70 Perez out of the way, Mendoza wished to establish himself as a leader
who was a family man with a son he could be proud of, one who could
be counted on to capture the imagination of the younger and more
idealistic elements in the People's Freedom Party. The fact that the
mother was a dance hall hostess in a dubious club was of little
75 consequence. No one troubled about such things these days. But a son –
such as Mario – that was something different.

Mario was an intelligent boy and took his responsibilities seriously.
Although he had no inkling of the plot against Perez, he was prepared to
defend his father to the death. When therefore, glancing upward, he
80 caught the glint of a rifle in the evening sun, he did not hesitate. It took
him less than two seconds to raise his own gun and fire. He was an
excellent shot. Toni, shot through the head, fell and rolled grotesquely –
bump – bump – bump – down the steep side of the hill into the gulley.

Seeing what had happened, Tomas slipped and slithered down the
85 other side of the hill, unnoticed by the men bending over Toni's body.
Shaking with passion, he shot Mario in the back. The boy fell in a
crumpled heap on Toni. Horrified, Mendoza turned, recognised Tomas
and cried out, 'Merciful God, what have you done, Tomas? You have
killed my son!'
90 'He killed my friend,' said Tomas, the rage in him giving way to
despair. 'Only I had the right. Now kill me if you wish, I am ready.'

Exercise 1

1 Describe briefly the main features of the scene in which this story is set.
2 Give your impression of Tomas.
3 Why is the young terrorist, Toni, represented as an idealist?
4 What conclusion do you draw from the phrase, 'he was not only useful but
   expendable' (lines 17–18)?
5 Can you find any similarities between the 'different objectives' of Tomas and
   Toni?
6 How did the People's Freedom Party plan to take control of the capital?
7 What were Tomas's first reactions on sighting Toni?
8 What do you learn about 'Toni' from the phrase 'conditioned only to distrust
   those he had been taught to distrust' (lines 52–3)?
9 How did the two men communicate with each other?
10 Say why you think Mendoza had made a point of being accompanied by his son.
11 Describe how Toni met his death.
12 '... Only I had the right' (line 91).
   What did Tomas imply by this statement?

The story of Tomas and Toni shows how a strong relationship built up between two
men who had never seen each other before, and one of whom was prepared to kill the
other. Read or listen now to two short poems, each of which offers guide-lines to a
lover on how their relationship may be kept constant and untroubled. The first, from a
man to a woman, is anonymous but can be found in John Wilbye's 'Second Set of
Madrigals', 1609.

Reader Love not me for comely grace,
For my pleasing eye or face,
Nor for any outward part.
No, nor for a constant heart:
    For these may fail or turn to ill,
    So thou and I shall sever:
Keep, therefore, a true woman's eye,
And love me still but know not why –
    So hast thou the same reason still
        To doat upon me ever!

Vocabulary notes – *comely* : pleasant to look at; *doat* (dote): be infatuated with; *hast thou* : you have

And here is a poem by Christina Rossetti, one of the Pre-Raphaelite poets of the nineteenth century.

Reader When I am dead, my dearest,
Sing no sad songs for me;
Plant thou no roses at my head,
    Nor shady cypress tree:
Be the green grass above me
    With showers and dewdrops wet:
And if thou wilt, remember,
    And if thou wilt, forget.
I shall not see the shadows,
    I shall not feel the rain;
I shall not hear the nightingale
    Sing on, as if in pain;
And dreaming through the twilight
    That doth not rise nor set
Haply I may remember
    And haply may forget.

Vocabulary notes – *haply* : perhaps; *thou wilt* : you will; *That doth* : that does;
Doth : poetic and biblical form of 'does': *He/she/it doth*

Exercise 2

1 Read or listen to the first poem again and then see if you can 'translate it' into modern English, using the sort of phrases a young man might use today.
2 Read or listen to the second poem again and repeat it. Say briefly what you think the poet is trying to tell her lover.
3 What do you like or dislike about the sentiments expressed in these poems?
4 How do you think a constant relationship with a man or woman is best maintained?

ORAL SKILLS B

Dialogue

Listen to the following dialogue.

Child	What does 'highbrow' mean, Gran?
Grandmother	Oh, it's knowing a lot about music and art and books and things like that and being clever enough to enjoy them, too.
Child	Are you highbrow, Gran?
5 Grandmother	Heavens, no! I never was much of a reader. Those old writers are too long-winded for me. Your Aunt Polly is, though. To tell you the truth, she made rings round your Dad when she was at school. Ought to have gone to university, only of course your grandad wouldn't hear of it. Made her go into the shop. I told
10	him at the time, 'She'll be a square peg in a round hole,' I said, but he wouldn't listen. But I was right because – well, to cut a long story short, she married the first man that asked her just to get away from the shop and that only lasted three years till he was off to New Zealand with another woman.
15 Child	I'm glad you're not highbrow, Gran. I'm glad Dad isn't either. Didn't Dad like school?
Grandmother	Oh, he liked it all right, but he was a bit of an all-rounder, you see. What I mean is, he did average well in most things, but he was never top of his class like Polly. I suppose the long and the
20	short of it is, he was lazy.
Child	Dad? Lazy?
Grandmother	Not really lazy, just not interested perhaps. Not that it mattered in the long run. He's done all right for himself. If you ask me, I don't think they ever quite got the measure of him at school.
25 Child	What do you mean, 'got the measure of him'?
Grandmother	They didn't take the trouble to find out what he could really do, that's what I mean. He's clever, your dad, in his own way.
Child	Have you got the measure of me, Gran?
Grandmother	I shouldn't be surprised. Now stop asking questions and go and
30	get the draughts board. We've just got time for a game before your mum comes in.
Child	I beat you last time, didn't I, Gran?
Grandmother	Hm – well – I'm going to beat you this time, so then we'll be all square. Go and get the board.

Listen again. Match these expressions to their meaning in the dialogue. Put the letter of your choice in the box.

☐	**1** *highbrow*	*A*	verbose/taking too long to say something simple
☐	**2** *long-winded*	*B*	to give a brief account of
☐	**3** *made rings round*	*C*	intellectual/interested in intellectual subjects
☐	**4** *a square peg in a round hole*	*D*	equal
☐	**5** *to cut a long story short*	*E*	the real reason
☐	**6** *an all-rounder*	*F*	a person who is doing a job for which he is totally unsuited
☐	**7** *the long and the short of it*	*G*	understood what he was really like
☐	**8** *in the long run*	*H*	was much cleverer than/knew much more than

☐	**9**	*got the measure of him*	*I*
☐	**10**	*all square*	*J*

9 *got the measure of him* — *I* as it turned out eventually/taking future events into account

10 *all square* — *J* a person who is fairly good at most things but does not excel at any one thing

Exercise 1

Choosing the most suitable expression from those given, re-phrase the following statements, keeping as closely as possible to the original meaning.

1 Without bothering too much about the details, this is what happened.
2 John has never been able to cope with that job.
3 I do wish Professor Brown wouldn't give such tedious explanations.
4 He may say he doesn't like London, but the real reason he's moving to Edinburgh is to get away from his mother-in-law.
5 I don't think I shall ever really understand my boss.
6 Peter was quite good at most things at school, but not brilliant.
7 Taking everything into consideration, I think Charles will eventually do quite well out of that new project.
8 You lent me £5 last month, but if I pay our fares to Brighton, I shan't owe you anything.
9 Sarah says she hates people who pretend to be intellectual.
10 I may be studying Domestic Economy, but my sister-in-law knows infinitely more than I do about running a house.

ORAL SKILLS **C**

Talking about Relationships

Exercise 1

Group work.

Consider the following relationships and then discuss what you think is the main cause of the trouble and how it should best be dealt with.

1 Mrs Brown is a middle-aged widow who bought a house for her married son, on condition that she occupied two rooms. She has no job and doesn't like living by herself. However, her daughter-in-law obviously resents the situation and makes her feel very much in the way.
2 At twenty-five, John has been appointed as Sales Manager for a large firm, but the older sales representatives object to him introducing new sales techniques and ignore his instructions. In consequence he is beginning to lose confidence in his own judgment.
3 Joan and Mary were at school together and are now sharing a flat in London. They have always been very good friends. Mary is engaged to Jim, a young man they have both known since they were children. Recently Mary has discovered that Joan has been going out with him. She is very distressed and cannot understand why Joan has not mentioned it.
4 Johnnie, aged nine, has a slight stammer. This has recently got much worse and he has begun to invent excuses for not being able to go to school. His mother suspects that the other children are bullying him.

ORAL SKILLS **D**
Photograph for Discussion

Look at this picture and be prepared to talk about it.

Questions

1 Describe the people in the picture.
2 What does the woman seem to be doing?
3 Does the child seem to be enjoying herself?
4 What do you think the woman is making?

Topics

The relationship between the old and the young.
Learning crafts and skills.
Family life.

ORAL SKILLS **E**

Reading Aloud

Look at this passage. Be prepared to answer some questions about it and then to read it aloud.

Judging from your c.v., you seem to have had considerable experience in marketing in a junior managerial capacity. I must tell you, however, that we are not looking for an administrator but for someone who is prepared to get out into the field and, if necessary, make snap decisions on the spot. The job involves considerable travelling abroad. You must be prepared to use your own initiative and, above all, be able to form a good relationship with people of widely differing cultures and creeds.

Who do you think the speaker is?
Who is he talking to?
What is he talking about?
What are the main points he outlines?

USE OF ENGLISH **A**

Revision of Clauses

A Simple Sentence consists of one sentence with **Subject** and **Verb,** or two or more such simple sentences joined by *and*/*but*/*or* :

They have been married for twenty-five years and their silver wedding anniversary is on August 24.
They may get married this summer or they may wait till Christmas.
They got married last year but they still haven't found a house.

A Compound Sentence is made up of a principal sentence – the **Main Clause** – with one or more sentences – **Subordinate Clauses** – which give us additional information about the Subject, Verb or Object or help us to identify it in the same way as adjectives and adverbs do. A clause can also act as the Subject or Object of a verb and this is called a **Noun Clause.**

Make sure that the **Subordinate Clauses** (like the Participle Phrases, Reminder 6, page 186) are put in the correct place and introduced by the right kind of word.

Noun Clauses
I don't know *what he will do next* (object of 'know')
We can't understand *why he is late* (object of 'understand')

Relative/Adjectival Clauses
Introduced by Relative Pronouns/Adverbs
1   The man *who fired at the President* was arrested the same day.   (which man?)
     The cafe *where we had lunch* was very crowded.   (which cafe?)
2   I enjoyed reading the book (*that*) *John lent me.*   (which book?)

Relative/Adjectival Clauses refer to **Nouns** and if they are precisely defining the noun, that is telling us exactly *which person* or *which thing* is being talked about, then 'that' can be used instead of 'who'/'which'. 'That' can also be omitted, if liked, except when it represents the subject of the sentence.

Examples

The man *that* fired at the President was arrested the same day.
I enjoyed reading the book *John lent me*.

Sometimes this kind of clause is not intended to tell us *which* person or thing, but simply to describe him/her/it or give us some interesting or additional information about the Noun. In this case the clause must always be put between *commas* or the sense may be changed. 'That' cannot be substituted for the relative pronoun that introduces it.

Examples

The picture, *which was by an unknown artist of the seventeenth century,* was found lying under some papers in the attic.

This tells us something additional about the picture.

But N.B. The picture (*that*) *John gave us for a wedding present* was stolen but the one (that) I inherited from my grandmother wasn't taken.

Here the two clauses define exactly which picture was stolen and which wasn't. They are not separated from their nouns by commas.

Exercise 1   Who/Which/What/Whose/That/Why/Where/When

Insert the correct Relative Pronoun/Adverb in the following sentences. Insert any necessary *Commas.*

1   The girl .... had been left an orphan was brought up in a Home.
2   The girl .... you were talking to is my sister.
3   Have you received the letter .... I posted yesterday?
4   The letter .... was written in a thin, spidery writing had been pressed between the leaves of a Bible .... had belonged to my great-grandmother.
5   The man .... enormous frame seemed to fill the doorway stood staring at us without speaking.
6   My elder brother .... is studying to be a doctor is coming to England next year.
7   It is uncertain .... he will return.
8   Peter told me .... he doesn't want to stay on at university, but I don't think .... he really knows .... he wants to do.
9   The men .... had been lying in wait for several days timed their attack very carefully.
10   Have you any idea .... Mary refuses to speak to that nice young man .... she met at your party?
11   My friend .... lives in Spain is coming to stay with us this summer.
12   The lectures .... Professor Hughes gave on psychology were extremely interesting.

Adverbial Clauses

| Place | *where/in which* | We visited Blenheim Palace, *where* Winston Churchill was born. |
| Time | *when/before/until/as soon as* *while/during/after/since* | She left home *when* she was sixteen. He telephoned for an ambulance *as soon as* he saw the accident. I have lived here *since* I was a child. |

Unit eight

Reason	*because/since/for/as*	They only stayed two days in the hotel *because* it was so expensive. *Since* it was so expensive, they only stayed two days in the hotel.
Purpose	*so that/in order that*	I am bringing my camera *so that* I can take a lot of photographs. The prisoner's head was covered with a blanket *in order that* no one would be able to see his face. (See also 'Infinitives', Unit 6, page 165)
Result	*so/with the result that*	He saved regularly all his working life, *so* he was able to retire in comfort. She studied very hard, *with the result that* she got excellent marks in the examination.
Concession	*although/though/notwith-* *standing the fact that/* *in spite of the fact that*	*Although* I don't like Robert Jones, I must admit he is a good speaker. *In spite of the fact* that he stutters, he is a very amusing speaker.
Comparison	*as ... as/not so ... as/* *as much ... as/more than*	My husband doesn't take *as much* interest in politics *as* he used to. I like detective stories *more than* I like Westerns.
Condition	*if/so long as/provided* *that/unless*	He may come *if* he has time. The children may look round the museum *so long as* they don't touch anything.

Exercise 2

Join the following facts into a **Compound Sentence** using the words given and making any necessary changes.

1 The Police were convinced Harris had committed the crime.
They did not arrest him.
They did not have enough evidence.

ALTHOUGH   BECAUSE

2 The local residents have decided to present a petition to the Minister of the Environment.
They have been suffering considerable inconvenience from aircraft noise.
The new airport was opened in 1977.

SINCE   WHO

3 George Jepson became interested in community relations.
He was a boy living in the dockside area of Liverpool.
He vividly remembers the lack of amenities for young people.
He had to play in the streets.
There was constant danger from traffic.

WHEN   AND   AS   WHERE

4 He lived at home.
He left home at fourteen.
His father married again.

TILL   WHEN

5 Her husband died.
The old lady lived alone.
She bought a parrot.
She saw the parrot in a pet shop.
It used such bad language.
The neighbours complained.

AFTER   SO   BUT   WHICH   THAT

6 He was studying in London.
He met the well-known politician, Geoffrey Barnes.
Geoffrey Barnes' personality made such a deep impression on him.
He decided to go into politics himself.

WHILE   WHOSE   THAT

7 They first met in the summer of 1966.
Neither of them could speak a word of the other's language.
They married.
They had known each other for six weeks.
They were extremely happy.

THOUGH   WHEN   AFTER   AND

8 How can I explain?
I read Mary's letter to John.
I was afraid.
It might contain bad news.

THAT   BECAUSE

9 Alan was appointed as Personnel Manager.
He had not had much experience.
He was sympathetic to other people's problems.

BUT   SO

10 The poems are by Robert Frost.
You are reading them.
Robert Frost is an American poet.

WHICH   WHO

11 Mrs Brown was always owing money on her household bills.
Her husband gave her a very good housekeeping allowance.
She was always buying new clothes.
She already had more clothes than she could wear.

IN SPITE OF THE FACT THAT   BECAUSE   ALTHOUGH

12   I shall telephone him.
      I shall finish my letters first.
      He can't complain.
      I haven't let him know.
      The contract has fallen through.

      AS SOON AS   SO THAT   THAT

Inversion

Occasionally the position of Subject and Verb in a clause in *inverted*, that is *changes place*, in order to give emphasis or dramatic effect. In the main inversion is limited to:

1   **Adverb Clauses** with: *hardly/scarcely/never/no sooner ... than*
2   **Conditional Clauses** in which *'if'* is replaced by *had ... but/had ... only/should*
3   **Clauses** containing an *Adjective* preceded by *'so'*, i.e. *so great, so little*, etc.
     In this case a Participle Adjective such as *surprised, annoyed*, etc. changes to the Noun form: *surprise, annoyance*.

In *spoken English* such inversions sound pompous and awkward and even in *written English* the normal *Subject + Verb* is usually preferable. However, the student should be able to make such inversions, if required to do so in an examination. They are usually associated with a *Past Tense*.

Examples

Hardly had he left the building, when the bomb went off.
Scarcely had I opened the door, before he attacked me.
Never have I seen such a terrible sight!
No sooner had she turned the corner, *than* the car hit her.
Had he but known her true character, he would never have married her.
Had I only told them the truth, this would never have happened.
Should the river flood, the sirens will sound.
So great was his astonishment, that he was speechless.
So little did I know of her private life, that I was unable to tell the detectives anything.

N.B. *'did I know'* replacing the uninverted form, *I knew*

Exercise 3

Rewrite the following sentences, inverting subject and verb and making any necessary changes.

1   He had hardly sat down before his wife started complaining.
     ....

2   They had no sooner entered the house than the lights fused.
     ....

3   If Clara had only known how troublesome the children would be, she would never have agreed to look after them.
     ....

4   I understood so little about astronomy, that the lecture was completely beyond me.
     ....

5   He was so annoyed that he refused to have anything more to do with her.
     ....

6 If we had been told how difficult the climb would be, we would never have attempted it.

....

7 If she decides to leave her husband, who will look after the children?

....

8 They had scarcely decided to be more tolerant of each other, than they began quarrelling again.

....

9 If you happen to see Mr Jones, tell him I'll ring him at 3 o'clock.

....

10 I had hardly finished reading Joan's letter, than she arrived.

....

11 He was so disappointed about not getting the job, that he began to think he was unemployable.

....

12 If only you had told us you were coming, we would have met you at the airport.

....

WRITTEN SKILLS **A**

Description

'Man is a knot, a web, a mesh into which relationships are tied, only those relationships matter.'

('Flight to Arras' Saint-Exupery, *1942*)

Describing something, whether telling someone about it or writing about it, often isn't very easy; and it doesn't matter whether you are describing a person, a place or a thing – it just isn't easy to capture it in words. For example, try describing something simple like a ball-point pen to the other students in your class and see how many of them can guess what you are describing. (Don't cheat and just say it's a thing for writing with, but really think about a pen – its colour, shape, the material it's made of, size etc.) It's not so easy to remember exactly what something looks like if it's not in front of you, is it? So now you've discovered the number one rule for effective description – accurate observation. Let's consider ways of improving your ability to describe things; here are a few points to help you.

Relationships with things and places

1 Observe closely

You can train yourself to do this – start looking at perfectly ordinary things as though you had never seen them before and imagine how you would describe them. Be precise, don't vaguely describe any chair for example, but choose a particular one, perhaps the one you are sitting on – the secret is to be able to actually visualise the object you are thinking of. That is your first step in factual description. Try describing the following.

The chair you're sitting on   The book you're using
The room you're in   The college/school/place you study at

Use simple language and just give a factual description. Consider how simply the author described a jellied-eel stand in the following extract from 'A Kid for Two Farthings' by Wolf Mankowitz.

Tubby Isaacs' eel and pie stall in the East End of London.

'Near Alf's stall there was a jellied-eel stand with a big enamel bowl of grey jellied eels, small bowls for portions, a large pile of lumps of bread, and three bottles of vinegar. There were also orange and black winkles in little tubs and large pink whelks. People stood around shaking vinegar on their eels and scooping them up with bread. A little thin man in a white muffler ladled out portions.'

The author has used simple language and yet he has made us quite clearly *see* the eel stand as the child in the book did. How has he achieved it? Well, firstly, he has visualised the scene clearly in his mind's eye and then he has picked out the principal objects and described them by using simple adjectives of colour or size; big enamel bowl ... small bowls ... large pile ... lumps of bread ... little tubs ... thin man ... grey jellied eels ... orange and black winkles ... pink whelks ... a white muffler. Secondly, he has made us *feel* the scene by the effective use of two verbs 'scooping' and 'ladling'. Do you think your feeling about the scene would have been the same if the author had used '*getting* them up with bread' or '*giving* out portions'? So here we have some more points to add to our list.

2 Pick out details

Having observed closely, we should now pick out details which particularly interest us. In the 'eel stand' extract the child was interested in what there was to eat, how people were eating, what the food looked like and the relative sizes and colours. Other people observing the scene might have been interested in the cost, hygiene, feelings of the people eating, etc. – they would have picked out different details to describe. This how Charles Dickens described a different scene connected with eating; notice what interested him.

> 'Mr Grazinglands looked in at a pastrycook's window, hesitating as to the expediency of lunching at that establishment. He beheld nothing to eat, but butter in various forms, slightly charged with jam, and languidly frizzling over tepid water. Two ancient turtle-shells, on which was inscribed the legend, 'SOUPS', decorated a glass partition within, enclosing a stuffy alcove, from which a ghastly mockery of a marriage-breakfast spread on a rickety table, warned the terrified traveller. An oblong box of stale and broken pastry at reduced prices, mounted on a stool, ornamented the doorway; and two high chairs that looked as if they were performing on stilts, embellished the counter. Over the whole, a young lady presided, whose gloomy haughtiness as she surveyed the street, announced a deep-seated grievance against society, and an implacable determination to be avenged.'

The scene Dickens has conjured up is in complete contrast to the boy's view of the jellied-eel stand – there everything had a positive value, the food was desirable, brightly coloured, people were eating, the little man was busy serving; but Dickens' attitude to the pastrycook's is distrustful from the beginning (notice the use of 'hesitating') and develops through a feeling of distaste to almost revulsion by the end. All the adjectives have a limiting or negating effect: tepid water ... ancient turtle-shells ... stuffy alcove ... ghastly mockery ... rickety table ... terrified traveller ... stale and broken pastry ... gloomy haughtiness ... deep-seated grievance ... implacable determination – an effect carried through by the adverbs and verb forms: slightly charged ... languidly frizzling ... warned ... mounted ... embellished ... presided ... surveyed ... to be avenged – nothing has life or colour and there is no feeling of action or movement. The language used is far more complicated than in 'A Kid for Two Farthings' but this is intentional as we are given a man's view of, and attitude to, a scene.

By expressing his character's attitude to the situation, Dickens has added another dimension to his descriptive passage, which takes us to our third point.

3 Expressing an attitude

We have seen so far, how a scene can be described through close observation, how it can be conveyed vividly by picking out details and how a character's attitude can add to the description. In the following extract from 'Titus Groan' by Mervyn Peake, a kitchen is described almost entirely through the attitude towards it of the character (Mr Flay).

> 'As Mr Flay entered the great kitchen the steaming, airless concentration of a ghastly heat struck him. He felt that his body had received a blow. Not only was the normal sickening atmosphere of the kitchen augmented by the sun's rays streaming into the room at various points through the high windows, but, in the riot of festivities, the fires had been banked dangerously.... Mr Flay, wiping away with the back of his claw-like hand, the perspiration that had

already gathered on his brow, allowed his eyes to travel sourly around. Everything was confusion, but behind the flux of the shifting figures and the temporary chaos of overturned mixing tables, of the floor littered with stock-pots, basting pans, broken bowls and dishes, and oddments of food, Mr Flay could see the main fixtures of the room and keep them in his mind as a means of reference, for the kitchen swam before his eyes in a clammy mist.'

We've come a long way from the boy's simple, delighted description of food in the first extract to Mr Flay's jaundiced view of the 'great kitchen'. No mention is made of food except for the 'oddments' on the floor, Mr Flay's impression is only of 'heat', 'confusion', 'chaos'. The author is less interested in just describing the kitchen to his readers than in conveying what impression Mr Flay had of it – and what effect the kitchen had on Mr Flay. Consider how the author paints his depressing scene. What effect do the adjectives and adverbs have? What is achieved by the use of the verbs 'banked', 'littered' and 'swam'? Are there any other verbs that you know which would be as effective?

Exercise 1

1 Describe, as seen by a young child:

a A playground in the park
b A sweetshop
c A fruit or vegetable stall in the market

2 Give an adult person's description of:

a A deserted farmhouse
b A picturesque bay
c An almost empty café

Remember not to use too many adjectives – a few used effectively are better than whole batteries cancelling each other out.

There is one other point you could take into consideration when describing a scene and that is:

4 Writing from a point of view

In other words, what angle you wish to view the scene from. For example, you might like to consider it

a as though seen for the first time
b as seen by a foreigner
c seen anew (perhaps a place visited after many years absence)

Here are various writers' approaches to describing a place, written from different points of view. Notice how they achieve their effects and how they use adjectives, adverbs and verbs and what other kind of language they use.

'Often and often Nicholas had pictured to himself what the lumber-room might be like, that region that was carefully sealed from youthful eyes and concerning which no questions were ever answered. It came up to his expectations. In the first place it was large and dimly lit, one high window opening on to the forbidden garden being its only source of illumination. In the second place it was a storehouse of unimagined treasures.... First and foremost there was a piece of framed tapestry that was evidently meant to be a firescreen. To

Nicholas it was a living breathing story; he sat down for many golden minutes and took in all the details....

But there were other objects of delight and interest claiming his instant attention; there were quaint twisted candlesticks in the shape of snakes, and a teapot fastened like a china duck, out of whose open beak the tea was supposed to come. How dull and shapeless the nursery teapot seemed in comparison! And there was a carved sandalwood box packed tight with aromatic cotton-wool, and between the layers of cotton-wool were little brass figures, hump-necked bulls, and peacocks and goblins, delightful to see and handle. Less promising in appearance was a large square book with plain black covers; Nicholas peeped into it, and behold, it was full of coloured pictures of birds. And such birds!... here were herons and bustards, kites, toucans, tiger-bitterns, brush turkeys, ibises, golden pheasants, a whole portrait gallery of un-dreamed-of creatures. And as he was admiring the colouring of the mandarin duck, the voice of his aunt in shrill vociferation of his name came from the gooseberry garden outside.'

('The Lumber-room' Saki, *1914*)

'How it had changed Eustace mused, and meanwhile his steps were bringing him nearer to the red-capped Third Shelter and the cliff's edge. The hedgerow which used to cling to it so tenaciously had disappeared, a casualty of the erosion that was slowly eating away the face of the cliff. Far below, no doubt, among the debris of boulders that buttressed the great wall, could be found fragments of quickset, brittle, dried and dead, that the birds used for their nests. Never mind; some time the ancient landmark had to go, and it had been, he remembered, a trap for paper-bags and other litter. There was no railing now, it had gone the same way as the hedge, and the remains of the old one – a post here and there and a spar or two sticking out into space – were scantier than they used to be. High time that the Urban District Council, which flaunted their names and notices everywhere, took the matter in hand and put up a proper fence, even if it did fall down after a few years, for the place was not really safe.'

('Eustace and Hilda' L. P. Hartley, *1952*)

'The country of Brobdingnag is well inhabited, for it contains fifty one cities, near an hundred walled towns, and a great number of villages. To satisfy my curious reader, it may be sufficient to describe Lorbrulgrud. This city stands upon almost two equal parts on each side of the river that passes through. It contains above eighty thousand houses. It is in length three glonglungs (which make about fifty four English miles) and two and a half in breadth....

The king's palace is no regular edifice, but an heap of buildings about seven miles round: the chief rooms are generally two hundred and forty foot high, and broad and long in proportion. The kitchen is indeed a noble building, vaulted at top, and about six hundred foot high. The great oven is not so wide by ten paces as the cupola at St Paul's: for I measured the latter on purpose after my return. But if I should describe the kitchen-grate, the prodigious pots and kettles, the joints of meat on the spits, with many other particulars; perhaps I should be hardly believed; at least a severe critick would be apt to think I enlarged a little, as travellers are often suspected to do.'

('Gulliver's Travels' Jonathan Swift, *1726*)

(Brobdingnag is an imaginary country whose inhabitants are giants.)

Exercise 2

Write one or two paragraphs describing
1 A house, or a room in a house, as you first saw it
2 A foreign country or town
3 A place in the countryside or by the sea which you visit after many years away

Relationships with people

The same principles of writing can be applied in the description of people: they can be described factually; or with certain points picked out; as seen through the eyes of the author or a character in the book, who has a certain attitude to them; or as viewed subjectively. Here is a completely factual description first of all.

1 Factual

'Missing boy: John Smith, 9 years old, missing since 7 p.m. Sunday 8 June. 4ft. 6ins., slim build, round face, light brown hair with fringe, large upper front teeth. Last seen wearing dark blue polo-neck sweater, with off-white collar, cuffs and waistband, long blue trousers, black shoes.'

Notice how careful observation is the most important point to remember in factual description.

2 Highlighted

Certain characteristics of appearance or personality are picked out and highlighted. Here is Charles Dickens again with his description of Uriah Heep. Notice how he plays up the two images of length and a reddish colour.

'I saw a cadaverous face appear at a small window on the ground floor, and quickly disappear. The low arched door then opened, and the face came out. It was quite as cadaverous as it had looked at the window, though in the grain of it there was that tinge of red which is sometimes to be observed in the skins of red-haired people. It belonged to a red-haired person – a youth of fifteen, as I take it now, but looking much older – whose hair was cropped as close as the closest stubble; who had hardly any eyebrows, and no eyelashes, and eyes of a red-brown, so unsheltered and unshaded, that I remember wondering how he went to sleep. He was high-shouldered and bony; dressed in decent black, with a white wisp of neckcloth; buttoned up to the throat; and had a long, lank, skeleton hand, which particularly attracted my attention, as he stood at the pony's head rubbing his chin with it, and looking up at us in the chaise.'

('David Copperfield' *1850*)

3 Impression

Sometimes the description of a character is less straightforward and includes the impression made on the viewer. Two contrasting pieces show this effect. First, the effect of the duchess on the jeweller; he is completely submerged in the images of brilliant, flashing colours and drowned in the relentless waves of her presence.

'And Oliver, rising, could hear the rustle of the dress of the duchess as she came down the passage. Then she loomed up, filling the door, filling the room with the aroma, the prestige, the arrogance, the pomp, the pride of all the dukes and duchesses swollen in one wave. And as the wave breaks, she broke, as she sat down, spreading and splashing and falling all over Oliver Bacon, the great jeweller, covering him with sparkling bright colours, green, rose, violet; and odours; and iridescences; and rays shooting from fingers, nodding from plumes, flashing from silk; for she was very large, very fat, tightly girt in pink taffeta, and past her prime. As a parasol with many flounces, as a peacock with many feathers, shuts its flounces, folds its feathers, so she subsided and shut herself as she sank down in the leather armchair.'

('The Duchess and the Jeweller', Virginia Woolf *1944*)

'Something of daylight still lingered, and the moon was waxing bright: I could see him plainly. His figure was enveloped in a riding cloak, fur collared and steel clasped; its details were not apparent, but I traced the general points of middle height, and considerable breadth of chest. He had a dark face with stern features and a heavy brow; his eyes and gathered eyebrows looked ireful and thwarted just now; he was past youth, but had not reached middle age; perhaps he might be thirty-five. I felt no fear of him, and but little shyness.'

('Jane Eyre', Charlotte Bronte *1847*)

In the second passage Charlotte Bronte builds up her picture of Mr Rochester quite logically, progressing from his clothes to his face and age (which were of more importance to her) and then on to her reaction to him (how he affected her); the most important of all.

4 Subjective

Some descriptions are presented so subjectively that the details are fragmented or incomplete, the writer being more interested in the feelings of his characters and how they interact than external details. Here a young man remembers his mother and his description of her is mixed up with emotional memories and half-understood feelings.

'He had vague memories of somewhere else, a dim room, a window looking down on white buildings, and of someone else who talked to forgotten people and who was his mother. He could not recall her features very distinctly, but he remembered with extreme definition a white dress she wore, with a pattern of little sprigs of flowers and little bows upon it, and a girdle of straight-ribbed white ribbon about the waist. Linked with this, he knew not how, were clouded half-obliterated recollections of scenes in which there was weeping, weeping in which he was inscrutably moved to join.'

('Kipps', H. G. Wells *1905*)

5 Character

Here, the writer is as interested in indicating character as in describing appearance.

'Two young men came down the hill of Rutland Square. One of them was just bringing a long monologue to a close. The other, who walked on the verge of the path and was at times obliged to step on to the road, owing to his companion's rudeness, wore an amused listening face. He was squat and ruddy. A yachting cap was shoved far back from his forehead and the narrative to which he listened made constant waves of expression break forth over his face from the corners of his nose and eyes and mouth. Little jets of wheezing laughter followed one after another out of his convulsed body. His eyes, twinkling with cunning enjoyment, glanced at every moment towards his companion's face. Once or twice he rearranged the light waterproof which he had slung over one shoulder in toreador fashion. His breeches, his white rubber shoes and his jauntily slung waterproof expressed youth. But his figure fell into rotundity at the waist, his hair was scant and grey and his face, when the waves of expression had passed over it, had a ravaged look.'

('Two Gallants' from 'Dubliners', James Joyce *1916*)

What kind of character do you think this man has? How has Joyce indicated it?

Exercise 3

Write some descriptive studies of the following people – they could be purely factual. Show how they affect others. Be subjective or concentrate on character, but try and write some of each kind of description.

In the Cambridge Proficiency examination you are often asked to describe a scene or person in a photograph, so the above pictures can be used for oral description practice as well as written work.

WRITTEN SKILLS **B**
Narrative

This really only means telling a story or relating some kind of action. In talking about writing descriptions of places and people we have seen that adjectives and adverbs have played a large part in achieving effects. Now when we come to look at narrative writing we will find that verbs play an important part.

Stories, which can be fact or fiction, are generally based on some kind of plan and of course include some kind of description which helps to set the scene or introduce the characters. A good story often looks something like this.

Introduction	...	Development	...	Excitement	...	Climax	...	Ending
A	...	**B**	...	**Suspense**	...	**C**	...	**D**

The most interesting or exciting part of the story should fall between B and C, but don't concentrate all your efforts there and ignore the other parts; a good story should be well thought out from beginning to end.

A Introduction   The first sentence should suggest that the story is going to be worth reading; you can't expect your readers to continue if they are bored to start with! Possible beginnings could be: 'From the very first day of our journey we felt that all was not well'; 'I warned him, but he wouldn't listen to me'. But get a book of short stories and see how good writers introduce their subject. Here are a few examples: 'There were 26 of us, 26 human machines boxed up in a damp basement' (Gorky); 'And after all the weather was ideal' (Katherine Mansfield); 'When I was a kid I longed for a dovecot' (Isaac Babel); 'It started one Saturday' (V. S. Pritchett); 'I had never seen Joseph Leborgne at work before' (Georges Simenon); 'Halloa! Below there!' (Dickens).

As you can see most of the openings are stating facts, except for Dickens', but in an interesting enough way for you to want to read on.

B Development   Now the story starts to move: perhaps a plan of action is made ... a decision taken. The point of the story begins to emerge: the journey becomes difficult ... the travellers move into dangerous territory.... The reader should by now be absorbed and working towards the suspense with the writer.

Suspense   The most gripping part of the story, the cliff-hanger episode – will the travellers be able to extricate themselves from the danger?

C Climax   At this point the excitement ends, quite suddenly, almost unexpectedly – the travellers have a hairbreadth escape.... The reader can breathe again; he knows what happened. The story should then move quickly on to D.

D Ending   The story can now be rounded off, perhaps by making a comment or giving a moral or adding some information about what happened afterwards. It should not be too prolonged – the travellers vowed never to use that route again.

Remember, as with other types of composition, work out your basic plan before you start writing, don't get your characters to the suspense point and then wonder what to do with them. Also, keep your narrative fairly short as you are writing to a time-limit of approximately an hour in the examination.

Narratives are usually written in a past tense as the writer is either relating something factual from his past or telling a fictional story where his characters are looking back. The verbs generally play a large part in the writing as they move the action along and are therefore particularly important in the middle suspense/climax section of the story.

Unit eight

Exercise 1

1 Here is the beginning of a story. Continue it in any way you wish, but try and make it interesting.

The three children walked slowly along the beach. They were roughly the same height and probably the same age too: about twelve. The one in the middle, though, was a little smaller than the other two.

Apart from the three children, the whole long beach was deserted, except for a dark blur in the far distance. The children were strangely quiet, moving forward in a straight line with rapid even steps, calm, holding hands, taking no notice of the tracks they were carving with precision in the sand.

They drew nearer the dark shape, their eyes flickered uneasily. ...

2 This time the suspense part of the story is given. See if you can give it a beginning and an ending.

But somehow she could not scream. She was too frightened even for that. She stood still and listened. Was he moving stealthily across the carpet? She thought – no, she couldn't be sure. Anything might be happening. He might strike her from above – with one of those heavy boots perhaps. The light switch was near the door – or was it? Why did nothing seem to be happening? The suspense was intolerable. She moved. ...

3 And finally, here is an ending. See if you can fit a middle and a beginning to it.

... I never did find out what he meant.

You will notice that in many of the narratives you are expected to convey what the characters felt as well as the action that was happening to them, so try to imagine the scene or situation clearly before you begin writing; record any impressions or thoughts which might flit through your mind or your character's mind. Try to capture the feeling of being there and then convey it to your readers. A good way to train yourself is to try and remember something clearly from your childhood – when you learnt to ride a bike or swim – then try to recreate the feelings and impressions. In the following extract a schoolboy, Tom Brown, remembers what it was like on his first coach journey in 1820.

'It was a dark ride on top of the Tally-ho, I can tell you, in a tight Petersham coat, and your feet dangling six inches from the floor. Then you knew what the cold was, and what it was to be without legs, for not a bit of feeling had you in them after the first half-hour. ... But it had its pleasures, the cold dark ride. First there was the consciousness of silent endurance – of standing out against something and not giving in. Then there was the music of the rattling harness, and the ring of the horses' feet on the hard road, and the glare of the bright lamps through the steaming hoarfrost, over the leader's ears into the darkness; and the cheery toot of the guard's horn, to warn some drowsy pikeman, or the ostler at the next change; and the looking forward to daylight, – and last, but not least, the delight of returning sensation in your toes.'

('Tom Brown's Schooldays', Thomas Hughes *1820*)

Exercise 2

Describe

1 Your first car journey
2 Your reactions to starting in a new English class
3 Your feelings when you discovered you could swim, *or* when you first fell in love.

In the Cambridge Proficiency examination you generally have the choice of two descriptive compositions, one of which may be narrative/description, so here is a choice. Do not spend more than one hour on any composition.

Exercise 3

1 Describe

either A train journey back to your home town
or A dangerous situation you found yourself in and how you felt

2 Describe

either Market day in a small village
or I had never felt so excited before....

WRITTEN SKILLS **C**
Reading Comprehension

Exercise

Read the following passages and then answer the questions. Choose A, B, C or D for your answer.

First Passage

Extract 1

In any relationship the worst pitfall is possessiveness. You must never think you own the other person just because you are their parent, their marriage partner or you pay them to work for you. You must accept that they will always be themselves and that nothing you can do will alter this fact. You can give advice if it is asked for but you should never impose it. People usually only ask for advice that they hope to find palatable. Phrases such as 'You'll be making a great mistake if ...', or 'Of course, if I were you I'd ...' suggest criticism, even censure. The important thing to remember is that it is another person and not you who is making the decision.

Extract 2

Sometimes when you are being considered for a job you may be asked to take a personality test. This means that your prospective employer is trying to assess what kind of person you are, whether you can work well under stress, how you express youself and, most important, how you get on with other people. Part of a personality test may take the form of a group discussion or role-play. Here it is important not to try to impose your views on the other members of the group, to avoid getting argumentative or start talking about something totally irrelevant. There is no reason why you can't say what you think, so long as you say it pleasantly and do not totally rule out any opinion which differs from your own.

Extract 3

Any relationship with children must be based on truth and dignity. Children are not impressed by adults who are trying to impress them and they resent being talked down to or treated by strangers as some form of household pet to be rewarded for good behaviour and punished for misdemeanours. Children should be treated as people in their own right. This is probably why the relationship between children and the very old is often so successful. Elderly people often find themselves being treated in much the same way as children and equally resent it.

1 In extract 1, why is possessiveness considered damaging to personal relationships?

    A It alters the other person's personality
    B It degrades the relationship
    C It disregards the personality of the individual
    D It is an expression of self-love

2 Extract 2 is probably taken from

    A a set of IQ tests
    B a guide for school-leavers
    C a manual for employers
    D an article on sociology

3 Extracts 1 and 3 emphasise the need for

    A respect for the individual
    B unsolicited advice
    C differences of opinion
    D lack of judgement

4 Extract 3 suggests that children and old people often get on well together because they

    A distrust other people
    B are ignored by other age groups
    C have similar reactions
    D feel isolated from others

5 Extracts 1, 2 and 3 all imply the importance of

    A self respect
    B understanding
    C flexible opinion
    D self-examination

Second Passage

Following is an extract from a collection of essays, 'Friends in Council' by Sir Arthur Helps (1813–1875).

On the Art of Living with Others

Not to interfere unreasonably with others, not to ridicule their tastes, not to question and re-question their resolves, not to indulge in perpetual comment on their proceedings, and to delight in their having other pursuits than ours, are all based upon a thorough perception of the simple fact that they are not we.

5   Another rule for living happily with others is to avoid having stock subjects of disputation. It mostly happens, when people live much together, that they come to have certain set topics, around which, from frequent dispute, there is such a growth of angry words, mortified vanity, and the like, that the original subject of difference becomes a standing subject for quarrel; and there is a tendency in all

10 minor disputes to drift down to it....

If you would be loved as a companion, avoid unnecessary criticism upon those
with whom you live. The number of people who set themselves up as judges is
very large in any society. Now it would be hard for a man to live with another who
was always criticising his actions, even if it were kindly and just criticism. It would
15 be like living between the glasses of a microscope. But these self-elected judges,
like their prototypes, are very apt to have the persons they judge brought before
them in the guise of culprits.

One of the most provoking forms of the criticism above alluded to is that which
may be called criticism over the shoulder. 'Had I been consulted,' 'Had you
20 listened to me,' and such short scraps of sentences may remind many of us of
dissertations which we have suffered and inflicted, and of which we cannot call
to mind any soothing effect.

Another rule, is not to let familiarity swallow up all courtesy. Many of us
have a habit of saying to those with whom we live such things as we say about
25 strangers behind their backs. There is no place, however, where real politics is of
more value than where we mostly think it would be superfluous. You may say
more truth, or rather speak out more plainly, to your associates, but not less
courteously than you do to strangers.

1   We understand that a good relationship with those we live with should be based on
   A   a readiness to praise rather than criticise
   B   a reluctance to make fun of one another
   C   the acceptance of human individuality
   D   the policy of non-interference

2   The writer tells us that disharmony in the home is often caused by
   A   arguing for the sake of argument
   B   always reverting to a favourite argument
   C   being too ready to take offence
   D   not knowing the cause of the disagreement

3   According to the passage, a man who is constantly criticised is likely to feel
   A   the need for self-examination
   B   like a scientific specimen
   C   like a scientific instrument
   D   exposed to the public gaze

4   What do you understand by the phrase 'criticism over the shoulder' (line 19)?
   A   calling attention to advice not taken
   B   reminding someone to follow certain advice
   C   finding fault with advice given
   D   listening to uncalled for advice

5   The writer says that in the art of living together
   A   rudeness should not be excused on the grounds of familiarity
   B   people should not use familiar forms of address
   C   truth is more important than politeness
   D   plain speaking is another name for rudeness

REMINDER **8**

Commonly Confused Verbs

Don't make a mistake
With **bring, fetch** and **take**

Students often find some difficulty in distinguishing between **bring, fetch** and **take,** although in English they have very distinct meanings.

Bring   To take something/someone to another place/person because you have been asked or told to do so

Fetch   To go and get something which you have left in another place and now need; to go to another place and get something which is there and take it back to another person

Take   To decide, unasked, to take something/someone to another place because it seems to you necessary, sensible, or just a good idea

Consider the following examples.

Bring   John's records are rather out of date and he thinks it would be nice if Mary *brought* some of her newer ones to his party.
'Will you *bring* some of your new records, Mary?'

Fetch   When Mary gets to John's party, she realises she has forgotten to bring her new records. As she lives quite near she says she will go home and *fetch* them.
'I'll go home and *fetch* them, John.'

Take   Mary has been invited to John's party. She knows his records are rather out-of-date so she thinks it would be a good idea *to take* some of her new ones.
'I'm going *to take* some of my new records to John's party.'

N.B. 'Get' can often be substituted for 'fetch' but not for 'bring' or 'take'.

Exercise 1

Complete the following sentences with the correct form of *bring, fetch* or *take* and any necessary additions.

1   My camera's broken. Would .... yours tomorrow?
2   I'm sure it isn't going to rain, so .... my raincoat.
3   Ask Elizabeth if .... my glasses from upstairs.
4   John .... his car on holiday because he dislikes driving long distances.
5   Why .... with you last Sunday? You could have bathed in the lake.
6   If they .... a tent, they wouldn't have had to sleep in the car.
7   Can you stop in the High Street? I .... my coat from the dry cleaner's.
8   I wish .... some warm clothes when I went to Sweden. I had no idea it would be so cold.
9   I asked Mary .... the photographs of her holiday, but I expect she'll forget.
10   I shan't be a minute. I'm just .... the guide book I left on my dressing table.

Say and **tell**
Are hard as well

Say   is to make a simple statement of fact or ask a simple question. The statement
        does not necessarily have to be addressed to any particular person, but if it is,
        it is followed by 'to'.
        'I think it's going to rain,' *he said.*
        'I like your new dress,' *he said to her.*
        'Would you like to come to the cinema with me tonight?' *he said.*

Tell is to give instructions, orders or information to another person and *must* be
        followed by a **Person Object** except in the expressions:
        To tell the truth/to tell a lie/to tell a story
        (See also Unit six, Infinitives, page 165)
        It is more often used in indirect than in direct speech.
        He told us to be at the station by 12 o'clock.
        He told me that he was going to America in the autumn.
        He never *tells* a lie.
        He told an amusing story about his adventures in Canada.

Exercise 2

Complete the following sentences with the correct form of *say* or *tell* with any
necessary additions.
1   The tour organiser .... to assemble in the hotel lobby at 9 o'clock.
2   John .... history at Liverpool University next year.
3   He .... before, but I don't think he is telling the
    truth now.
4   My mother always .... not to speak to strangers in the street.
5   'Are you really going to America next summer?' he ....
6   I don't know how many times I .... not to borrow my car without
    asking.
7   When I asked him, one of them .... he had only been in England
    three days.
8   The sergeant .... to wait until he gave the order to fire.
9   'English must be a very difficult language to learn,' ....
10 They .... two hours at the airport before their
    flight was called.

Make and do
Have problems too

Generally speaking, **make** refers to a particular action and **do** to a general one.
For example, we 'make the beds', but 'do the housework'. Obviously both verbs have
a very wide use, but following are some of the commoner examples of differences
between them.

Make a mistake	Do the homework
Make a cake	Do the cooking
Make a dress	Do the sewing
Make the plates dirty	Do the washing up
Make a call	Do some telephoning
Make an effort	Do your best

Unit eight

Now here are a few of the very many verbal expressions used with *make* and *do*

To *make up* :	**1** use cosmetics	To *do up* :	**1** fasten
	2 invent		**2** renovate
	3 prepare a compound	To *do out* :	to clean thoroughly
	4 resolve a quarrel		(house, room, etc.)
To *make out* :	**1** assert	To *do for* :	exterminate/cause the
	2 distinguish/understand		end or downfall of
	3 prepare a bill/list		
To *make for* :	go in the direction of		
To *make do with* :	be obliged to use a substitute		

Exercise 3

Complete the following sentences with a suitable form of *make* or *do* with any necessary additions.

1   How many .... in your homework yesterday?
2   I don't know if I can help Mary, but ....
3   The headmaster .... the timetable for next term.
4   It's a nice house, but .... before we move in.
5   We had forgotten to buy any butter, so we .... margarine.
6   If you take it to the chemist, he .... for you.
7   If only he ...., he would have passed the exam easily.
8   I .... this cupboard. It's full of rubbish.
9   He said he .... the signature at the end of the letter.
10   I'm afraid this scandal .... his political career.

Appendix

Unit one / Dialogue

Annie		It's a super evening, isn't it?
Joe		I'll say. Sky's covered in stars. Looks like someone's left all the lights on. Shouldn't like to pay that electricity bill.
Annie		Well, I don't suppose you'll have to. Hey, what's that?
Joe	*5*	What's what?
Annie		That sort of big orange blob over there.
Joe		I can't see any orange blob.
Annie		Yes, you can. Look up there.
Joe		Oh, yes, now I've got it. That's not a blob. Looks more like a soup plate
	10	wrong way up, only it's got a kind of aerial or something sticking out of the top.
Annie		It looks ever so funny. What on earth can it be, Joe?
Joe		How should I know? Probably some new plane or other they're testing at the Research Centre. Whatever it is, it's not much to look at.
Annie	*15*	I think it's a bit scarey. It's all yellowy now. I think it's getting bigger. Oh Joe, do you – do you think it's one of those UFO things?
Joe		What do you mean? A Flying Saucer? 'Course not. There's no such thing. Anyway, it's gone now.
Annie		It must've landed or something behind those trees. It couldn't just –
	20	well – *disappear*, could it?
Joe		Well, if it's landed, you'd better look out. Any minute now we'll be surrounded by little green men with ray guns saying 'Take me to your Leader'.
Annie		Don't, Joe. I didn't like the look of it one little bit. I'm glad it's gone.
Voice	*25*	Good evening. I am Oris. Would you be kind enough to take me to your Leader?

Unit one / Passage 1

Jane	Do you know what, Tom, it won't be long before we'll all be travelling to space in a cable car!
Tom	A cable car? What do you mean – a sort of ski lift?
Jane	Well, yes, I suppose so.
Tom	You must be joking. Where on earth did you get that idea from?
Jane	Oh, I've just been reading it in a book called *Apes to Astronauts* by Adrian Berry. He's the Science correspondent of *The Daily Telegraph* so he should know what he's talking about. He says – wait a minute, I've got it here, page 28 – 'A Cable Car to the Heavens'.
Tom	Oh, honestly, Jane! You surely don't believe all that stuff you read in those sci-fi books.
Jane	It's not science fiction. It's fact. Hang on, I'll read you what he says: The space writer, Arthur C. Clarke, to whose inspiration we owe the communication satellite, recently outlined a proposal for a new means of space travel which, he admitted, 'is so outrageous that many of you may consider it not even science fiction, but pure fantasy.' Shall I go on?
Tom	No, just tell me how he thinks it could be done.
Jane	Well, it sounds quite simple really. One end of a cable, 23,000 miles long –
Tom	How long?
Jane	23,000 miles. Do listen. One end of a cable, 23,000 miles long, would be attached to a point on the Earth's equator and the other to a satellite in geostationary orbit.
Tom	So?
Jane	The cable would be absolutely tight between the two points and the elevator would travel up and down, carrying people and freight. According to Arthur Clarke, it's the only way to travel in space without using rocket engines – which would make it much more economical. I wonder if it would be more comfortable.
Tom	It sounds pretty uncomfortable to me, and heaven knows what speed it'd be travelling at. What would happen if the cable broke?
Jane	Oh, he explains all that. Apparently the most likely place for it to break would be at or near the ground, and if that happened, it wouldn't fall down, it would fall upwards.
Tom	Upwards? Mm – yes – I suppose it would.
Jane	Yes, sounds funny, doesn't it? Something falling upwards. Anyway, it wouldn't matter too much either if the cable broke away from the high end. It'd remain rigid until it could be reattached to the satellite. I don't quite see why.
Tom	Well, it would be the pull of gravity from above. Anyway, who'd want to be stuck in an elevator attached to a rigid cable thousands of miles up in space? I suppose he doesn't say what would happen if it broke in the middle.
Jane	Actually he does. He says it would be dangerous if the break occurred at any altitude up to 15,000 miles because the bit attached to the Earth would – what does he say? Oh, yes – 'collapse and wrap itself round the equator like a whiplash'.
Tom	Whiplash?

Jane You know, the long bit of cord or leather on a whip. Anyway, even that would only be really catastrophic if the cable was made of steel or some other metal. Metals are much too heavy. The cable would have to be made of some material that's very light and extremely strong and can endure 3,000 miles of vertical suspension without snapping.

Tom But I thought you said the cable would be 23,000 miles long.

Jane I did, but the 3,000 miles 'breaking length' is because of gravity.

Tom Well, all I can say is, you'll never catch me going to space in a cable car. I'd rather keep my feet on the ground, thank you very much.

Unit one / Passage 2

At a small village in the south-east of England sightings of UFOs are regularly reported by dedicated amateurs whose findings are reported to world-wide inter-planetary associations. Armed with binoculars, cameras and recording equipment, an increasingly large number of people from all walks of life spend hours watching
5 and waiting in damp fields and hedgerows for the appearance of these apparently benevolent visitors from space. Photographs, purporting to be authentic, are produced showing objects of the familiar Flying Saucer pattern and others, long and cigar-shaped, looking something like the early airships. It is further said that anyone visiting this village soon becomes aware of the scent of sweet-smelling
10 flowers and that there is a peculiar sense of tranquillity and fellowship among the inhabitants.

The village is one of the most ancient in England. Since earliest times it has had mystical associations. The origin of its name, 'Warminster' is variously interpreted as *'the place at the nunnery by the stream'* or *'the place of waters where the blue*
15 *sky-god was worshipped in a green place where a dragon protected the spirit of a chief in his grave'*. However that may be, it is certainly built over water courses forming a kind of network beneath the ground. Some people hold the theory that there is a kind of subterranean energy beneath the surface. No evidence has so far been produced to support this theory, but the sightings of UFOs continue. Strange
20 flashes of light in the sky, clusters of rainbow-coloured lights, forming and re-forming in geometrical shapes, circles and triangles, balls of fire and floating bubbles – all manner of unidentified flying objects appearing and disappearing apparently at will, leaving no trace except an occasional indentation in the ground.

Who and what are these things? Why, if they are intelligently controlled, do
25 they spend so much of their time hovering over this obscure village? And still a further question arises between the observers and their strange visitors – who is watching whom?

Unit one / Lecture

Do UFOs really exist? This question divides people into two sharply opposing camps – the believers and the non-believers. The former are quite convinced that extra-terrestrials exist and travel around the universe in Flying Saucers. The non-believers are sure that the only form of life exists here on Earth and that any
5   UFO sightings can be scientifically explained as purely terrestrial phenomena. So let's take the believers first and see what evidence they have to support their belief.

For many years there have been reports of strange flying objects, and in 1947 the name of Unidentified Flying Objects, or UFOs was given to these phenomena.
10 Many of the reports of UFOs have a curious similarity: the objects are generally described as disc- or cigar-shaped. In daylight they appear silvery, often luminous or surrounded by an aura; at night they have the appearance of bright lights often yellowy-red in colour. They are said to travel at high speed and accelerate rapidly – frequently disappearing suddenly. A sound described as a low hum or swish has
15 been heard when the UFOs appear and they sometimes stop and hover or rotate over certain spots as though observing something.

These reports have come from all types of people; policemen, farmers, walkers, aircraft pilots, children, housewives; in fact no-one class can be selected as being particularly susceptible to sightings. Perhaps, though, the most convincing
20 evidence has come from the aircraft pilots whose visual sightings have been supported by radar tracking. Most radar operators have compared the UFOs on their radar screens to large aircraft, although they have an unexpected manner of simply vanishing, unlike a normal aircraft. Certain photographic evidence of UFOs has also been produced, although many of the prints are unclear or blurred.

30   But the most astonishing reports have been of close encounters with UFOs. Dr Hynek, Director of the Center for UFO Studies in Illinois, USA has classified these encounters as of three kinds. A close encounter of the first kind is when a witness reports seeing a UFO within a few hundred metres – often when it has landed on the ground. A close encounter of the second kind is when the UFO
35 has left a physical trace, such as an indentation or scorching of the ground, a burnt area of vegetation or broken telephone wires or tree branches. A close encounter of the third kind is when people report actual contact with alien beings; here the descriptions vary widely from reports of normal-looking humans, generally wearing unusual clothes or speaking a strange language, to those little
40 green men with four legs. This third kind of encounter is the most difficult to believe in, although many of the witnesses appear to be sensible men and women not given to lying.

From all the different kinds of report there seems to emerge a general pattern of UFOs. There is a high level of agreement on the shape, colour, movement and
45   sound of UFOs, but far less coherence when describing extra-terrestrial beings. Actual evidence of the existence of UFOs is very slight, however, and according to the unbelievers, doesn't exist.

In fact, the unbelievers state quite categorically that all UFOs have a scientific explanation. They are either natural phenomena such as ball lightning, marsh
50   gas, comets or northern lights or they are aircraft seen from an unusual angle. Unbelievers also suggest UFOs might be planes or rockets which are on Government secret lists and therefore of designs unknown to the public. They discount the evidence of radar sightings as the screens sometimes show up radar shadows or mirages of things which do not exist. Photographs are dismissed as
55   fakes or as pictures of aircraft taken from unusual angles. Finally the three types of close encounter are discounted by the non-believers as hoaxes, hallucinations or people misinterpreting information. The first encounter can be accounted for in the same way as a Flying Saucer seen in the air – as a natural phenomenon. The second kind of encounter usually has a natural cause: the heat marks
60   resulting from fires caused by lightning or people's carelessness, the telephone wires and branches being blown down by high winds and the indentations resulting from subsidence of the land. The third kind of encounter is generally disbelieved because no photographic or taped evidence exists. It is also felt that the witnesses may have been suffering from abnormal mental or physical states
65   at the time.

So to sum up – it is very difficult to say whether UFOs definitely exist or not. The evidence for their existence is rather weak, but on the other hand, there are certain strange phenomena which cannot be explained scientifically at the moment. Perhaps we can leave the subject with a quote from Dr Hynek: 'Maybe the whole
70   phenomenon is not as mysterious as we think, after all a hundred years ago we knew nothing about nuclear energy – maybe our scientific knowledge is just not advanced enough to explain UFOs.' In the meantime reports will continue to pour into the Center for UFO Studies and spotters all over the world will continue to watch the sky for signs of men from outer space.

Unit three / Intensive Listening

	Tony	What would you say, Mr Murray, are the main reasons that so much of our wildlife will have died out by the end of the next few decades?
	Richard	Well, Tony, we can't of course rule out the effect of urbanisation due to the spread of population but, apart from that, I believe there are two
5		reasons which, in a way, are like the opposite ends of a piece of string. If you tie a knot in that piece of string, you end up with a circle and whichever way you go round it's going to turn out to be the same.
	Jenny	I don't think I quite get that, Mr Murray.
	Richard	Well, let's put it another way. It's rather like a film – you've got the
10		Good Guys and the Bad Guys – they're pulling in opposite directions but when it comes to the final showdown, it's hard to make out which is which.
	Tony	What are your two reasons, Mr Murray?
	Richard	I call them Greed and Caring.
15	Jenny	Greed and Caring?
	Richard	Yes, I know they don't seem to have much to do with one another, but think about it. The motive of greed is pretty obvious. In the course of the next few months, thousands of baby seals will be bludgeoned to death before they are even weaned from their mothers. What for? For
20		the sale of their skins at inflated prices to please the vanity of a few and line the pockets of the killers. Crocodiles will be slaughtered to provide shoes and handbags for the rich, gorillas, tigers, leopards and rhino will be hunted for senseless sport or poached in defiance of regulations – their skins, their horns, their magnificent heads will be used as trophies
25		to decorate someone's living-room floor or walls …
	Jenny	That's terrible.
	Richard	Yes, but it's not all. The whale, probably the most impressive and certainly one of the most intelligent sea mammals in creation, will be cruelly hunted and harpooned to make more money for the profiteers.
30		The dolphin, the sailor's friend, will be indiscriminately battered to death at so much a head on the grounds that it is taking away the livelihood of a few fishermen by consuming the fish in its natural habitat.
	Tony	But surely, Mr Murray, we do have to keep warm, we need whale oil
35		and ambergris, fishermen have to make a living …
	Richard	Part of what you say is true, of course, Tony, but we shall have to enforce far stricter controls if future generations are not to find themselves in a world devoid of wildlife as we know it.
	Jenny	Well, I see what you mean about fur coats and crocodile handbags, Mr
40		Murray, but I don't understand what you mean by 'Caring'. That can't be bad, surely. I mean, I thought we were supposed to be living in a 'caring society'.
	Richard	Well, so we do, in a way. The trouble is, there are so many well-intentioned people who start out with the best possible motives of
45		trying to protect or immunise us from this, that or the other in the most effective way at the quickest possible rate – but in their enthusiasm, they lose sight of the long-term consequences. It's only very gradually that the danger to other forms of life, including humans, comes out –

50   not to say, leaks out – and by that time it will probably be too late to do much about it. Take insecticides, for instance.

Jenny   But insecticides protect crops from pests, they destroy disease-carrying mites and creepy-crawlies like cockroaches – even the ordinary housewife will usually keep some form of spray in her cupboard.

Richard   True, but Nature has a way of developing her own immunity against
55   insecticides and other pest controls, with the result that the biologists are driven to inventing stronger and stronger compounds which, though they may annihilate the pest, nevertheless permeate the environment, are assimilated by plant and animal life, become absorbed by the soil. Countless innocent creatures, the beaver or the mole, for example,
60   many of whom were performing a useful task in the natural control of pests, will die from the effects or be rendered sterile. An even more alarming prospect is that as these poisons enter the foods we eat and consequently our own systems, they will find their way into the body cycle of the pregnant mother and into her milk, offering incalculable
65   risks to the unborn or newly born infant. In spite of all our technological expertise, our time is running out; we are virtually destroying ourselves.

Unit three / Listening Comprehension

(Doorbell rings)
(Door opens)

Woman   Yes?

Man   Oh, good morning, Madam. I'm from Pestaway Market Research. I'm doing consumer research in this area. I wonder if you'd mind telling me – do you use Pestaway in your home?

Woman   Pestaway? Oh – the insecticide thing. Well, yes, as a matter of fact, I do.

Man   What do you use it for, Madam? Fleas, ants, cockroaches, woodworm?

Woman   Oh, cockroaches. This is an old house, you see, and we often get cockroaches in the kitchen. I tried scrubbing and disinfecting but it didn't seem to be much good, and then I heard a commercial about Pestaway, so I thought I'd try that.

Man   Was that on TV?

Woman   No, it was radio – one of those early morning shows.

Man   You heard it advertised on the radio. Fine. And you say you use it in the kitchen. Do you use it anywhere else in the house? In the bathroom, say?

Woman   Oh, no we've never had any trouble anywhere else. We get the odd wasp in the summer sometimes, but I don't bother about them. It's the cockroaches I don't like – nasty, creepy-crawly things.

Man   And you find Pestaway does the trick?

Woman   Well, yes, it's quite good. It gets rid of most of them.

Man   How long have you been using it, Madam?

Woman   Oh, let's see – about two years now, I think.

Man   About two years. And how often do you find you have to spray?

Woman   Oh, I give the kitchen a good spray round the skirtings and under the stove – you know – about every six weeks.

Man	Every six weeks or so. I see. Where do you buy your Pestaway, Madam? Supermarket? Chemist?
Woman	Oh, no. I get it at the little shop at the end of this street. They stock practically everything. It means taking a bus if I want to go to the supermarket.
Man	Well, thank you very much, Madam. Oh, could I have your name please?
Woman	Mrs Egerton – Mary Egerton – that's E-G-E-R-T-O-N.
Man	E-G-E-R-T-O-N. And the address is 12, Holly Crescent, Peterford?
Woman	That's right.
Man	Might I ask your age, Madam?
Woman	Oh – well – er – just put down I'm over fifty.
Man	As you like, Mrs Egerton. And occupation – housewife?
Woman	Well, I used to be a telephonist before I married. I had a very good job with the Post Office, but what with a husband to look after and four children to bring up, it doesn't leave you much time, does it?
Man	Occupation – 'housewife'. Well, thank you very much for your time, Madam. You've been most helpful …

Unit four / Listening Comprehension

George Barker	Hello, Charles, I didn't know you went in for jogging.
Charles Evans	Oh, yes, George, I've been doing it for over a month now – twice round the park before breakfast every day. It's amazing what it does for one. I feel fitter now than I've felt for years.
5 **George Barker**	Hmm, well, it's all right, I suppose, so long as you don't overdo it. I find exercising Lulu is about as much as I can manage these days.
Charles Evans	Lulu?
George Barker 10	Well, she's the wife's really. She's over there chasing that Great Dane. She gets a bit overexcited when she sees something ten times her size. Still, the wife thinks it does her good. She's terribly overweight, you see.
Charles Evans	Your wife? But last time I saw her, she said the doctor thought she was still a bit underweight after her operation.
15 **George Barker**	Not my wife, the dog. The trouble is she overeats. She's got a positive passion for cream cakes and – I say, do you have to keep jogging up and down like that? You don't want to overstrain yourself, not at your time of life.
Charles Evans 20	Oh, I don't think that's very likely. Still, perhaps I will sit down a moment and get my second wind. I am a bit out of breath. It's not that I'm not fit, it's just that we've had rather a rush on at work lately.
George Barker 25	Been overworking, have you? Now, that's something I make a point of never doing. A man who's overtired doesn't do his work well. It affects his judgment; he gets things out of perspective.
Charles Evans	You may be right. I did find it rather an effort getting up early this morning.
George Barker	It's always an effort with me.

Unit five / Listening Comprehension

Hello and welcome to 'Stranger Than Fiction' – the family quiz programme in which you – and I do mean *you* – take part! First of all, I know you are all waiting to know the result of last week's competition in which we asked listeners to send in 'Stranger Than Fiction' news stories. All the entries were so good it was a difficult job trying to pick the best, but here they are! And here are the members of our panel to read them to you.

We are going to keep you guessing for a few more minutes before we tell you which one won. There is a second and third prize of £250 and £100 each and the lucky winner takes home £500!

Number 1! The Benedictine monks of Prinknash Abbey in the West of England have been engaged to make 500 stone jugs to hold altogether 80 gallons of the North Sea. These will be presented to VIPs at the Houston Offshore Technology Conference. They will be labelled 'Genuine North Sea' and the idea of the jugs is to remind visitors to this showplace of the world's oil industry how the engineering and technical problems of the hostile North Sea environment have been overcome by a British firm.

Number 2! A Yorkshire company has just won a contract to supply 52 tons of bubblegum to Egypt. The first container was dispatched from the Sheffield factory to Alexandria last month, carrying $7\frac{1}{2}$ tons. By the time the contract is finished early next year, Sheffield will have produced a rope of gum 117 miles long – more than enough to stretch the length of the Suez Canal.

Number 3! The Crocker National Bank on the west coast of America has attracted 120 million dollars in the past two months by banking on every grown-up's teddy bear nostalgia. They are giving away a bear for every 300 dollars invested in a savings account. The money has been pouring in so fast that they have had to issue a 'bear with us' announcement while delivery of bears is speeded up to their branches. More than 100,000 bears have been given away already.

And here comes
Number 4! US millionaire Daniel Ludwig, at 80 possibly one of the richest men in the world, is now awaiting the completion of a most extraordinary project. Two floating factories, a prefabricated cellulose plant and a complete power plant, have reached the coast of Brazil after having crossed the ocean all the way from Japan. They are now travelling up the Amazon to Ludwig's 400-million-acre estate, the Jari Forestry and Ranching Company, which is one of the biggest development projects in the Amazon region.

Unit six / Listening Comprehension

Mr Harris	Of course the public playhouses in Shakespeare's time weren't built in the way most of them are today. They were square like the 'Fortune' theatre or octagonal like the 'Globe'.
John	Octagonal? You mean it was eight-sided?
Mr Harris	That's right. There was an unroofed yard in the centre for the groundlings.
Mary	What are groundlings, Mr Harris?
Mr Harris	Oh, they were the common people, Mary – servants, artisans, people who were considered vulgar and noisy by the wealthier patrons who took care not to mix with them.
Peter	Where did the rich people sit then?
Mr Harris	Oh, well, the yard was surrounded by tiers of covered galleries.
Mary	But where was the stage?
Mr Harris	The main stage was a large platform about four to five feet high. It jutted forward from the actors' dressing room at the back to about thirty feet into the centre of the yard.
Susan	Was there a curtain, Mr Harris?
Mr Harris	No, Susan. You see the platform was surrounded on three sides so it couldn't be curtained off. It was usually left bare.
John	But how did the audience know what the scene was supposed to be?
Mr Harris	They learnt that from the actors' speeches, and sometimes there was music or noises off.
Susan	Noises off?
Mr Harris	Drums or cannon effects to show there was a battle in progress – that sort of thing. Actually, the Elizabethan theatre was very adaptable. At the back of the main stage there were two doors and between them a curtained alcove which they used for interior scenes. Above this, with two windows on either side, there was a balcony stage. This also had a curtain which could be drawn aside so the balcony could serve as the battlements of a castle or a bedroom.
Mary	Like the balcony scene in *Romeo and Juliet*.
Mr Harris	That's right. But that wasn't all. Above the balcony there was a musicians' gallery. A painted canopy, raised on two pillars, represented the heavens, and on top of this there was a hut for stage properties and below the platform there was a space for 'hell'.
Peter	What did they want all that for?
Mr Harris	Well, they both had trapdoors so that they could achieve spectacular effects.
Peter	What sort of spectacular effects?
Mr Harris	Oh, the magical appearance of ghosts, devils or gods from above or below.
Mary	It sounds a bit like a pantomime. What sort of costumes did they wear?
Mr Harris	The costumes were very elaborate and expensive and of course they added to the general visual effect. All the same it was a very intimate theatre, in spite of its pageantry. The actor stood next to the groundlings and none of the spectators were ever more than a short distance away. As I said the groundlings could be very noisy and unruly, so the success of the play depended very largely on the eloquence of the actors. They *had* to be good.

Susan	I wish I could have acted in one of those plays.
Mr Harris	I'm afraid even if you'd been alive then, you wouldn't have been able to, Susan. All the women's parts were played by boys.

Unit seven / Dialogue (1)

Magistrate	If I understand you correctly, Mr Savage, you were driving well within the speed limit when you were stopped by the Police.
Savage	That's right. I always keep to the limit in Downside Road because there's a school slap on the corner of the first turning and I
5	wouldn't want to run the risk of hitting one of the kids, now would I?
Magistrate	But Mr Savage, the Police stopped you at 11 p.m. You're surely not suggesting that children of any age would be likely to be leaving school at such a late hour. I cannot find that your assertion provides any conclusive proof that you were driving within the limit.
10 **Savage**	Proof? Well, it's not exactly proof, I grant you, but it sort of backs me up, if you know what I mean.
Magistrate	I'm afraid I do not know what you mean.
Savage	Well, I go by the speedometer, don't I? That's what a speedometer's for, isn't it, to tell you how fast you're going. I mean a machine
15	can't lie, can it? People can, but not machines.
Magistrate	'Machines' as you call them are not necessarily infallible guides, Mr Savage. They sometimes go wrong. In any case according to the Police testimony you were driving at more than sixty miles an hour in such a manner as to cause a danger to the public. 'Weaving from
20	side to side like a go-go dancer' is what I think the Police Constable said.
Savage	Very funny, sir. Still, the steering wheel has been playing up a bit lately, I'll admit that. I said to the wife only the other day I'd better have it seen to, but she said put it off till we went on holiday so –
25 **Magistrate**	Quite so, Mr Savage. Now, I understand that when the Police stopped you, you refused to take a breathalyser test. Why was that?
Savage	Well, I hadn't been drinking, had I? Half a lager and lime at The Feathers – you must be joking.
Magistrate	It is not my habit to make jokes in court, Mr Savage, and the report
30	I have here shows that subsequent tests indicated that you had taken considerably more than a lager and lime.
Savage	You don't want to take any notice of that, sir. They're just trying to put it over on me – me and all the others they stop when they've nothing better to do. If you ask me the Police ought to be
35	protecting innocent people from vandals and muggers, instead of picking on innocent drivers –
Magistrate	Kindly lower your voice, Mr Savage. This is a court of law not a theatrical presentation. Now, if you would care to listen to this report, I will read it out to you....

Unit seven / Dialogue (2)

1 Magistrate In view of the fact that you have no previous convictions, I am going to put you on probation for six months, but I warn you that I shall not take such a lenient attitude if you are brought before me again. A young man of your age and intelligence should know better than to spend his time jumping out of doorways and menacing elderly people.

2 Minister of Education During the next three years we propose to abolish both the CSE and GCE examinations, the pass grades of which have given rise to considerable confusion, particularly among employers. We shall be substituting a single examination with a wider range of grades at Pass level. Naturally, this will take a year or two to effect, but I should like to add that we are not taking this step lightly and the decision has been taken after the most careful consultation with head teachers, prominent industrialists and members of the university examining boards.

Index

Index